직독직해로 읽는
비밀의 화원
The Secret Garden

직독직해로 읽는
비밀의 화원
The Secret Garden

개정판 1쇄 발행 2016년 12월 20일
초판 1쇄 발행   2010년 10월 10일

원작	프랜시즈 호즈슨 버넷
역주	더 콜링(김정희, 박윤수, 권나연, 이성진, 이은신)
디자인	DX
일러스트	정은수
발행인	조경아
발행처	랭귀지북스
주소	서울시 마포구 포은로2나길 31 벨라비스타 208호
전화	02.406.0047
팩스	02.406.0042
이메일	languagebooks@hanmail.net
홈페이지	www.languagebooks.co.kr
등록번호	101-90-85278
등록일자	2008년 7월 10일
ISBN	979-11-5635-043-9 (13740)
가격	13,000원

ⓒ LanguageBooks 2010

잘못된 책은 구입한 서점에서 바꿔 드립니다.
www.languagebooks.co.kr에서 MP3 파일을 다운로드 할 수 있습니다.

이 도서의 국립중앙도서관 출판예정도서목록(CIP)은 서지정보유통지원시스템 홈페이지(http://seoji.nl.go.kr)와
국가자료공동목록시스템(http://www.nl.go.kr/kolisnet)에서 이용하실 수 있습니다. (CIP제어번호 : CIP2016006149)

직독직해로 읽는
비밀의 화원
The Secret Garden

프랜시스 호즈슨 버넷 원작
더 콜링 역주

Language Books

머리말

"어렸을 때 누구나 갖고 있던 세계명작 한 질,
그리고 TV에서 하던 세계명작 만화에 대한 추억이 있습니다."

"친숙한 이야기를 영어 원문으로 읽어 봐야겠다고 마음 먹고 샀던 원서들은
이제 애물단지가 되어 버렸습니다."

"재미있는 세계명작 하나 읽어 보려고 따져 보는 어려운 영문법,
모르는 단어 찾느라 이리저리 뒤져 봐야 하는 사전,
몇 장 넘겨 보기도 전에 지칩니다."

영어 독해력을 기르려면 술술 읽어가며 내용을 파악하는 것이 중요합니다. 현재 수능 시험에도 대세인 '직독직해' 스타일을 접목시킨 **〈직독직해로 읽는 세계명작 시리즈〉**는 세계명작을 영어 원작으로 쉽게 읽어갈 수 있도록 안내해 드릴 것입니다.

'직독직해' 스타일로 읽다 보면, 영문법을 들먹이며 따질 필요가 없으니 쉽고, 끊어 읽다 보니 독해 속도도 빨라집니다. 이 습관이 들여지면 어떤 글을 만나도 두렵지 않을 것입니다.

명작의 재미를 즐기며 영어 독해력을 키우는 두 마리의 토끼를 잡으세요!

PREFACE

〈직독직해로 읽는 세계명작 시리즈〉의 세 번째 책에서도 변함없이 함께해 준 오랜 친구 윤수와 즐겁게 작업에 동참해 줬던 성진 그리고 은신 씨, 나연 씨, 정성스럽게 작업해 주신 일러스트레이터 은수 씨, 늘 꼼꼼하게 챙겨 주시는 디자인 DX, 이 책이 출판될 수 있도록 늘 든든하게 지원해 주시는 랭귀지북스에 감사의 마음을 전합니다.

마지막으로 내 삶의 소망 되시는 하나님께 영광을 올려 드립니다.

더 콜링 김정희

목차

Chapter 1 THERE IS NO ONE LEFT 8
track 02

Chapter 2 MISTRESS MARY QUITE CONTRARY 22
track 03

mini test 1 44

Chapter 3 THE CRY IN THE CORRIDOR 46
track 04

mini test 2 64

Chapter 4 THE KEY TO THE GARDEN 66
track 05

mini test 3 82

Chapter 5 THE ROBIN WHO SHOWED THE WAY 84
track 06

mini test 4 104

★ 원작 〈비밀의 화원〉에는 영국 요크셔 지방의 사투리가 많이 나오는데, 이 책에 나온 사투리의 특징은 '를 사용하여 말을 줄인다는 점입니다. 또한 you는 tha(영어 고어의 thou에서 변형)로 표현됩니다.
본 책은 독해 실력 기르기를 위한 책이므로 매끄러운 번역보다는 문장의 이해에 중심을 두었습니다. 따라서 사투리의 경우 편의상 모두 표준말로 번역했습니다.

Chapter 6 DICKON 106
track 07

mini test 5 136

Chapter 7 "I AM COLIN" 138
track 08

mini test 6 172

Chapter 8 MAGIC 174
track 09

mini test 7 204

Chapter 9 IN THE GARDEN 206
track 10

mini test 8 246

The Secret Garden을 다시 읽어 보세요 248

1

THERE IS NO ONE LEFT
아무도 남지 않았다

When Mary Lennox was sent / to Misselthwaite Manor / to live with her uncle / everybody said / she was the most disagreeable-looking child / ever seen. It was true, too. She had a little thin face / and a little thin body, / thin light hair / and a sour expression. Her hair was yellow, / and her face was yellow / because she had been born / in India / and had always been ill / in one way or another. Her father had held a position / under the English Government / and had always been busy / and ill himself, / and her mother had been a great beauty / who cared only / to go to parties / and amuse herself / with gay people. She had not wanted a little girl / at all, / and when Mary was born / she handed her over / to the care of an Ayah, / who was made to understand / that if she wished to please the Mem Sahib / she must keep the child out of sight / as much as possible.

manor 저택, 영지 | disagreeable-looking 불쾌하게 생긴, 못생긴 | sour expression 뽀로통한 표정 | amuse oneself 즐기다 | gay 쾌활한, 명랑한 | Ayah 인도의 원주민 하녀, 또는 유모 | please 기쁘게 하다 | as much as possible 할 수 있는 한 많이

8   The Secret Garden

So / when she was a sickly, fretful, ugly little baby / she
그래서 그녀가 골골거리고, 까다롭고, 못생긴 갓난아기였을 땐

was kept out of the way, / and when she became a sickly,
집안 구석에서 자라게 했고, 그녀가 골골거리고, 까다로운 어린애로 자라자

fretful, toddling thing / she was kept out of the way also.
여전히 집안의 구석에 방치되었다.

She never remembered / seeing familiarly anything / but
그녀는 전혀 기억에 없었다 무엇인가를 친숙하게 바라본 경험이

the dark faces of her Ayah and the other native servants, /
보모와 다른 원주민 하인들의 까무잡잡한 얼굴 밖에는,

and as they always obeyed her / and gave her her own way
그리고 이들은 항상 그녀의 말을 들어줬고 제멋대로 하도록 놔두었기 때문에

/ in everything, / because the Mem Sahib would be angry
무엇이든, 사히브 부인이 화를 낼까 봐

/ if she was disturbed by her crying, / by the time she was
아이가 울어대서 방해가 되면, 6살 되던 무렵엔

six years old / she was as tyrannical and selfish a little pig
그녀는 폭군의 이기적인 돼지새끼 같았다

/ as ever lived. The young English governess / who came
이런 아이는 처음이라고 할 만큼. 젊은 영국인 가정교사는 그녀에게 가르치러 온

to teach her / to read and write / disliked her so much /
읽기와 쓰기를 그녀에게 질려서

that she gave up her place / in three months, / and when
일을 그만두었다 석 달 만에,

other governesses came / to try to fill it / they always went
그리고 다른 가정교사들이 왔을 땐 그 자리를 채우기 위해 그들은 달아나기 일쑤였다

away / in a shorter time than the first one. So if Mary had
첫 번째 가정교사보다 더 빨리. 그래서 메리가 결심하지 않았

not chosen / to really want to know / how to read books /
으면 진정으로 알고 싶다고 책 읽는 법을

she would never have learned her letters / at all.
글자도 배우지 못했을 것이다 전혀.

---

fretful 까다로운, 불평이 많은 | toddling 아장아장 걷는 | dark 까무잡잡한 | native 원주민 | Sahib 과거형 인도에서 사회적 신분이 있는 유럽 남자에게 쓰던 호칭으로 Mem Sahib은 그 부인을, Missie Sahib은 그 자녀를 칭할 때 사용했다 | tyrannical 폭군의 | governess 가정교사 | letters 글자

One frightfully hot morning, / when she was about nine
어느 몹시 무더운 날 아침, 아홉 살 되던 때,
years old, / she awakened / feeling very cross, / and she
  메리는 깨어났다 불쾌한 기분으로,
became crosser still / when she saw / that the servant who
그리고 더욱 기분이 나빠졌다 알았을 때 서 있는 하인이
stood / by her bedside./ was not her Ayah.
  침대 옆에 보모가 아니었음을.
"Why did you come?" / she said to the strange woman. "I
"왜 네가 여기에 왔지?" 낯선 하녀에게 말했다.
will not let you stay. Send my Ayah to me."
"여기 있지 마. 내 보모 오라고 하란 말이야."
The woman looked frightened, / but she only stammered
하녀는 겁에 질린 얼굴이었지만, 더듬거리기만 했다
/ that the Ayah could not come / and when Mary threw
  보모가 올 수 없다고 그리고 메리가 격노하며
herself into a passion / and beat and kicked her, / she
  하녀를 때리고 걷어차자,
looked only more frightened / and repeated / that it was not
하녀는 더욱 겁먹은 표정을 지으며 되풀이하기만 했다 불가능하다고
possible / for the Ayah to come / to Missie Sahib.
  보모가 오는 것이 사히브 아씨에게.
There was something mysterious / in the air / that morning.
왠지 이상했다 분위기가 그 날 아침에는.
Nothing was done in its regular order / and several of the
아무것도 평소처럼 되지 않았고 몇몇 원주민 하인들은
native servants / seemed missing, / while those whom
  보이지 않는 듯했다. 반면에 메리 눈에 띈 하인들은
Mary saw / slunk or hurried about / with ashy and scared
  살금살금 돌아다니거나 허둥댔다 잿빛으로 겁에 질린 얼굴로.

frightfully 끔찍하게 | cross 못마땅하다 | stammer 더듬거리며 말하다 | throw oneself into a passion 격노하다 | missing 행방불명의 | slunk (slink의 과거형) 살금살금 걷다 | ashy 재의, 잿빛의 | wander 돌아다니다 | pretend ~인 체하다 | blossoms 꽃 | heaps of earth 흙더미 | mutter 투덜대다 | worst 최악의

faces. But no one would tell / her anything / and her Ayah
하지만 아무도 이야기 해 주지 않았다 메리에게 아무것도 그리고 보모는 오지 않

did not come. She was actually left alone / as the morning
았다. 메리는 사실상 혼자 내팽개쳐졌다 아침이 다 가도록,

went on, / and at last / she wandered out into the garden
 그리고 결국 그녀는 화원에 들어가 어슬렁 거리며

/ and began to play / by herself / under a tree / near the
 놀기 시작했다 혼자서 나무 밑에서 베란다 근처의.

veranda. She pretended / that she was making a flower-
 그녀는 시늉을 했다 꽃밭을 만드는 것처럼

bed, / and she stuck big scarlet hibiscus blossoms / into
 그리고 커다란 진홍빛 히비스커스 꽃을 꽂았다

little heaps of earth, / all the time / growing more and
조그만 흙더미에, 그럴 때마다 점점 더 화가 치밀어 올라

more angry / and muttering to herself / the things she
 혼자 중얼거렸다 그녀가 할 말들과

would say / and the names she would call Saidie / when
 보모에게 퍼부을 욕을

she returned.
보모가 오면.

"Pig! Pig! Daughter of Pigs!" / she said, / because to call a
"돼지! 돼지! 돼지 새끼!" 그녀는 말했다. 왜냐하면 원주민을 돼지라고

native a pig / is the worst insult of all.
부르는 것은 가장 모욕적인 욕이었기 때문에.

Key Expression

by oneself =홀로, 혼자서

재귀대명사는 전치사와 결합하여 다양한 의미를 표현합니다.
by oneself (홀로, 혼자서)(=alone)
for oneself (혼자의 힘으로=without anyone's help)
of oneself (저절로)
beside oneself (제정신이 아니고)
to oneself (혼자 차지하는, 독점하는)
in itself (그 자체에, 본래)
between ourselves (비밀 이야기인데)

ex) She wandered out into the garden and began to play by herself under a tree near the veranda.
그녀는 정원에 들어가 어슬렁 거리며 베란다 근처 나무 밑에서 혼자서 놀기 시작했다.

She was grinding her teeth / and saying this / over and over again / when she heard her mother come out / on the veranda / with someone. She was with a fair young man / and they stood talking together / in low strange voices. Mary knew the fair young man / who looked like a boy. She had heard / that he was a very young officer / who had just come from England.

The child stared at him, / but she stared most / at her mother. She always did this / when she had a chance to see her, / because the Mem Sahib / — Mary used to call her that / oftener than anything else — / was such a tall, slim, pretty person / and wore such lovely clothes. Her hair was like curly silk / and she had a delicate little nose / which seemed to be disdaining things, / and she had large laughing eyes. All her clothes were thin and floating, / and Mary said / they were "full of lace." They looked fuller of lace / than ever / this morning, / but her eyes were not

grind 갈다 | officer 장교 | curly 곱슬곱슬한 | delicate 섬세한 | disdain 경멸하다, 멸시하다 | full of lace 레이스 투성이 | imploringly 애원하듯이 | tremble 떨리다 | wrung (wring의 과거형) 쥐어 틀다 | silly 바보 같은 | clutch 꽉 붙잡다 | shiver (추위 또는 두려움으로) 떨다

laughing / at all. They were large and scared / and lifted
전혀. 어머니의 눈은 동그래져서 겁에 질려 있었고 간청하듯 올려다 봤다

imploringly / to the fair boy officer's face.
젊은 소년 장교의 얼굴을.

"Is it so very bad? Oh, is it?" Mary heard her say.
"그 정도로 매우 나빠요? 아, 그런 거예요?" 메리는 어머니가 말하는 것을 들었다.

"Awfully," / the young man answered / in a trembling
"끔찍하게요," 젊은 장교는 대답했다 떨리는 목소리로.

voice. "Awfully, / Mrs. Lennox. You ought to have gone to
"끔찍하게요, 레녹스 부인. 부인께서는 산으로 들어가셨어야 했습니다

the hills / two weeks ago."
2주 전에."

The Mem Sahib wrung her hands.
사히브 부인은 두 손을 꼭 쥐었다.

"Oh, / I know I ought!" / she cried. "I only stayed / to go to
"오, 그랬어야 한다는 걸 알아요!" 그녀는 소리쳤다. "난 남아 있었어요

that silly dinner party. What a fool I was!"
그 바보 같은 만찬 파티에 참석하느라. 내가 얼마나 어리석었는지!"

At that very moment / such a loud sound of wailing broke
그 순간 큰 울음 소리가 터져 나와서

out / from the servants' quarters / that she clutched the
하인들이 머무는 곳으로부터 사히브 부인은 젊은 장교의 팔을 움켜잡

young man's arm, / and Mary stood shivering / from head
았고 메리도 떨며 서 있었다 머리에서 발끝까지.

to foot. The wailing grew / wilder and wilder.
울음 소리는 커졌다 점점 더 사납게.

Key Expression

ought to[should] have p.p. : ~했어야 했는데

ought to have p.p. '~했어야 했는데'라는 뜻으로 과거에 하지 않은 일에 대한 유감, 후회, 비난을 담고 있는 표현입니다. ought to 대신에 should를 사용해도 같은 의미가 됩니다.

ex) You ought to have gone to the hills two weeks ago.
    당신은 2주 전에 산으로 갔어야만 했어요.

"What is it? What is it?" Mrs. Lennox gasped.
"무엇이죠?   무엇이죠?"   사히브 부인은 숨을 거칠게 몰아쉬며 소리쳤다.

"Someone has died," / answered the boy officer. "You
"누군가가 죽었어요,"   소년 장교가 말했다.   "말하지 않으

did not say / it had broken out among your servants."
셨잖아요   그게 댁의 하인 가운데 발병했다는 것을.

14   The Secret Garden

"I did not know!" / the Mem Sahib cried. "Come with me! Come with me!" / and she turned / and ran into the house. After that, / appalling things happened, / and the mysteriousness of the morning / was explained to Mary. The cholera had broken out / in its most fatal form / and people were dying like flies. The Ayah had been taken ill / in the night, / and it was because she had just died / that the servants had wailed / in the huts. Before the next day / three other servants were dead / and others had run away / in terror. There was panic on every side, / and dying people in all the bungalows. During the confusion and bewilderment / of the second day / Mary hid herself in the nursery / and was forgotten by everyone. Nobody thought of her, / nobody wanted her, / and strange things happened / of which she knew nothing. Mary alternately cried and slept / through the

---

appalling 섬뜩하게 하는 | cholera 콜레라 | fatal 치명적인 | wail 울부짖다 | bungalow 인도에서 유래된 주위에 베란다가 있는 작은 목조 단층집 | bewilderment 당황함 | nursery 아이 방, 육아실 | alternately 번갈아가며

hours. She only knew / that people were ill / and that she heard / mysterious and tightening sounds. Once / she crept into the dining-room / and found it empty, / though a partly finished meal was on the table / and chairs and plates looked / as if they had been hastily pushed back / when the diners rose suddenly / for some reason. The child ate some fruit and biscuits, / and being thirsty / she drank a glass of wine / which stood nearly filled. It was sweet, / and she did not know / how strong it was. Very soon / it made her intensely drowsy, / and she went back to her nursery / and shut herself in / again, / frightened by cries she heard / in the huts / and by the hurrying sound of feet. The wine made her so sleepy / that she could scarcely keep her eyes open / and she lay down on her bed / and knew nothing more / for a long time. Many things happened / during the hours / in which she slept so heavily, / but she was not disturbed / by the wails

---

crept (creep의 과거형) 살금살금 기다 | hastily 황급히 | drowsy 졸음이 오는 | scarcely 거우, 간신히

The Secret Garden

and the sound of things / being carried in and out of the bungalow.

When she awakened / she lay and stared at the wall. The house was perfectly still. She had never known it / to be so silent / before. She heard / neither voices / nor footsteps, / and wondered / if everybody had got well of the cholera / and all the trouble was over. She wondered also / who would take care of her / now her Ayah was dead. There would be a new Ayah, / and perhaps she would know some new stories. Mary had been rather tired of the old ones.

Key Expression

neither A nor B : A도 B도 아닌

neither A nor B는 둘 다 아니다라는 뜻으로 짝을 이루어 쓰이는 상관접속사입니다.
상관접속사의 A와 B에는 같은 형태의 단어나 구, 절이 온다는 점에 주의하세요.
또한 neither A nor B 구문이 주어로 쓰일 경우에는 뒤에 오는 B에 인칭 및 수를 일치시켜야 합니다.

ex) She heard neither voices nor footsteps.
 그녀는 목소리도 발자국 소리도 듣지 못했다.

still 정지한 | footsteps 발자국

She did not cry / because her nurse had died. She was not
그녀는 울지 않았다 보모의 죽음으로 인해. 그녀는 정이 많은 아이

an affectionate child / and had never cared much for any
가 아니었고 그 누구를 좋아한 적도 없었다.

one. The noise and hurrying about and wailing / over the
시끄러움과 야단 법석과 울음 소리가 콜레라로 인한

cholera / had frightened her, / and she had been angry /
그녀를 두렵게 했고, 그녀는 화가 나 있었다

because no one seemed to remember / that she was alive.
아무도 기억하지 못하는 것 같아 그녀가 살아있다는 것을.

Everyone was too panic-stricken / to think of a little girl
모두가 너무나도 겁에 질려 있어서 작은 여자 아이를 생각하지 못했다

/ no one was fond of. When people had the cholera / it
아무도 좋아하지 않는. 사람들이 콜레라에 걸리면

seemed that they remembered nothing / but themselves.
아무것도 기억하지 못하는 것처럼 보였다 자기 자신들 밖에는.

But if everyone had got well again, / surely someone
그러나 만일 모두가 다 낫는다면, 분명 누군가가 기억할 것이고

would remember / and come to look for her.
그리고 그녀를 찾으러 올지도 몰랐다.

But no one came, / and as she lay waiting / the house
하지만 아무도 오지 않았다, 그리고 누워서 기다리는 동안

seemed to grow more and more silent. She heard
집안은 점점 더 조용해지는 것 같았다. 어떤 소리를 들었다

something / rustling on the matting / and when she looked
깔개 위에 부스럭거리는 그리고 아래를 내려다 보자

down / she saw a little snake gliding along / and watching
작은 뱀 한 마리가 미끄러지듯 지나가는 것을 보았다 그리고 그녀를 쳐다보는

her / with eyes like jewels. She was not frightened, /
것을 보석 같은 눈으로. 그녀는 겁이 나지 않았다,

because he was a harmless little thing / who would not
그것은 해가 없는 작은 동물이었기 때문에 그녀를 해치지 않을

hurt her / and he seemed in a hurry / to get out of the
그리고 그것은 바쁜 듯이 보였다 방에서 빠져 나가려고.

affectionate 정이 많은 | panic-stricken 공포에 휩싸인, 당황한 | fond of 호감을 갖다, 좋아하다 | get well 병이 낫다 | | rustle 바스락거리다 | harmless 해가 없는

The Secret Garden

room. He slipped under the door / as she watched him.
뱀은 문 밑으로 빠져나갔다   그녀가 보고 있는 동안.

"How queer and quiet it is," / she said. "It sounds / as if
"어찌나 이상하게도 조용한지,"   그녀가 말했다.   "들리는 것 같아

there were no one in the bungalow / but me and the snake."
집안에 아무도 없는 것처럼   나와 뱀을 빼고는."

Almost the next minute / she heard footsteps in the
바로 그 다음 순간   그녀는 저택에서 발소리를 들었다.

compound, / and then on the veranda. They were men's
그리고 베란다에서도.   남자들의 발자국이었다.

footsteps, / and the men entered the bungalow / and talked
그리고 그들이 집 안으로 들어와서   나지막한 목소리로

in low voices. No one went / to meet or speak to them / and
이야기를 나누었다.   아무도 가지 않았다   그들을 만나거나 그들에게 말을 걸기 위해

they seemed to open doors / and look into rooms.
그리고 그들은 문을 열고   방들을 기웃거리는 듯 보였다.

"What desolation!" / she heard one voice say. "That pretty,
"이렇게 황폐할 수가!"   한 목소리가 말하는 것을 들었다.   "그렇게 예쁘고도,

/ pretty woman! / I suppose the child, too. I heard there was
예쁜 부인이!   그 아이도 그렇게 되었나 봐.   아이가 하나 있다고 들었어,

a child, / though no one ever saw her."
아무도 그녀를 보지는 못했지만."

> ### Key Expression!
>
> **nothing but = only**
> nothing but은 '단지 ~밖에, ~뿐'의 의미로 only와 같은 뜻으로 쓰이는 숙어입니다.
> 비슷한 형태의 anything but은 '결코 ~가 아닌'의 의미로 never의 의미이니 혼동하지 않도록 하세요.
>
> ex) When people had the cholera it seemed that they remembered nothing but themselves.
> 사람들이 콜레라에 걸리면 자기 자신들 밖에는 아무 것도 기억하지 못하는 것처럼 보였다.

queer 괴상한, 이상야릇한 | no one ~ but me 나 외에는 아무도 없다 | compound (저택의) 구내 울타리 친 주택 지구 | desolation 황폐함, 쓸쓸함

Mary was standing / in the middle of the nursery / when
메리는 서 있었다 자기 방 가운데에 그들이 문을 열

they opened the door / a few minutes later. She looked
었을 때 몇 분 후에. 그녀는 못생기고, 불만이

an ugly, cross little thing / and was frowning / because
가득 찬 어린 아이로 보였다 그리고 인상을 찌푸리고 있었다

she was beginning to be hungry / and feel disgracefully
배가 고파오기 시작했고 무시 당했다는 것이 수치스러워서.

neglected. The first man who came in / was a large officer
첫 번째 들어온 남자는 덩치 큰 장교였다

/ she had once seen / talking to her father. He looked tired
그녀가 한 번 본 적 있는 아버지에게 이야기 하고 있는 모습을. 그는 지치고 고통스러운

and troubled, / but when he saw her / he was so startled /
듯 보였는데, 메리를 보자 너무 놀라서

that he almost jumped back.
거의 뒤로 나자빠질 뻔 했다.

"Barney!" / he cried out. "There is a child here! A child
"버니!" 그는 소리쳤다. "여기 애가 있어! 애가 혼자 있다고!

alone! In a place like this! Mercy on us, / who is she!"
이런 곳에 말이야! 맙소사, 이 애는 누구야!"

"I am Mary Lennox," / the little girl said, / drawing herself
"난 메리 레녹스에요." 여자 아이가 말했다, 몸을 꼿꼿이 세우며.

up stiffly. She thought / the man was very rude / to call her
그녀는 생각했다 그 남자가 매우 예의 없다고 아버지의 집을 말

father's bungalow / "A place like this!" "I fell asleep / when
하다니 "이런 곳에!"라고. "나는 잠들었어요

everyone had the cholera / and I have only just wakened up.
모두가 콜레라에 걸렸을 때 그리고 이제 막 일어났어요.

Why does nobody come?"
왜 아무도 오지 않는 거죠?"

"It is the child / no one ever saw!" / exclaimed the man,
"그 아이야 아무도 보지 못했다는!" 그 남자가 탄성을 질렀다.

---

frowning 눈살을 찌푸리다 | disgracefully 불명예스럽게 | trouble 걱정스럽다, 불안하다 | stiffly 뻣뻣하게 | rude 무례하다 | exclaim 감탄하다

The Secret Garden

/ turning to his companions. "She has actually been
그의 동료들을 돌아보며. "이 아이는 정말 잊혀졌던 거라고!"
forgotten!"

"Why was I forgotten?" / Mary said, / stamping her foot.
"내가 왜 잊혀졌죠?" 메리가 말했다, 발을 동동 구르며.

"Why does no one come?"
"왜 아무도 오지 않는 거예요?"

The young man / whose name was Barney / looked at her
젊은이는 버니라는 이름의 매우 슬픈 듯 그녀를 바라

very sadly. Mary even thought / she saw him wink his eyes
보았다. 메리는 생각할 정도였다 그가 눈을 깜빡이는 것을 보았다고

/ as if to wink tears away.
깜빡여서 눈물을 감추려는 듯.

"Poor little kid!" / he said. "There is nobody left / to come."
"가엾은 꼬마야!" 그가 말했다. "아무도 남지 않았다 올 사람은."

It was in that strange and sudden way / that Mary found out
그렇게 이상하고 갑작스럽게 메리는 알아차렸다

/ that she had neither father nor mother left; / that they had
그녀에겐 아버지도 어머니도 남아 있지 않다는 것을; 그들은 죽어서

died / and been carried away / in the night, / and that the
실려 나갔고 밤 사이에, 몇 명의 원주민 하인들도

few native servants / who had not died / also had left the
죽지 않은 집을 떠났다는 것을

house / as quickly as they could get out of it, / none of them
빠져나갈 수 있는 한 최대한 빨리, 아무도 기억하지도 못

even remembering / that there was a Missie Sahib. That was
한 채 사히브 아씨가 남아 있다는 것을. 그게 이유였다

why / the place was so quiet. It was true / that there was
집이 그렇게도 조용했던. 사실이었다 집에 아무도 없다는 것은

no one in the bungalow / but herself and the little rustling
그녀 자신과 바스럭거리는 작은 뱀 밖에는.

snake.

stamp 발을 구르다 | poor 가엾은

2

MISTRESS MARY QUITE CONTRARY
심술궂은 메리 아가씨

Mary had liked / to look at her mother / from a distance /
메리는 좋아했었다   어머니를 보는 것을   멀리 떨어져서

and she had thought her very pretty, / but as she knew very
그리고 그녀가 매우 아름답다고 생각했었다.   하지만 어머니에 대해 별로 알지 못

little of her / she could scarcely have been expected / to
해서   거의 할 것 같지 않았다   어머니를

love her / or to miss her very much / when she was gone.
사랑하거나   어머니를 그리워하는 것을   돌아가셨을 때.

She did not miss her at all, / in fact, / and as she was a self-
메리는 어머니를 전혀 그리워하지 않았다,   실제로,   그리고 자기 밖에 모르는 아이였기

absorbed child / she gave her entire thought to herself, / as
때문에   자신에 대해서만 생각했다,

she had always done. If she had been older / she would no
항상 그래왔듯이.   나이가 좀 더 들었더라면   그녀는 틀림없이 매우 걱

doubt have been very anxious / at being left alone in the
정했을 것이다   세상에 외톨이로 남는 것을,

world, / but she was very young, / and as she had always
하지만 그녀는 매우 어렸고,   항상 누군가의 보살핌을 받아 왔기 때문에,

been taken care of, / she supposed she always would be.
계속 그럴 거라고 생각했다.

What she thought was / that she would like to know / if she
그녀가 생각했던 것은   알고 싶다는 것이다

was going to nice people, / who would be polite to her / and
자신이 좋은 사람들에게 가는지,   자신에게 친절하고

give her her own way / as her Ayah and the other native
마음대로 하게 놔 두는   보모와 다른 원주민 하인들이 했던 것처럼.

servants had done.

---

quite contrary 심술궂은 | self-absorbed 자기 밖에 모르는

She knew / that she was not going to stay / at the English
메리는 알았다   머물지 않으리라는 것을   이 영국인 목사의 집에서

clergyman's house / where she was taken at first. She did
                  그녀가 처음 받아 들여진.   메리는 그곳에

not want to stay. The English clergyman was poor / and
머물고 싶지 않았다.   목사는 가난했고

he had five children / nearly all the same age / and they
아이가 다섯 명 있었는데   모두 나이대가 비슷한

wore shabby clothes / and were always quarreling / and
그들은 낡은 옷을 입고   항상 다투면서

snatching toys from each other. Mary hated their untidy
서로에게서 장난감을 빼앗아 갔다.   메리는 그 어수선한 집이 싫어서

bungalow / and was so disagreeable to them / that after
           그들에게 무뚝뚝하게 대했고

the first day or two / nobody would play with her. By the
하루 이틀이 지나자   아무도 그녀와 놀지 않았다.

second day / they had given her a nickname / which made
이튿날이 되어서는   그녀에게 별명을 붙여 주었다

her furious.
그녀를 몹시 화나게 만들었던.

Key Expression

다양한 뜻을 가진 as

as는 접속사와 전치사로 '~때, ~때문에, ~과 같이, ~함에따라서, 마치 ~인 것처럼' 등 다양한 의미로 쓰입니다.

ex) She did not miss her at all, in fact, and as she was a self-absorbed child
(~때문에)
she gave her entire thought to herself, as she had always done.
(~것처럼)
실제로, 그녀는 어머니를 전혀 그리워하지 않았다, 그리고 자기 밖에 모르는 아이였기 때문에 항상 그래 온 것처럼 자신에 대해서만 생각했다.

---

clergyman 목사 | **shabby** 해진, 허름한 | **quarrel** 다투다 | **snatching** 빼앗다, 잡아 채다

It was Basil / who thought of it first. Basil was a little boy
배질이었다 그것을 처음 생각한 사람은. 배질은 작은 소년이었다

/ with impudent blue eyes / and a turned-up nose, / and
건방져 보이는 파란 눈과 들창코를 가진, 그리고 메리

Mary hated him. She was playing by herself / under a
는 배질을 싫어했다. 메리는 혼자 놀고 있었다 나무 아래에서,

tree, / just as she had been playing the day / the cholera
그 날처럼 콜레라가 발병했던.

broke out. She was making heaps of earth / and paths for
메리는 흙무더기를 쌓고 화원으로 가는 길을 만들

a garden / and Basil came / and stood near to watch her.
고 있었고 배질이 다가와서는 옆에 서서 그녀를 지켜보았다.

Presently he got rather interested / and suddenly made a
이내 흥미를 느꼈는지 갑자기 제안을 하나 했다.

suggestion.

"Why don't you put a heap of stones there / and pretend
"저기다가 돌무더기를 쌓는 건 어때 바위 화원처럼 말이야?"

it is a rockery?" / he said. "There in the middle," / and he
배질이 말했다. "거기 가운데 말야," 그가 메리 위

leaned over her / to point.
로 몸을 숙였다 방향을 가리키기 위해.

"Go away!" / cried Mary. "I don't want boys. Go away!"
"저리 가!" 메리가 소리를 질렀다. "난 난 남자 애들이 싫어. 저리 가!"

For a moment / Basil looked angry, / and then he began to
잠시 동안 배질은 화가 난 듯이 보였다, 그리고는 놀리기 시작했다.

tease. He was always teasing his sisters. He danced round
배질은 항상 자기 누이들을 못살게 굴었다. 배질은 메리 주변을 빙글빙글

and round her / and made faces / and sang and laughed.
돌며 춤을 추고 얼굴을 찌푸린 채 노래하며 깔깔댔다.

impudent 건방진, 뻔뻔스러운 | turned-up nose 들창코 | heap of earth 흙무더기 | presently 이내, 곧 | make a suggesion 제안을 하다

The Secret Garden

"Mistress Mary, quite contrary, /
"심술궂은 메리 아가씨,

How does your garden grow?
화원은 잘 자라고 있나요?

With silver bells, / and cockle shells, /
은방울과,   조가비와,

And marigolds all in a row."
금잔화가 줄지어 있는."

He sang it / until the other children heard and laughed,
배질은 노래했다   다른 아이들도 듣고 깔깔 웃어댈 때까지;

too; / and the crosser Mary got, / the more they sang /
그리고 메리가 짜증을 내면 낼수록,   그들은 더욱 노래를 불러댔다

"Mistress Mary, quite contrary"; / and after that / as long
"심술궂은 메리 아가씨"라고;   그리고 그 이후

as she stayed with them / they called her / "Mistress Mary
메리가 아이들 곁에 있기만 하면   그들은 불렀다   "심술궂은 메리 아가씨"라고

Quite Contrary" / when they spoke of her to each other, /
메리에 대해 이야기를 나누거나,

and often when they spoke to her.
종종 메리에게 말을 걸 때에도.

"You are going to be sent home," / Basil said to her, / "at
"너는 집으로 가게 될 거야,"   배질이 메리에게 말했다.

the end of the week. And we're glad of it."
"이번 주말에.   그래서 기뻐."

Key Expression

the+비교급 ~, the+비교급 … : ~하면 할수록 더욱 …하다

'the + 비교급' 뒤에는 '주어 + 동사'의 절이 와서 '(주어)가 ~하면 할수록, 더욱 (주어)가 …하다'로 해석합니다.

ex) The crosser Mary got, the more they sang
메리가 짜증을 내면 낼수록, 그들은 더욱 노래를 불러댔다.

---

all in a row 줄지어 있는 | cross 심술을 내다 | snap (눈이 노여움을 나타내어) 번쩍 빛나다 | desolate 황량한, 적막한 | hunchback 곱사등이 | horrid 무서운

"I am glad of it, too," / answered Mary. / "Where is home?"

"She doesn't know where home is!" / said Basil, / with seven-year-old scorn. "It's England, / of course. Our grandmama lives there / and our sister Mabel was sent to her / last year. You are not going to your grandmama. You have none. You are going to your uncle. His name is Mr. Archibald Craven."

"I don't know anything about him," / snapped Mary.

"I know you don't," / Basil answered. "You don't know anything. Girls never do. I heard father and mother / talking about him. He lives in a great, big, desolate old house / in the country / and no one goes near him. He's so cross / he won't let them, / and they wouldn't come / if he would let them. He's a hunchback, / and he's horrid."

"I don't believe you," / said Mary; / and she turned her back / and stuck her fingers in her ears, / because she would not listen / any more.

But she thought over it / a great deal / afterward; / and
하지만 메리는 그 말에 대해 다시 생각했다   여러 번   나중에;

when Mrs. Crawford told her / that night / that she was
그리고 크로포드 부인이 메리에게 말했을 때   그 날 밤

going to sail away to England / in a few days / and go
배를 타고 영국으로 가게 된다고 했다   며칠 안에   고모부에게로,

to her uncle, / Mr. Archibald Craven, / who lived at
아치벌드 크레이븐 씨는,   미셀스와이트 저택에 살고 있는,

Misselthwaite Manor, / she looked so stony and stubbornly
메리는 돌처럼 굳어서 완전히 무관심해 보여서

uninterested / that they did not know / what to think about
그들은 몰랐다   그녀에 대해 무슨 생각을 해야 할지.

her. They tried to be kind to her, / but she only turned her
그들은 메리에게 친절하려고 노력했다,   하지만 메리는 고개를 돌려버렸다

face away / when Mrs. Crawford attempted to kiss her,
크로포드 부인이 그녀에게 입맞춤하려고 했을 때,

/ and held herself stiffly / when Mr. Crawford patted her
그리고 몸을 뻣뻣하게 세웠다   크로포드 씨가 어깨를 토닥거리자.

shoulder.

"She is such a plain child," / Mrs. Crawford said pityingly,
"저 애는 참 못생겼네요,"   크로포드 씨 부인이 동정하는 투로 말했다,

/ afterward. "And her mother was such a pretty creature.
나중에.   "엄마는 참 예뻤었는데.

She had a very pretty manner, too, / and Mary has the
참 예의도 바른 사람이었는데,   메리는 가장 미운 짓만 하네요

most unattractive ways / I ever saw in a child. The children
내가 본 아이들 중에서.

call her 'Mistress Mary Quite Contrary,' / and though it's
애들이 메리를 '심술궂은 메리 아가씨'라고 부른다죠,   그건 장난이겠지만,

naughty of them, / one can't help understanding it."
이해가 가네요."

---

stubbornly 고집스럽게 | stiffly 뻣뻣하게, 딱딱하게, 완고하게 | pat 가볍게 두드리다 | plain 꾸밈이 없는, 못생긴 |
pityingly 동정하며 | jump out of his skin 놀라 자빠질 뻔 하다

"Perhaps / if her mother / had carried her pretty face and her pretty manners / oftener into the nursery / Mary might have learned / some pretty ways too. It is very sad, / now the poor beautiful thing is gone, / to remember / that many people never even knew / that she had a child at all."

"I believe / she scarcely ever looked at her," / sighed Mrs. Crawford. "When her Ayah was dead / there was no one / to give a thought to the little thing. Think of / the servants running away / and leaving her all alone / in that deserted bungalow. Colonel McGrew said / he nearly jumped out of his skin / when he opened the door / and found her standing by herself / in the middle of the room."

Key Expression

can't help ~ing : ~하지 않을 수 없다

조동사 can을 이용한 숙어 표현으로 '~하지 않을 수 없다', 즉 '할 수밖에 없다'는 뜻입니다.
같은 의미로 can't but + 동사원형이 있습니다. 표현에 따른 동사 형태에 주의하세요.

ex) Though it's naughty of them, one can't help understanding it.
그것은 장난이었겠지만, 이해하지 않을 수 없네요.

Mary made the long voyage to England / under the care of
메리는 영국으로의 긴 여행을 했다 　　　　　　　　　어느 장교 부인의 보살핌을 받으며,

an officer's wife, / who was taking her children / to leave
　　　　　　　　자신의 자녀들을 데리고 가던

them in a boarding-school. She was very much absorbed in
기숙학교에 보내기 위해.　　　　　　그녀는 정신이 팔려 있어서

/ her own little boy and girl, / and was rather glad to hand
자신의 어린 아들 딸에만,　　　　　메리를 넘기게 되자 기뻐했다

the child over / to the woman / Mr. Archibald Craven sent
　　　　　　　부인에게　　　　아치벌드 크레이븐 씨가 보낸,

to meet her, / in London. The woman was his housekeeper /
　　　　　　런던에서.　　　그 여자는 그의 가정부였고

at Misselthwaite Manor, / and her name was Mrs. Medlock.
미셀스와이트 저택의,　　　　　　이름은 메들록 부인이었다.

She was a stout woman, / with very red cheeks / and sharp
그녀는 덩치 큰 여자였다,　　　매우 붉은 빰과　　　　매서운 검은 눈을

black eyes. She wore a very purple dress, / a black silk
가진.　　　그녀는 진한 자주색 드레스를 입고,　　　검정색 실크 망토를 걸치고

mantle / with jet fringe on it / and a black bonnet / with
　　　　아랫단에 술이 달린　　　　　그리고 검은 보닛을 썼다

purple velvet flowers / which stuck up and trembled / when
자주색 벨벳 꽃 장식이 달린　　　매달려 흔들거리던

she moved her head. Mary did not like her at all, / but as she
부인이 머리를 움직일 때마다.　　메리는 메들록 부인이 전혀 마음에 들지 않았지만, 사람들을 마음

very seldom liked people / there was nothing remarkable in
에 들어한 적이 거의 없기 때문에　　　그렇게 특별한 것이 아니었다;

that; / besides / which it was very evident / Mrs. Medlock
　　　　게다가　　분명해 보였다　　　　　　메들록 부인이 메리를 마음

did not think much of her.
에 들지 않은 것은

"My word! She's a plain little piece of goods!" / she said.
"맙소사!　　이 아이는 정말 못생겼네요!"　　　　메들록 부인이 말했다.

"And we'd heard / that her mother was a beauty. She hasn't
"듣기로는　　　아이 어머니는 미인이었다던데.　　　　　어머니한테 미모는

---

boarding-school 기숙학교 | absorb (관심을) 빼앗다, 빠지게 만들다 | housekeeper 가정부 | stout 덩치 큰, 건장한 | mantle 망토 | fringe 모양을 내기 위한 술 | bonnet 턱 밑에 끈을 매는 여성용 모자 | remarkable 주목할 만한, 특별한

30   The Secret Garden

handed much of it down, / has she, / ma'am?"
거의 물려 받지 못한 모양이네요. 그렇죠, 부인?"

"Perhaps / she will improve / as she grows older," / the
"아마도 좋아지겠죠 성장하면서,"

officer's wife said good-naturedly. "If she were not so
장교 부인이 온화하게 말했다. "혈색이 저렇게 나쁘지 않고

sallow / and had a nicer expression, / her features are
표정이 좀 더 밝았더라면, 외모도 꽤 괜찮을거예요.

rather good. Children alter so much."
아이들은 많이 변하잖아요."

"She'll have to alter a good deal," / answered Mrs.
"아주 많이 변해야겠네요," 매들록 부인이 대답했다.

Medlock. "And, there's nothing likely to improve
"그리고, 나아질 것은 없을 것 같지만

children / at Misselthwaite / —— if you ask me!" They
미셀스와이트에 있다고 해서 — 물어보신다면!" 그들은 생각했다

thought / Mary was not listening / because she was
메리가 듣지 않는다고 약간 멀리 떨어져 있었기 때문에

standing a little apart from them / at the window of the
호텔 창가에

private hotel / they had gone to. She was watching / the
그들이 도착한. 메리는 보고 있었다

passing buses and cabs and people, / but she heard quite
지나가는 버스들과 택시들 그리고 사람들을, 하지만 그녀는 매우 잘 들렸고

well / and was made very curious about her uncle / and
고모부가 어떤 사람인지 매우 궁금해졌다

the place he lived in. What sort of a place was it, / and
그리고 그가 사는 집도. 그곳은 어떤 곳일까,

what would he be like? What was a hunchback? She had
그리고 그는 어떤 사람일까? 곱사등이가 뭐지? 한 번도 곱사

never seen one. Perhaps / there were none in India.
등이를 본적이 없었다. 어쩌면 인도에는 곱사등이가 하나도 없었는지도 모른다.

---

hand down 물려 받다 | good-naturedly 온화하게 | sallow 혈색이 나쁜, 약간, 누런, 병색이 보이는 | feature 이목구비 alter 변하다

Since she had been living / in other people's houses / and
살게 된 이후   다른 사람들의 집에서

had had no Ayah, / she had begun to feel lonely / and to
보모까지 없었기 때문에,   메리는 외로움을 타기 시작했고

think queer thoughts / which were new to her. She had
이상한 생각을 하게 되었다   그녀에게 새로운.   그녀는 궁금해하

begun to wonder / why she had never seemed to belong
기 시작했다   왜 자신이 누군가의 아이같아 보이지 않았는지

to anyone / even when her father and mother had been
    부모님이 살아계실 때 조차도.

alive. Other children seemed to / belong to their fathers
다른 아이들은 ~처럼 보였다   아빠와 엄마의 아이들처럼,

and mothers, / but she had never seemed to / really be
    하지만 메리에게는 없었던 것 같다   진정 누군가의 사랑

anyone's little girl. She had had servants, / and food and
스러운 딸이었던 적이.   하인이 있었고,   음식과 옷도 있었지만,

clothes, / but no one had taken any notice of her. She did
    아무도 그녀를 알아보지 않았다.

not know / that this was because she was a disagreeable
메리는 몰랐다   자신이 못생겼기 때문이라는 것을;

child; / but then, / of course, / she did not know / she was
하지만 그 때,   물론,   그녀는 몰랐다   자신이 못생긴

disagreeable. She often thought / that other people were,
아이라는 것도.   그녀가 종종 생각했다   다른 사람들이 못생겼다고,

/ but she did not know / that she was so herself.
    하지만 알지 못했다   자신이 바로 그렇다는 것은.

She thought / Mrs. Medlock the most disagreeable
메리는 생각했다   메들로 부인이 가장 못생긴 사람이라고

person / she had ever seen, / with her common, highly
    지금까지 본 사람 중에,   평범하고 진한 얼굴에,

colored face / and her common fine bonnet. When the
    흔한 보닛을 쓰고 있는.   다음 날

---

belong to ~ 의 것이다, ~에 속하다, 소속이다 | disagreeable 무뚝뚝한, 싫어하는 | carriage 객실 | not in the least 전혀 | stand no nonsense 허튼 짓을 용납 않다 | dare 감히 ~ 하다, ~ 할 엄두를 내다

next day / they set out on their journey to Yorkshire, /
요크셔로 가기 위해 여행을 떠났다,

she walked through the station to the railway carriage /
메리는 역을 지나쳐 객실로 걸어갔다

with her head up / and trying to keep as far away from
고개를 꼿꼿이 세운 채   그리고 부인으로부터 멀리 떨어지려 했다

her / as she could, / because she did not want / to seem to
가능한 한 멀리,   왜냐하면 원하지 않았기 때문에   자신이 메들록 부인

belong to her. It would have made her angry / to think /
의 아이처럼 보이는 것을. 그 사실은 메리를 화나게 만들었다   생각하는 것은

people imagined / she was her little girl.
사람들이 상상했다고   자신이 그녀의 딸이라고.

But Mrs. Medlock was not in the least disturbed / by
하지만 메들록 부인은 전혀 신경 쓰지 않았다

her and her thoughts. She was the kind of woman / who
메리나 그녀의 생각을.   그녀는 그런 여자였다

would "stand no nonsense from young ones." At least, /
"어린 것들의 허튼 행동을 용납하지 않겠다"는.   적어도,

that is what she would have said / if she had been asked.
그렇게 말했을 것이다   누군가 그녀에게 물어봤다면.

She had not wanted to go to London / just when / her
그녀는 런던으로 가기를 원치 않았었다.   막 ~할 때

sister Maria's daughter was going to be married, / but
자신의 딸 마리아가 결혼하려고,   하지만 그녀

she had a comfortable, well paid place / as housekeeper
는 편안하고 보수가 좋은 직장이 있었고

at Misselthwaite Manor / and the only way / in which she
미셀스와이트 저택의 가정부라는   그리고 유일한 방법은   그 직업을 지키기 위한

could keep it / was to do at once / what Mr. Archibald
즉시 실행하는 것이었다   아치빌드 크레이븐 씨가 그녀에게 시킨

Craven told her to do. She never dared / even to ask a
일을.   그녀는 감히   질문조차도 할 수 없었다.

question.

"Captain Lennox and his wife / died of the cholera," /
"레녹스 대령과 부인이   콜레라에 걸려 죽었소,"

Mr. Craven had said / in his short, cold way. "Captain
크레이븐 씨가 말했었다 늘 그렇듯 짧고 냉정하게. "레녹스 대령은 나의 부

Lennox was my wife's brother / and I am their daughter's
인의 동생이니   내가 그 딸의 후견인이지.

guardian. The child is to be brought here. You must go to
       그 아이를 이곳으로 데려와야 하오.   런던으로 가서

London / and bring her yourself."
    그녀를 내게 데려 오시오."

So she packed her small trunk / and made the journey.
그래서 그녀는 작은 가방을 싸서   여행을 떠났다.

Mary sat in her corner / of the railway carriage / and
메리는 구석에 앉았는데   기차 객실에

looked plain and fretful. She had nothing / to read or to
못생기고 조바심내는 듯 보였다. 메리는 아무것도 없었다 읽을 것도 볼 것도,

look at, / and she had folded her thin little black-gloved
        그래서 검은 장갑을 낀 작고 앙상한 손을 포개놓았다

hands / in her lap. Her black dress / made her look yellower
무릎에.   메리의 검은 드레스로 인해   이전보다 더 노랗게 보였고,

than ever, / and her limp light hair straggled / from under
        힘없는 옅은 머리카락은 들어졌다

her black crepe hat.
크레이프 모자 밑으로.

"A more marred-looking young one / I never saw in my
"이렇게 버릇없어 보이는 아이는   내 평생에 본적이 없네,"

life," / Mrs. Medlock thought. (Marred is a Yorkshire word
  메들록 부인은 생각했다. (Marred란 요크셔 사투리로

/ and means spoiled and pettish.) She had never seen a
  '버릇없다'는 뜻이다).   그녀는 아이를 본 적이 없었다

child / who sat so still / without doing anything; / and at
    그렇게 꼼짝않고 앉아서 아무것도 안 하는;   그리고는 결국에

---

guardian (부모가 사망한 아동의) 후견인 | fretful 조바심치는 | fold 접다 | straggle 제멋대로 자라나다 | crepe 크레이프, 주름진 비단의 일종 | marred 요크셔 사투리로 응석받이 그리고 심통을 부린다는 뜻 | spoil (아이를) 응석받이로 키우다 | pettish 심술을 부리는 | brisk 딱딱한, 사무적인

34 The Secret Garden

last / she got tired of watching her / and began to talk / in a
메들록 부인은 메리를 지켜보는 것에 지쳐서 　　　　말문을 열었다

brisk, hard voice.
딱딱하고 거친 목소리로.

"I suppose / I may as well tell you something about / where you are going to," / she said. "Do you know anything / about your uncle?"

"No," / said Mary.

"Never heard / your father and mother talk about him?"

"No," / said Mary frowning. She frowned / because she remembered / that her father and mother had never talked / to her about anything / in particular. Certainly / they had never told her things.

"Humph," / muttered Mrs. Medlock, / staring at her queer, unresponsive little face. She did not say any more / for a few moments / and then she began again.

> ### Key Expression
>
> **may as well : ~하는 것이 낫다**
> may as well 은 '~하는 것이 낫다'로 had better와 같은 의미로 쓰입니다. 비슷한 형태의 may well은 '~하는 것이 당연하다'의 의미이니 혼동하지 않도록 주의하세요.
>
> ex) I suppose I may as well tell you something about where you are going to.
>   내 생각에는 아가씨가 갈 곳에 대해 얘기해 주는 게 좋겠네요.
>   I suppose you might as well be told something — to prepare you.
>   내 생각에는 아가씨가 미리 듣는 편이 편이 좋겠어요 — 마음의 준비를 위해서.

"I suppose / you might as well be told something / —— to
"내 생각에는   아가씨가 미리 듣는 편이 편이 좋겠어요   —— 마음의

prepare you. You are going to a queer place."
준비를 위해서.   매우 이상한 곳에 갈 테니까요."

Mary said nothing at all, / and Mrs. Medlock looked rather
메리는 아무 말이 없었고,   그래서 메들록 부인은 혼란스러웠다

discomfited / by her apparent indifference, / but, after
   메리가 무관심해 보이자,   하지만. 그녀는 숨을 한

taking a breath, / she went on.
번 들이쉬고는,   계속 했다.

"Not but that it's a grand big place / in a gloomy way, / and
"큰 저택이라서가 아니라   음울하게 보이는,

Mr. Craven's proud of it in his way / —— and that's gloomy
크레이븐 씨는 그 저택을 자랑스러워하고 있습니다   —— 물론, 충분히 음울하기는 하지요.

enough, too. The house is six hundred years old / and
   그 집은 600년이나 되었고

it's on the edge of the moor, / and there's near a hundred
황무지의 끝에 있어요,   방이 거의 100개나 되는데,

rooms in it, / though most of them's / shut up and locked.
   그 대부분은   닫히고 잠겨 있어요.

And there's pictures and fine old furniture / and things
그곳엔 그림과 오래된 고급 가구가 있고   오래 전부터 있었던 골동

that's been there for ages, / and there's a big park round
품들도 있어요,   그리고 집 주변엔 큰 공원이 있고

it / and gardens / and trees / with branches trailing to the
   화원들과   나무들이 있어요   나무가지가 땅으로 드리워진

ground / —— some of them." She paused / and took another
   —— 몇몇 나무들은."   메들록 부인은 잠시 쉬면서   한 번 더 숨을 들이

breath. "But there's nothing else," / she ended suddenly.
쉬었다.   "하지만 그 밖의 다른 것은 없어요,"   그녀는 서둘러서 말을 맺었다.

---

frown 인상을 찌푸리다 | unresponsive 둔감한 | discomfited 혼란스럽게 만들다(주로 수동형으로 쓰임) | apparent 분명한, ~인 것처럼 보이는, 겉보기에는 | indifference 무관심 | take a breath 숨을 들이쉬다 | moor 황무지 | trail (덩굴이) 뻗다, 옷자락이) 끌리다

Mary had begun to listen / in spite of herself. It all sounded so unlike India, / and anything new rather attracted her. But she did not intend to look / as if she were interested. That was one / of her unhappy, disagreeable ways. So she sat still.

"Well," / said Mrs. Medlock. "What do you think of it?"

"Nothing," / she answered. "I know nothing about such places."

That made Mrs. Medlock laugh / a short sort of laugh.

"Eh!" / she said, / "but you are like an old woman. Don't you care?"

"It doesn't matter" / said Mary, / "whether I care or not."

"You are right enough there," / said Mrs. Medlock. "It doesn't. What you're to be kept at Misselthwaite Manor for / I don't know, / unless because it's the easiest way. He's not going to trouble himself about you, / that's sure and certain. He never troubles himself / about no one."

in spite of oneself 자신도 모르게 | unlike ~ 와 다른, 다르게 | matter 중요하다, 문제가 되다 | what~for 왜 (=why) | trouble oneself about ~으로 고민하다 | talkative 말하기를 좋아하는, 수다스러운 | pass time 시간을 보내는 | at any rate 어쨌든, 적어도

38　The Secret Garden

She stopped herself / as if she had just remembered
메들록 부인은 말을 끊었다   무언가 생각이 난 것처럼

something / in time.
　　　　　마침.

"He's got a crooked back," / she said. "That set him
"그 분은 등이 굽었어요."   그녀가 말했다. "그래서 괴팍해지셨지요.

wrong. He was a sour young man / and got no good of all
젊었을 때는 퉁한 분이셨으니   돈과 넓은 집을 제대로 활용하지도

his money and big place / till he was married."
못했죠   결혼 전까지는."

Mary's eyes turned toward her / in spite of her intention
메리의 눈은 메들록 부인을 향했다   관심 있어 보이고 싶지 않았음에도 불구

not to seem to care. She had never thought of / the
하고.   메리는 한번도 생각해 본 적이 없었다

hunchback's being married / and she was a trifle
곱사등이가 결혼할 수 있다고   그래서 그녀는 약간 놀랐다.

surprised. Mrs. Medlock saw this, / and as she was a
메들록 부인은 이것을 보았고,   그녀는 말이 많은 여자였기에

talkative woman / she continued / with more interest.
　　　　　　　　말을 계속했다   더욱 신이 나서.

This was one way / of passing some of the time, / at any
이것도 한 방법이니까   시간을 보내는,   어떤 식으

rate.
로든.

Key Expression

as if 가정법 : 마치 ~인 것처럼

as if는 가정법의 특수한 형태로 '마치 ~인 것처럼'이란 의미로 쓰여요. 특히 be 동사의 경우 인칭에 관계없이 were를 쓴다는 점에 주의하세요.

as if 가정법 과거
→ 주절 현재시제, as if + 주어 + 과거동사/were (마치 ~인 것처럼)

as if 가정법 과거완료
→ 주절 과거/현재완료 시제, as if + 주어 + had p.p.(마치 ~였던 것처럼)

ex) But she did not intend to look as if she were interested.
　　그녀는 자신이 관심 있어 하는 것처럼 보이길 원하지 않았다.
　　She stopped herself as if she had just remembered something in time.
　　메들록 부인은 마치 무언가 생각이 난 것처럼 말을 끊었다.

"She was a sweet, pretty thing / and he'd have walked
부인은 친절하고 아름다운 분이었어요   주인님은 온 세상을 돌아 다니셨을 거에요

the world over / to get her a blade o' grass / she wanted.
풀 한 포기를 얻기 위해서   그녀가 원하는.

Nobody thought / she'd marry him, / but she did, / and
누구도 생각하지 못했어요. 부인이 주인님과 결혼할 거라고, 그런데 하셨어요,

people said / she married him / for his money. But she
사람들이 말하기를   부인이 결혼한 것은   돈 때문이라고 했죠.   하지만 그것 때문이

didn't / —— she didn't," / positively. "When she died —— "
아니었어요   — 그렇지 않았어요,"   정말로.   "부인이 돌아가시고 — "

Mary gave a little involuntary jump.
메리는 자기도 모르게 약간 움찔했다.

"Oh! Did she die!" / she exclaimed, / quite without
"저런! 돌아가셨다고!"   메리는 소리쳤다,   전혀 그럴 뜻이 없었지만,

meaning to. She had just remembered a French fairy story
메리는 프랑스 동화를 떠올렸다

/ she had once read / called "Riquet a la Houppe." It had
한 번 읽었던 적이 있는   "곱사등이 리퀘"라는 제목의.

been about a poor hunchback / and a beautiful princess
그건 불쌍한 곱사등이에 관한 이야기였다   아름다운 공주와

/ and it had made her / suddenly sorry for Mr. Archibald
그리고 그 이야기가 떠오르자   아치벌드 크레이븐 씨가 갑자기 불쌍하게 여겨졌다.

Craven.

"Yes, she died," / Mrs. Medlock answered. "And it made
"네, 부인은 돌아가셨어요,"   메들록 부인이 대답했다.   "그래서 주인님은 더 이상

him queerer / than ever. He cares about nobody. He won't
해지셨죠   이전보다.   그 분은 누구에게도 관심이 없답니다.   아무도 만나고 싶

see people. Most of the time / he goes away, / and when he
어 하지 않아요.   대부분   먼 곳으로 가 계세요,   그리고 미셀스와이트

is at Misselthwaite / he shuts himself up in the West Wing
에 계실 때면   서쪽 건물에 틀어박혀서

/ and won't let any one / but Pitcher see him. Pitcher's an
누구도 들이지 않아요   피처가 만나러 가는 것 외에는.   피처는 늙은 하인인데, /

old fellow, / but he took care of him / when he was a child /
주인님을 돌보았죠   주인님이 어렸을 때부터

and he knows his ways."
그래서 그는 주인님의 방식을 알고 있어요."

It sounded like something in a book / and it did not make
마치 어떤 책에 나오는 이야기 같았고   그것은 메리를 기분을 들뜨게 했다.

Mary feel cheerful. A house with a hundred rooms, /
                     100개나 되는 방이 있는 집,

nearly all shut up / and with their doors locked / —— a
거의 대부분은 닫혀 있고   잠겨진 채

house on the edge of a moor / —— whatsoever a moor was
— 황무지 끝에 있는 집   — 황무지가 뭐든 간에

/ —— sounded dreary. A man with a crooked back / who
  — 우울하게 들렸다.   등이 굽은 남자 또한

shut himself up also! She stared out of the window / with
자신도 문을 걸어 닫고 사는!   메리는 창 밖을 쳐다 보았다

her lips pinched together, / and it seemed quite natural /
입술을 꽉 다문 채,   자연스러워 보였다

that the rain should have begun to pour down / in gray
비가 쏟아지기 시작한 것이   회색빛으로 비스

slanting lines / and splash and stream down the window-
듬하게   창에 튀기고 물줄기를 이루며 흘러 내려가면서.

panes. If the pretty wife had been alive / she might have
        만약에 아름다운 부인이 살아 있었더라면   그녀가 그를 좀 더 밝게 만들

made things cheerful / by being something like her own
었지 모른다   메리의 어머니가 그랬던 것처럼

mother / and by running in and out / and going to parties
           안팎을 돌아다니며   파티들에 가기도 하면서

/ as she had done in frocks "full of lace." But she was not
 "레이스 투성이"의 옷을 차려 입고 하듯이.   하지만 그녀는 거기에 없었다

there / any more.
        더 이상.

---

sweet 달콤한, 귀여운, 상냥한, 좋은 | involuntary 자기도 모르게, 본의 아니게 | west wing 서쪽 부속 건물 |
cheerful 발랄한 | pinch 꼬집다, 물다 | slanting 비스듬한, 사선의 | splash 튀기다 | pane 창유리 | frocks
드레스

41

"You needn't expect to see him, / because ten to one you
주인님을 만나리라고는 기대하지 마세요, 십중팔구 만나지 못할테니까요,

won't," / said Mrs. Medlock. "And you mustn't expect
메들록 부인은 말했다. "그리고 기대하지 마세요

/ that there will be people to talk to you. You'll have
아가씨에게 말을 걸 사람이 있을 거라는 것을. 아가씨는 혼자 놀아야 하고

to play about / and look after yourself. You'll be told /
스스로를 돌봐야 할 거예요. 아가씨에게 알려 줄 거예요

what rooms you can go into / and what rooms you're to
어떤 방에 들어갈 수 있는지 어떤 방에서 멀리 떨어져 있어야 하는지.

keep out of. There's gardens enough. But when you're in
뜰에서는 마음대로 돌아다니세요. 하지만 집 안에 있을 때에는

the house / don't go wandering / and poking about. Mr.
여기저기 돌아다니지 마세요 기웃거리거나

Craven won't have it."
크레이븐 씨가 받아들이지 않을 거예요.

"I shall not want to go poking about," / said sour little
""여기저기 기웃거리고 싶지 않을 거예요," 뚱한 메리가 말했다.

Mary / and just as suddenly as she had begun to be
그리고 크레이븐 씨가 갑자기 불쌍해 보이기 시작했던 것처럼

rather sorry for Mr. Archibald Craven / she began to
메리는 불쌍하다는 생각을

cease to be sorry / and to think / he was unpleasant
갑자기 멈추었다 그리고 생각했다 그는 충분히 불쾌하다고

enough / to deserve all that had happened to him.
그에게 일어난 모든 일이 당연하다고 할 만큼.

---

ten to one 십중팔구 | keep out ~에 들어가지 않다, 막다 | poke about 어슬렁거리다 | deserve (마땅히) ~할 만하다 | streaming 흐름 | gaze out 바라보다

42 The Secret Garden

And she turned her face / toward the streaming panes of
그리곤 메리는 고개를 돌렸다   빗물이 흘러내리는 창문을 향해

the window / of the railway carriage / and gazed out at
기차 객실의   그리고 잿빛 폭우를 뚫어져라

the gray rain-storm / which looked / as if it would go on
쳐다보았다   ~으로 보이는

forever and ever. She watched it / so long and steadily /
끊임없이 계속 될 것 같이. 메리는 빗줄기를 보았고   오랫 동안 그리고 끊임없이 내리는

that the grayness grew heavier and heavier / before her
잿빛은 점점 더 짙어져 갔다   자신의 눈 앞에서

eyes / and she fell asleep.
     그리고 메리는 잠이 들었다.

Key Expression

enough to : ~하기에 충분한

enough to는 to 부정사를 사용한 관용 표현 중 하나로 아래와 같이 쓰입니다. 여기서 to 부정사는 앞의 형용사(부사)를 수식하는 부사적 용법으로 파악할 수 있습니다.

형용사[부사] + enough + to 부정사
= so + 형용사[부사] + that + 주어 + can (~할 만큼 충분히 ...하다)

ex) She began to cease to be sorry and to think
he was unpleasant enough to deserve
(=he was so unpleasant that he can deserve)
all that had happened to him.
그녀는 불쌍해 하는 것을 그만두고 그에게 일어난 이 모든 일이 당연할 만큼 불쾌한 사람이라고 생각하기 시작했다.

mini test 1

A. 다음 문장을 해석해 보세요.

(1) When Mary was born / she handed her over / to the care of an Ayah, / who was made to understand / that if she wished to please the Mem Sahib / she must keep the child out of sight / as much as possible.
→

(2) Nobody thought of her, / nobody wanted her, / and strange things happened / of which she knew nothing.
→

(3) I suppose / I may as well tell you something about / where you are going to.
→

(4) She did not intend to look / as if she were interested.
→

B. 다음 주어진 문장이 되도록 빈칸에 써 넣으세요.

(1) 따라서 메리가 정말 책 읽는 방법을 알고 싶다고 하지 않았다면 <u>그녀는 글자도 전혀 배우지 못했을 것이다</u>.

So if Mary had not chosen to really want to know how to read books _____ her letters at all.

(2) 당신은 2주 전에 산 위로 <u>갔어야만 했어요</u>.

You _____ the hills two weeks ago.

(3) 마치 이 저택에 나와 뱀 외에는 <u>아무도 없는 것처럼</u> 들렸다.

It sounds _____ in the bungalow but me and the snake.

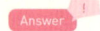

A. (1) 메리가 태어나자 그녀는 보모에게 넘겨져 돌봐졌으며, 보모는 사히브 부인을 기쁘게 하려면 아이를 되도록 눈에 보이지 않도록 해야 한다는 사실을 알아야만 했다. (2) 아무도 그녀를 생각하지 않았고, 그녀를 원하지도 않았으며, 그녀는 전혀 모르는 이상한 일들이 일어났다. (3) 당신이 향해 가는 곳에 대해 좀

(4) 그녀는 메들록 부인이 그가 <u>이제까지 보았던 가장 못생긴</u> 사람이라고 생각했다.
She thought Mrs. Medlock _____.

C. 다음 주어진 문구가 알맞은 문장이 되도록 순서를 맞춰 보세요.

(1) 그녀는 목소리도 발자국 소리도 듣지 못했다.
(heard / nor / voices / She / footsteps / neither)
→

(2) 그것이 바로 그 장소가 그토록 조용했던 이유였다.
(why / the place / so / That was / quiet / was)
→

(3) 그것을 처음 생각해낸 사람은 바로 배질이었다.
(who / Basil / It / it / first / thought of / was)
→

(4) 그것이 그를 전보다 더 이상하게 만들었다.
(than / him / It / ever / made / queerer)
→

D. 다음 단어에 대한 맞는 설명과 연결해 보세요.

(1) fretful　　▶　　◀ ① walk around in a casual way
(2) wander　　▶　　◀ ② speak very quietly
(3) desolation　▶　　◀ ③ a feeling of great unhappiness and hopelessness
(4) mutter　　▶　　◀ ④ worried or unhappy about something

Answer

말해주는 게 좋겠네요. (4) 그녀는 자신이 관심 있어 하는 것처럼 보이고 싶지 않았다. | B. (1) she would never have learned (2) ought to have gone to (3) as if there were no one (4) the most disagreeable person she had ever seen| C. (1) She heard neither voices nor footsteps. (2) That was why the place was so quiet. (3) It was Basil who thought of it first. (4) It made him queerer than ever. | D. (1) ④ (2) ① (3) ③ (4) ②

3

THE CRY IN THE CORRIDOR
복도에서 들리는 울음 소리

At first / each day which passed by for Mary Lennox /
처음에는   메리 레녹스가 보낸 하루 하루는

was exactly like the others. Every morning / she awoke in
다른 날들과 정확히 똑같았다.   매일 아침   휘장이 쳐진 방에서 일

her tapestried room / and found / Martha kneeling upon
어나   발견했다   마사가 깔개에 무릎을 꿇고 앉아서

the hearth / building her fire; / every morning / she ate her
불을 지피고 있는 것을;   매일 아침   아침 식사를 했다

breakfast / in the nursery / which had nothing amusing in
어린이 방에서   신기한 것이라고는 전혀 없는;

it; / and after each breakfast / she gazed out of the window
아침 식사 후에는   창 밖을 멍하니 바라보았다

/ across to the huge moor / which seemed to spread out
넓은 황무지 너머를   모든 지역에 다 퍼져 있는 듯 보이는

on all sides / and climb up to the sky, / and after she had
하늘까지 타고 오르는 듯이,   그렇게 잠시 동안 바라본 후

stared for a while / she realized / that if she did not go out
그녀는 깨달았다   만약에 밖으로 나가지 않는다면

/ she would have to stay in / and do nothing / —— and so
집 안에 계속 머물러야만 하고   아무것도 하지 말아야 한다는 것을   —그래서 메리

she went out. She did not know / that this was the best
는 밖으로 나갔다.   메리는 알지 못했다   이것이 가장 잘한 일임을

thing she could have done, / and she did not know that, /
또한 그녀가 몰랐던 것은,

when she began to walk quickly / or even run along the
자신이 빠르게 걷기 시작하거나,   길을 따라 달리기라도 할 때면

paths / and down the avenue, / she was stirring her slow
가로수 길 아래로,   느리게 흐르던 피를 뒤흔들어

blood / and making herself stronger / by fighting with the
자신을 튼튼하게 만들고 있다는 것이었다   바람에 맞서 달리는 것이

---

tapestried 태피스트리된, 직물로 짜여진 | build one's fire 불을 지피다 | spread out 뻗다, 퍼지다 | avenue 거리를 의미하지만, 나무가 우거진 저택의 진입로를 뜻하기도 함 | whipped 맺히도록 | dull 따분한, 흐릿한, 둔한

46   The Secret Garden

wind / which swept down from the moor. She ran only /
　　　　황무지를 훑고 지나가는.　　　　　　　　　　　메리는 단지 달렸을 뿐이었다

to make herself warm, / and she hated the wind / which
따뜻해지기 위해서,　　　　그리고 바람이 싫었기 때문에　　　얼굴을 빠르게 지

rushed at her face / and roared / and held her back / as if it
나가며　　　　　　　웅웅거리고　　　자신을 잡아당기는

were some giant / she could not see.
마치 무슨 거인인 것처럼　메리가 볼 수 없는.

But / the big breaths of rough fresh air / blown over the
하지만　거칠고 상쾌한 공기를 가득 들이마시고　　　히스 꽃 위로 내뿜자

heather / filled her lungs with something / which was good
무엇인가 그녀의 허파를 채웠고　　　　　　여위고 몸에 도움이 되는

for her whole thin body / and whipped some red color into
　　　　　　　　　　　　　　　　뺨을 붉게 물들였으며

her cheeks / and brightened her dull eyes / when she did not
　　　　　　　　　　명한 눈을 반짝이게 했다

know anything about it.
아무것도 모르고 있는 사이에.

Key Expression

가정법 과거 : ~한다면 ~할텐데

가정법 과거는 현재 사실에 반대되는 일을 가정하거나 현재의 소망을 이야기할 때 씁니다. 그 형태는 다음과 같아요.

If+주어+과거동사, ~주어+would[should/could/might]+원형동사
※ 이때, if절의 be동사는 주어의 인칭이나 수에 관계없이 were를 쓴다는 점을 잊지 마세요.

ex) She realized that if she did not go out she would have to stay in and do nothing.
그녀는 만약 밖으로 나가지 않는다면 계속 안에 머물러 있어야 하고 아무것도 하지 말아야 한다는 것을 깨달았다.

But after a few days / spent almost entirely out of doors / she wakened one morning / knowing what it was to be hungry, / and when she sat down to her breakfast / she did not glance disdainfully at her porridge / and push it away, / but took up her spoon / and began to eat it / and went on eating it / until her bowl was empty.

"Tha' got on well enough with that / this mornin', / didn't tha'?" / said Martha.

"It tastes nice today," / said Mary, / feeling a little surprised herself.

"It's th' air of th' moor / that's givin' thee stomach for tha' victuals," / answered Martha. "It's lucky for thee / that tha's got victuals / as well as appetite. There's been twelve in our cottage / as had th' stomach / an' nothin' to put in it. You go on playin' / you out o' doors every day / an' you'll get some flesh / on your bones / an' you won't be so yeller."

"I don't play," / said Mary. "I have nothing to play with."

disdainfully 경멸하며 | porridge 포리지(오트밀(귀리(oats)에 우유나 물을 부어 걸쭉하게 죽처럼 끓인 음식. 특히 아침 식사로 먹음)go on ~ing 계속 해서 ~하다 | victual 양식, 식품

"Nothin' to play with!" / exclaimed Martha. "Our children plays / with sticks and stones. They just runs about / an' shouts an' looks at things." Mary did not shout, / but she looked at things. There was nothing else to do. She walked round and round the gardens / and wandered about the paths in the park. Sometimes / she looked for Ben Weatherstaff, / but though several times / she saw him at work / he was too busy / to look at her / or was too surly. Once / when she was walking toward him / he picked up his spade / and turned away / as if he did it on purpose.

One place / she went to oftener / than to any other. It was the long walk / outside the gardens / with the walls round them. There were bare flower-beds / on either side of it / and against the walls / ivy grew thickly. There was one part of the wall / where the creeping dark green leaves / were more bushy than elsewhere. It seemed as if / for a long time / that

---

spade 삽 | bare 황량한, 맨-, 벌거벗은, 가장 기본적인 | ivy 담쟁이덩굴 | creeping 서서히 진행되는 | bushy 우거진 | clip 깎다, 손질되어 있다, 다듬어져 있다 | trim 다듬다, 손질하다, 잘라내다 | chirp 짹짹거림 | forward perched 몸을 앞으로 빼고 앉다 | robin 붉은가슴울새

part had been neglected. The rest of it had been clipped /
그 부분은 다듬어지지 않은 것처럼. 다른 곳들은 잘 손질되어 있었고,

and made to look neat, / but at this lower end of the walk /
깔끔해 보였다, 하지만 이 산책로 끝은

it had not been trimmed at all.
전혀 손질되어 있지 않았다.

A few days after / she had talked to Ben Weatherstaff, /
며칠 뒤 벤 웨더스태프와 이야기 한 후,

Mary stopped to notice this / and wondered why it was so.
메리는 이 사실을 발견하고 멈춰 서서 왜 그런지 궁금해 했다.

She had just paused / and was looking up at a long spray
그녀는 걸음을 멈추고 긴 담쟁이덩굴 가지를 바라보았다

of ivy / swinging in the wind / when she saw a gleam of
바람에 흔들거리는 주홍색이 언뜻 눈에 띄었을 때

scarlet / and heard a brilliant chirp, / and there, on the top
그리고 명랑하게 지저귀는 소리를 들었다, 그리고 그곳, 담장 위에,

of the wall, / forward perched / Ben Weatherstaff's robin
몸을 빼고 앉아 있었다 벤 웨더스태프의 붉은가슴울새가,

redbreast, / tilting forward to look at her / with his small
메리를 보려고 앞으로 몸을 숙이며 작은 머리를 옆으로 하고는.

head on one side.

Key Expression

too ~ to… : 너무 ~해서 …할 수 없다

too + ~(형용사) + to…(동사원형) 구문은 '너무 ~해서 …할 수 없다', 혹은 '…하기에는 너무 ~하다'라는 의미로 쓰입니다. 이때 문장의 주어와 to 부정사의 행위자가 다를 경우에는 '의미상 주어 for + 목적격'을 to 부정사 앞에 삽입합니다. 또한 이 구문은 so + 형용사 + 주어 + can't 구문을 사용해 절로 바꿀 수 있어요.

ex) He was too busy to look at her.
 그는 너무 바빠서 그녀를 볼 수 없었다
 (=He was so busy that he couldn't look at her.)

"Oh!" / she cried out, / "is it you / —— is it you?" And it did
"오!"   메리가 소리쳤다.   "너로구나?"   — 너지?"

not seem at all queer to her / that she spoke to him / as if
그녀에게는 전혀 이상하지 않았다   새에게 말을 건 것이

she were sure / that he would understand / and answer her.
확신하는 듯이   새가 알아 듣고   대답할 거라고.

He did answer. He twittered / and chirped / and hopped
새는 정말 대답했다.   지저귀고   짹짹거리며   담벼락을 따라 뛰어 다녔다

along the wall / as if he were telling her / all sorts of things.
   마치 그녀에게 알려 주려는 듯   여러 가지를.

It seemed to Mistress Mary / as if she understood him, /
메리에게는 보였다   새의 말을 이해한 듯,

too, / though he was not speaking in words. It was as if he
마찬가지로, 말로 이야기 한 것은 아니지만.   새가 이렇게 말한 것 같

said:
았다:

"Good morning! Isn't the wind nice? Isn't the sun nice?
"좋은 아침이야!   바람이 좋지 않아?   햇살이 좋지 않아?

/ Isn't everything nice? Let us both chirp / and hop and
 모든 것이 좋지 않아?   우리 같이 지저귀자   폴짝 뛰면서 지저귀자.

twitter. Come on! Come on!"
   어서!   어서!"

Mary began to laugh, / and as he hopped / and took little
메리는 웃기 시작했다,   그리고 새가 폴짝폴짝 뛰면서   담벼락을 따라 날자

flights along the wall / she ran after him. Poor little thin,
   새를 쫓아 달려갔다.   불쌍하고 작고 앙상한,

sallow, ugly Mary / —— she actually looked almost pretty /
누렇고 부은 얼굴의 못생긴 메리   — 사실 그녀는 예뻐 보였다

for a moment.
아주 잠시 동안.

"I like you! I like you!" / she cried out, / pattering down
"네가 좋아!   네가 좋아!"   메리가 소리쳤다,   길을 따라 달리면서;

the walk; / and she chirped / and tried to whistle, / which
   그리고 메리는 짹짹거리며   휘파람을 불어보려고 했다,

last she did not know / how to do in the least. But the robin
그러나 전혀 몰랐다   어떻게 해야 하는지.   하지만 붉은가슴 울새는

/ seemed to be quite satisfied / and chirped / and whistled back at her. At last / he spread his wings / and made a darting flight / to the top of a tree, / where he perched and sang loudly.

That reminded Mary / of the first time / she had seen him. He had been swinging on a tree-top / then / and she had been standing in the orchard. Now / she was on the other side of the orchard / and standing in the path outside a wall / —— much lower down / —— and there was the same tree / inside.

"It's in the garden / no one can go into," / she said to herself. "It's the garden without a door. He lives in there.

Key Expression

remind A of B : A에게 B를 상기시키다(생각나게 하다)

remind는 '상기시키다, 기억나게 하다'라는 동사입니다. 이를 remind A(사람) of B(사람 혹은 사물)와 같은 형태로 사용하면 유사한 점 때문에 '(주어가) A에게 B를 생각나게 하다'라는 의미가 됩니다.
한편 of B 자리에 to + 동사를 넣으면 '(해야 할 일을 잊지 않도록) A에게 B를 하라고 상기시키다'의 뜻으로 그 의미가 조금 다르답니다.

ex) That reminded Mary of the first time she had seen him.
그것은 메리에게 그녀가 그를 처음 만났던 순간을 생각나게 했다.

twitter 지저귀다 | patter 가볍게 걸어가다 | darting 쏜살같이 움직이는, 휙 움직이는 | orchard 과수원

How I wish I could see / what it is like!"
봤으면 좋으련만 어떻게 생긴 화원인지!"

She ran up the walk to the green door / she had entered
그녀는 초록색 문까지 달려갔다 첫 날 아침 지나갔던.

the first morning. Then she ran down the path / through
그리고 나서 길을 따라 달려 내려가서는

the other door / and then into the orchard, / and when she
다른 문을 통과하여 과수원 안으로 들어갔다, 그리고 멈춰 서서 올려다

stood and looked up / there was the tree / on the other side
보았을 때 거기에 나무가 있었다 담벼락 반대편에,

of the wall, / and there was the robin / just finishing his
그리고 그 나무에 붉은가슴울새가 있었다 이제 막 노래를 마치고는,

song and, / beginning to preen his feathers with his beak.
부리로 깃털을 다듬기 시작하는.

"It is the garden," / she said. "I am sure it is."
"그 화원이구나," 메리가 말했다. "그 화원이 분명해."

She walked round / and looked closely / at that side of the
메리는 주변을 돌면서 자세히 관찰했다

orchard wall, / but she only found / what she had found
과수원의 담벼락을, 하지만 발견했을 뿐이었다 예전에 보았던 것만

before / —— that there was no door in it. Then / she ran
— 거기에는 문이 없다는 사실을. 그리고 나서

through the kitchen-gardens again / and out into the walk
메리는 다시 텃밭을 통과하여 산책로로 달려가서

/ outside the long ivy-covered wall, / and she walked to
담쟁이덩굴로 덮힌 긴 벽의 바깥쪽, 그 길 끝까지 따라 걸어가며

the end of it / and looked at it, / but there was no door; /
살펴 보았다, 그렇지만 문은 없었다;

and then / she walked to the other end, / looking again, /
그리고는 반대편 끝까지 걸어가면서, 다시 살펴보았다,

but there was no door.
하지만 문은 없었다.

---

preen 몸치장을 하다, 단장하다 | kitchen-gardens 텃밭, 채마밭 | languid 힘없는, 나른한 | cobwebs 거미줄

"It's very queer," she said. "Ben Weatherstaff said there was no door and there is no door. But there must have been one ten years ago, because Mr. Craven buried the key."

This gave her so much to think of that she began to be quite interested and feel that she was not sorry that she had come to Misselthwaite Manor. In India she had always felt hot and too languid to care much about anything. The fact was that the fresh wind from the moor had begun to blow the cobwebs out of her young brain and to waken her up a little.

She stayed out of doors nearly all day, and when she sat down to her supper at night she felt hungry and drowsy and comfortable. She did not feel cross when Martha chattered away. She felt as if she rather liked to hear her, and at last she thought she would ask her a question. She asked it after she had finished her supper and had sat down on the hearth-rug before the fire.

"Why did Mr. Craven hate the garden?" / she said. She had made Martha stay with her / and Martha had not objected at all. She was very young, / and used to a crowded cottage / full of brothers and sisters, / and she found it dull / in the great servants' hall down-stairs / where the footman and upper-housemaids / made fun of her Yorkshire speech / and looked upon her as a common little thing, / and sat and whispered among themselves. Martha liked to talk, / and the strange child / who had lived in India, / and been waited upon by "blacks," / was novelty enough to attract her.

She sat down on the hearth herself / without waiting to be asked.

Key Expression

not~until…: …할 때까지는 ~하지 않다(직역) / …하고 나서야 비로소 ~하다(의역)

not~until… 구문은 '…하고 나서야 비로소 ~하다'라고 의역하면 자연스러워져요.

또한 이 구문은 강조를 위해 not until을 문장 앞으로 뺀 도치 구문이나 'It is ~ that' 강조구문으로도 자주 사용되니 헷갈리지 않도록 주의하세요.

ex) Mary did not know what "wutherin'" meant until she listened.
메리는 그 말을 듣기 전까지는 "wutherin'"의 의미를 몰랐다.
(=들은 후에야 비로소 알 수 있었다)

"Art tha' thinkin' about that garden yet?" / she said. "I
"아직도 화원에 대해서 생각하고 있어요?" 마사가 말했다.

knew tha' would. That was just the way with me / when I
"그럴 줄 알았지요. 저랑 똑같네요

first heard about it."
처음 화원에 대해 들었을 때랑"

"Why did he hate it?" / Mary persisted.
"그는 왜 싫어했던 건데?" 메리가 다그쳤다.

Martha tucked her feet under her / and made herself quite
마사는 다리를 쭈그리며 편안한 자세를 만들었다.

comfortable.

"Listen to th' wind / wutherin' round the house," / she
"바람 소리를 들어보세요 집 주위를 쌩쌩 불어대는," 마사가 말

said. "You could bare stand up on the moor / if you was
했다. "황무지에 똑바로 서 있지도 못할 거예요 오늘 같은 밤에 나

out on it tonight."
간다면."

Mary did not know / what "wutherin'" meant / until she
메리는 알지 못했다 "쌩쌩 불어댄다"는 말의 의미를 듣기 전까지는,

listened, / and then she understood. It must mean / that
그리고는 이해했다. 그건 아마도 의미일 것이다

hollow shuddering sort of roar / which rushed round and
공허하고 소름끼치는 으르렁거림이라는 집 주위를 소용돌이치는

round the house / as if the giant no one could see / were
마치 보이지 않는 거인이

buffeting it / and beating at the walls and windows / to
퇴격대고 벽과 창문들을 두들기면서

try to break in. But one knew he could not get in, / and
침입하려는 듯이. 하지만 거인이 침입하지 못할 것을 알고 있었고,

somehow it made one feel very safe / and warm inside a
어쩐지 그 사실에 안도감과 따뜻함을 느꼈다 방 안에서

room / with a red coal fire.
난로가 붉게 불타는.

object 반대하다 | footman 남자 하인, 남종 | upper-housemaid 고참 하녀 | common 흔한 | whisper 속삭이다
| novelty 새로움 참신함, 진기함 | tucked 접어 넣은 | hollow 속이 빈, 공허한 | shuddering 몸이 떨리는,
몸서리치는, 흔들리는 | roar 으르렁거리다, 울부다, 함성을 지르다 | buffeting 난타, 큰 진동

"But why did he hate it so?" / she asked, / after she had listened. She intended to know / if Martha did. Then Martha gave up / her store of knowledge. "Mind," / she said, / "Mrs. Medlock said / it's not to be talked about. There's lots o' things in this place / that's not to be talked over. That's Mr. Craven's orders. His troubles are none servants' business, / he says. But for th' garden / he wouldn't be like he is. It was Mrs. Craven's garden / that she had made / when first they were married / an' she just loved it, / an' they used to 'ttend the flowers themselves. An' none o' th' gardeners / was ever let to go in. Him an' her used to go in / an' shut th' door an' stay there / hours an' hours, / readin' and talkin'. An, she was just a bit of a girl / an' there was an old tree / with a branch bent like a seat on it. An' she made roses grow over it / an' she used to sit there. But one day / when she was sittin' there / th' branch broke an' she fell on th' ground / an' was hurt so bad / that next day she died. Th' doctors thought

/ he'd go out o' his mind an' die, too. That's why he
크레이븐 씨도 정신이 나가서 죽을 것 같다고. 그것이 크레이븐 씨께서 화원을 싫

hates it. No one's never gone in / since, / an' he won't let
어하시는 이유지요. 아무도 들어가본 적이 없어요 그 이후로는, 크레이븐 씨는 아무도 말하

anyone talk / about it."
지 못하게 하세요 그곳에 대해서."

order 명령, 순서 | 'ttend (→attend) 돌보다, 참석하다, 주의를 기울이다 | gardener 정원사

Mary did not ask any more questions. She looked at the
메리는 더 이상 묻지 않았다. 그녀는 붉게 타오르는 불을 바라

red fire / and listened to the wind "wutherin'." It seemed to
보면서 "쌩쌩 불어대는" 바람 소리를 들었다.

be "wutherin'" louder / than ever.
더 크게 "쌩쌩 불어대는" 것 같았다 이전보다 더.

At that moment / a very good thing was happening to her.
바로 그 순간 메리에게 좋은 일이 일어나고 있었다.

Four good things had happened to her, / in fact, / since she
네 가지의 좋은 일이 그녀에게 일어났다. 사실은,

came to Misselthwaite Manor. She had felt / as if she had
미셀스와이트 저택으로 온 이후로. 그녀는 느꼈다 자신이 붉은가슴울새를

understood a robin / and that he had understood her; / she
이해한다면 그 새도 메리를 이해할 거라고;

had run in the wind / until her blood had grown warm;
메리는 바람 속을 달렸었고 피가 따뜻해질 때까지;

/ she had been healthily hungry / for the first time in her
메리는 건강한 허기를 느꼈다 생애 처음으로;

life; / and she had found out / what it was to be sorry for
그리고 메리는 발견했던 것이다 누군가를 불쌍히 여긴다는 감정이 무엇인지.

some one.

But as she was listening to the wind / she began to listen to
하지만 바람 소리를 듣고 있을 때 뭔가 다른 소리가 들렸다.

something else. She did not know / what it was, / because
메리는 알지 못했다 그것이 무엇인지, 왜냐하면

/ at first / she could scarcely distinguish it / from the
처음에는 거의 구분할 수 없었기 때문에 바람 소리 자체와.

wind itself. It was a curious sound / —— it seemed almost
그것은 호기심을 끄는 소리였다 — 그 소리는 들렸다

/ as if a child were crying somewhere. Sometimes / the
마치 아이가 어디선가 울고 있는 것처럼. 때로는

wind sounded / rather like a child crying, / but presently
바람 소리가 들렸다 아이가 우는 소리처럼, 하지만 지금

be sorry for ~을 안쓰럽게 여기다, 안됐다고 여기다 | scarcely 거의 ~ 않은, 간신히 | distinguish 구별하다

Mistress Mary felt quite sure / this sound was inside the
메리는 꽤 확신할 수 있었다 이 소리가 집 안에서 들린다는 것을,

house, / not outside it. It was far away, / but it was inside.
집 밖이 아니라. 멀리서 들리는 소리였지만, 집 안에서 들리는 소리였다.

She turned round / and looked at Martha.
그녀는 돌아서서 마사를 바라 보았다.

"Do you hear any one crying?" / she said.
"누가 우는 소리 안 들리니?" 메리가 말했다.

Martha suddenly looked confused.
마사는 갑자기 당황한 듯 보였다.

"No," / she answered. "It's th' wind. Sometimes / it
"아니요." 마사가 대답했다. "바람 소리일 거예요. 때로는

sounds like / as if someone was lost on th' moor / an'
소리가 나죠 누군가가 황무지에서 길을 잃고 울고 있는

wailin'. It's got all sorts o' sounds."
것처럼. 여러 소리가 섞여 있으니까요."

Key Expression

감각동사&지각동사

감각동사는 5감을 나타내는 동사로, look/seem/appear(~처럼 보이다), smell(~같은 냄새가 나다), taste(~같은 맛이 나다), sound(~같이 들린다), feel(~같이 느껴진다)가 있어요. 2형식 동사이므로 우리말로 부사처럼 해석이 되어도 뒤에는 반드시 형용사가 옵니다.

한편 지각동사는 감각을 통한 인지를 표현하는 동사로 5형식에 쓰이는 동사입니다. 주로 보다(see, look at, watch), 듣다(hear, listen to), 느끼다(feel)가 있어요.

지각동사는 5형식 동사로, 다음과 같은 형태로 쓰입니다.
지각동사+목적어+목적보어 (동사원형/현재분사)
▶ 현재분사는 진행 중인 동사를 강조할 때 쓰임

ex) She listened to the wind "wutherin'". (지각동사)
    그녀는 바람이 "쌩쌩 불어대는" 것을 들었다
    Mistress Mary felt quite sure. (감각동사)
    메리는 꽤 확실하게 느꼈다
    "Do you hear any one crying?" (지각동사)
    "누군가가 울고 있는 게 들리니?"

"But listen," / said Mary. "It's in the house / —— down
"하지만 들어 봐,"   메리가 말했다.   "집 안에서 들리는 소리야   —— 저 긴 복도 어

one of those long corridors."
딘가에서."

And at that very moment / a door must have been opened
그리고 바로 그 때   문이 열렸음에 틀림없었다

/ somewhere down-stairs; / for a great rushing draft
아래층 어딘가에서;   왜냐하면 엄청난 강풍이 불어와서

blew / along the passage / and the door of the room they
복도를 따라   그들이 앉아 있던 방의 문이

sat in / was blown open with a crash, / and as they both
쾅하고 열렸기 때문에,   그들은 놀라서 벌떡 일어섰고

jumped to their feet / the light was blown out / and the
   불빛이 꺼졌다

crying sound was swept down the far corridor / so that it
그리고 그 울음 소리가 멀리 복도를 휩쓸고 지나갔다

was to be heard more plainly than ever.
이전보다 더 똑똑히 들리도록.

"There!" / said Mary. "I told you so! It is someone crying
"자 봐!"   메리가 말했다.   "내가 말했잖아!   누군가 우는 소리야

/ —— and it isn't a grown-up person."
—— 그리고 어른의 소리가 아니라고."

Martha ran and shut the door / and turned the key, /
마사는 달려가서 문을 닫고   열쇠를 돌렸다,

but before she did it / they both heard the sound of a
하지만 문을 닫기 전에   둘 다 소리를 들었다

door / in some far passage shutting / with a bang, / and
멀리 복도 어디선가 문이 닫히는 소리를   쾅하고,

then everything was quiet, / for even the wind ceased
그리고는 모든 것이 조용해졌다,   바람마저도 "쌩쌩 불어대기"를 멈췄기 때문에

"wutherin'" / for a few moments.
   잠시 동안.

---

great rushing draft 엄청나게 빠른 바람 | blow out 꺼지다 | swept down 급습하다, 휩쓸고 지나가다 | scullery-maid 부엌데기

The Secret Garden

"It was th' wind," / said Martha stubbornly. "An' if it wasn't, / it was little Betty Butterworth, / th' scullery-maid. She's had th' toothache all day."

But something troubled / and awkward in her manner / made Mistress Mary stare very hard at her. She did not believe / she was speaking the truth.

Key Expression

must have p.p : ~였음에 틀림없다

조동사 must는 '~임에 틀림없다'(강한 추측)과 '해야 한다'(의무)의 두 가지 뜻이 있습니다. 이때 강한 추측에 대한 과거 표현이 바로 must have p.p로 '~였음에 틀림없다'라는 의미입니다.

must have p.p : ~였음에 틀림없다(90% 이상 확신)
may have p.p : ~였을 것 같다
might have p.p : ~였을지도 모른다
≠ cannot have p.p : ~였을리가 없다

한편 강한 추측 표현인 must의 반대말은 must not이 아니라 cannot(~일리가 없다)입니다. 따라서 must have p.p가 부정문에 쓰이려면 cannot have p.p의 형태로 쓰여야 합니다.

ex) And at that very moment a door must have been opened somewhere downstairs.
그리고 바로 그때 아래층 어딘가에서 문이 열렸음에 틀림없었다.

mini test 2

A. 다음 문장을 해석해 보세요.

(1) After she had stared / for a while / she realized / that if she did not go out / she would have to stay in / and do nothing.
→

(2) Though several times / she saw him at work / he was too busy / to look at her / or was too surly.
→

(3) It seemed as if / for a long time / that part had been neglected.
→

(4) The fact was / that the fresh wind from the moor / had begun to blow the cobwebs / out of her young brain / and to waken her up a little.
→

B. 다음 주어진 문장이 되도록 빈칸에 써 넣으세요.

(1) 그는 일부러 그러는 것처럼 자신의 삽을 들고 돌아섰다.

He picked up his spade and turned away _____ _____.

(2) 메리는 듣기 전까지는 "wutherin"이 무슨 의미인지 알지 못했으며, 그 후에 이해했다.

Mary _____ she listened, and then she understood.

(3) 그녀는 마치 그녀가 붉은가슴울새를 이해하고 새도 자신을 이해하는 것처럼 느꼈다.

She had felt _____.

A. (1) 잠시 동안 응시한 후 그녀는 자신이 밖으로 나가지 않는다면 안에 머물러서 아무것도 하지 않을 거란 사실을 깨달았다. (2) 그녀는 몇 번이나 그가 일하는 모습을 보았지만, 그는 너무 바빠서 혹은 너무 무례하여 그녀를 바라보지 않았다. (3) 오랫동안 그 부분은 방치되어 온 것처럼 보였다. (4) 사실은 황무지로

(4) 그 순간, 아래층 어딘가에서 문이 <u>열렸음에 틀림없었다</u>.

At that very moment a door _____ somewhere down-stairs.

C. 다음 주어진 문구가 알맞은 문장이 되도록 순서를 맞춰 보세요.

(1) 다른 할 일이 없어요.
(was / to / nothing / There / else / do)
→

(2) 그것은 메리에게 그녀가 그를 처음 보았던 때를 생각나게 했다.
(the first time / Mary / him / had seen / she / reminded / That / of)
→

(3) 그것은 아무도 들어갈 수 없는 정원 안에 있어.
(the garden / no one / It's / go into / can / in)
→

(4) 누군가 울고 있는 게 들리니?
(any one / you / Do / crying? / hear)
→

D. 다음 단어에 대한 맞는 설명과 연결해 보세요.

(1) hearth ▶   ◀ ① sit down lightly on the edge of something
(2) neglect ▶   ◀ ② fail to look after properly
(3) perch ▶   ◀ ③ the floor of a fireplace
(4) corridor ▶   ◀ ④ a long passage in a building or train

부터의 신선한 바람이 그녀의 머리 속에 쳐진 거미줄을 날려버리고 그녀를 깨운 것이었다. | B. (1) as if he did it on purpose (2) did not know what "wutherin" meant until (3) as if she had understood a robin and that he had understood her (4) must have been opened | C. (1) There was nothing else to do. (2) That reminded Mary of the first time she had seen him. (3) It's in the garden no one can go into. (4) Do you hear any one crying? | D. (1) ③ (2) ② (3) ① (4) ④

4

THE KEY TO THE GARDEN
화원의 열쇠

Two days after this, / when Mary opened her eyes / she sat
이런 일이 있고 이틀이 지난 후,   메리는 눈을 뜨자마자

upright in bed immediately, / and called to Martha.
자리에서 벌떡 일어나 앉아,   마사를 불렀다.

"Look at the moor! Look at the moor!"
"황무지를 봐!   황무지 좀 보라고!"

The rainstorm had ended / and the gray mist and clouds /
폭풍우가 그치고   잿빛 안개와 구름이

had been swept away / in the night / by the wind. The wind
휩쓸려 사라졌다   밤 동안   바람에 의해.   바람이 그치자

itself had ceased / and a brilliant, deep blue sky / arched
  밝고 푸른 하늘이   아치처럼 높이 펼쳐

high / over the moorland. Never, never / had Mary dreamed
져 있었다   황무지 위로.   절대, 절대로   메리는 상상해 본 적이 없었다

of / a sky so blue. In India / skies were hot and blazing;
  하늘이 이렇게 푸르리라고. 인도에서는   하늘이 덥고 타는 듯 했다;

/ this was of a deep cool blue / which seemed to almost
  하지만 이곳의 하늘은 깊고 시원하게 푸르렀다   반짝이듯이

sparkle / like the waters of some lovely bottomless lake,
  아름답고 헤아릴 수 없이 깊은 호수처럼,

/ and here and there, / high, high in the arched blueness
  그리고 여기 저기에,   아치를 이룬 높디 높은 하늘에

/ floated small clouds / of snow-white fleece. The far-
  작은 구름들이 떠 다녔다   눈처럼 하얀 솜털같은.

reaching world of the moor itself / looked softly blue /
저 멀리 보이는 황무지 세계 자체는   부드러운 푸른빛으로 보였다

instead of gloomy purple-black / or awful dreary gray.
음울한 어두운 자줏빛이나   지독하게 음산한 잿빛이 아니라.

---

upright 반듯하게, 꼿꼿이 | mist 안개, 연무 | sweep away 휙 지나가다 | cease 멈추다 | arch 둥근 곡선을 그리다 | blazing 타는 듯한, 강렬한 | sparkle 번쩍이다 | fleece 양털, 또는 그와 같이 부드러운 직물
grin 미소 | heel 발꿈치

66   The Secret Garden

"Aye," / said Martha / with a cheerful grin. "Th' storm's
"그렇네요," 마사가 말했다 환하게 웃으며. "폭풍우가 잠시 멎었

over for a bit. It does like this / at this time o' th' year.
네요. 이래요 일 년 중 지금 이맘 때면.

It goes off in a night / like it was pretendin' / it had
하룻밤 만에 사라지죠 시늉하고 있었던 것처럼 이곳에 없었고

never been here / an' never meant to come again. That's
다시는 오지 않을 것처럼.

because th' springtime's on its way. It's a long way off
봄이 오고 있는 거죠. 아직은 멀었지만,

yet, / but it's comin'."
그래도 봄은 오고 있지요."

"I thought / perhaps it always rained / or looked dark / in
"생각했어 아마도 늘 비가 오거나 어두침침한 곳이라고

England," / Mary said.
영국은," 메리는 말했다.

"Eh! No!" / said Martha, / sitting up on her heels /
"아니에요! 그렇지 않아요!" 마사가 말했다, 일어나 그녀의 발꿈치에 앉으면서

among her black lead brushes. "Nowt o' th' soart!"
검은 재를 쓸어내던 중에. "절대 글치 않쉬!(절대 그렇지 않아요!)"

Key Expression

부정어에 의한 도치 구문

강조를 위해 부정어 혹은 부정의 의미를 가진 부사어가 문장의 맨 앞에 위치하면 뒤따르는 주어와 동사의 어순이 도치됩니다. 도치할 때에는 조동사나 be동사가 있을 경우 이를 앞으로 빼며 일반동사는 do 동사를 이용합니다.

부정의 단어, 부사구, 부사절　　　+ 조동사 + 주어 + 동사
(no, not, nor, never,
hardly, few, little 등)　　　　　　+ have/has/had(완료시제) + 주어 + p.p
　　　　　　　　　　　　　　　　+ be동사 + 주어
　　　　　　　　　　　　　　　　+ do동사 + 주어 + 동사원형(일반동사일 경우)

ex) Never had Mary dreamed of a sky so blue.
절대로 메리는 하늘이 그렇게 푸르리라고 상상하지 못했다.

"What does that mean?" / asked Mary seriously. In India
"그게 무슨 뜻이지?" 메리가 진지하게 물었다. 인도에서는

/ the natives spoke different dialects / which only a few
원주민들이 다른 사투리로 말했다 몇몇 사람들만 알아들을 수 있는,

people understood, / so she was not surprised / when
그래서 그녀는 놀라지 않았다

Martha used words / she did not know.
마사가 단어를 사용했을 때 그녀가 알지 못하는.

Martha laughed / as she had done / the first morning.
마사가 웃었다 그녀가 그랬듯이 첫 날 아침에.

"There now," / she said. "I've talked broad Yorkshire
"이것 보세요." 그녀가 말했다. "요크셔 지방 사투리로 또 말해버렸네요

again / like Mrs. Medlock said I mustn't. 'Nowt o' th'
메들록 부인이 하면 안 된다고 했는데. '절대 글치 않슈'는 '절대로

soart' means 'nothin'-of-the-sort,'" / slowly and carefully,
그런 것이 아니다,'라는 뜻이에요." 천천히 또박또박 말하면,

/ "but it takes so long to say it. Yorkshire's th' sunniest
"그런데 말하는데 너무 오래 걸리잖아요. 요크셔는 세상에서 가장 화창한 곳이에요

place on earth / when it is sunny. I told thee / tha'd like
맑은 날에는. 말씀 드렸잖아요 황무지를 좋아하게

th' moor / after a bit. Just you wait / till you see th' gold-
될 거라고 조금 지나면. 조금만 기다리세요 황금빛 가시금작화를 볼 때까지

colored gorse blossoms / an' th' blossoms o' th' broom, /
양골담초 꽃이랑,

an' th' heather flowerin', / all purple bells, / an' hundreds
히스 꽃이랑, 보랏빛 종처럼 생긴, 수백 마리 나비들이 날아

o' butterflies flutterin' / an' bees hummin' / an' skylarks
다니고 꿀벌이 노래하며 종달새가 하늘 높이 날아

soarin' up / an' singin'. You'll want to get out on it / as
올라 노래하는 것을요. 그러면 나가고 싶어질 거예요 해가 뜨자

sunrise / an' live out on it / all day / like Dickon does."
마자 그리고 밖에서 살고 싶을 거예요 하루 종일 디콘처럼요."

"Could I ever get there?" / asked Mary wistfully, / looking
"내가 정말 거기 가 볼 수 있을까?" 메리가 생각에 잠겨 물었다.

---

dialects 방언, 사투리 | thee you의 고어체 | gorse 가시금작화 | flutter (날개를) 파닥거리다 | heavenly 천상의 | cottage 시골집, 오두막 | polishing 광을 내는 | rub 문지르다 | grate (난로 등의) 쇠살대

68　The Secret Garden

through her window / at the far-off blue. It was so new /
창 밖을 바라보며   저 멀리 펼쳐진 푸른 빛을.   그것은 너무나 새로웠고

and big and wonderful / and such a heavenly color.
넓고 멋졌으며   천상의 색과 같았다.

"I don't know," / answered Martha. "Tha's never used
"모르겠네요,"   마사가 대답했다.   "아가씨는 다리를 써 본 적이 없으

tha' legs / since tha' was born, / it seems to me. Tha'
니까요   태어날 때부터,   저한테는 그렇게 보이네요.

couldn't walk five mile. It's five mile to our cottage."
아가씨는 5마일도 못 걸을 거예요.   우리 오두막까지는 5마일이네요."

"I should like to see your cottage."
"너희 오두막집을 보고 싶어."

Martha stared at her / a moment curiously / before she
마사는 메리를 빤히 쳐다보다가   잠시 호기심 어린 눈으로

took up her polishing brush / and began to rub the grate
광내는 솔을 들고는   난로의 쇠살대를 문지르기 시작했다.

again. She was thinking / that the small plain face / did
그녀는 생각했다   작고 못생긴 얼굴이

not look quite as sour / at this moment / as it had done
그리 심술궂어 보이진 않는다고   지금 이 순간은   그랬던 것처럼

/ the first morning she saw it. It looked just a trifle like
처음 만났던 날 아침에.   그 얼굴은 약간 비슷해 보였다

little / Susan Ann's / when she wanted something very
동생인 수잔 앤과   뭔가를 엄청 원할 때의.

much.

Key Expression

비인칭 주어 it

글을 읽을 때 it이 나오면 습관적으로 '그것'이라고 해석하게 되는데요. it이 시간, 요일, 날짜, 날씨, 계절, 온도, 거리, 명암 등을 나타낼 때 이를 비인칭주어라고 부르며 이때의 it은 따로 해석하지 않습니다.

ex) It takes so long to say it 그것을 말하는 데 그렇게 오래 걸렸다 (시간)
　　 It is sunny. (날씨가) 맑다 (날씨)
　　 It's five mile to our cottage. 우리 오두막까지는 5마일이에요. (거리)
　　 It's my day out today. 오늘은 제 쉬는 날이에요. (날짜)

"I'll ask my mother about it," / she said. "She's one o' them / that nearly always sees a way / to do things. It's my day out today / an' I'm goin' home. Eh! I am glad. Mrs. Medlock thinks a lot o' mother. Perhaps she could talk to her."

"I like your mother," / said Mary.

"I should think tha' did," / agreed Martha, / polishing away.

"I've never seen her," / said Mary.

"No, tha' hasn't," / replied Martha.

She sat up on her heels again / and rubbed the end of her nose / with the back of her hand / as if puzzled for a moment, / but she ended quite positively.

"Well, / she's that sensible / an' hard workin' / an' good-natured / an' clean / that no one could help likin' her / whether they'd seen her or not. When I'm goin' home

---

day out 쉬는 날 | puzzle 어리둥절하다 | good-natured 착한 | crossing 건너다 | reflectively 생각에 잠겨

70　The Secret Garden

to her / on my day out / I just jump for joy / when I'm crossin' the moor."

"I like Dickon," / added Mary. "And I've never seen him."

"Well," / said Martha stoutly, / "I've told thee / that th' very birds likes him / an' th' rabbits an' wild sheep an' ponies, / an' th' foxes themselves. "I wonder," / staring at her reflectively, / "what Dickon would think of thee?"

"He wouldn't like me," / said Mary / in her stiff, cold little way. "No one does."

Martha looked reflective again.

"How does tha' like thysel'?" / she inquired, / really quite / as if she were curious to know.

Key Expression

whether ~ or not : ~이든 아니든

whether는 문장 끝에 or not을 동반하여 '~이든 아니든'이라는 의미의 부사절, 혹은 '~인지 아닌지'라는 의미의 명사절을 이끄는 접속사입니다.

ex) No one could help liking her whether they'd seen her or not.
그녀를 보았든 보지 않았든 간에 누구도 그녀를 좋아하지 않을 수 없었어요.

Mary hesitated a moment / and thought it over.
메리는 잠시 망설이다가 곰곰이 생각했다.

"Not at all — really," / she answered. "But I never
"전혀 — 정말로," 그녀가 대답했다. "하지만 한 번도 생각해 본 적

thought of that before."
이 없어."

Martha grinned a little / as if at some homely recollection.
마사는 살짝 미소지었다 집에서의 추억을 떠올리는 듯.

"Mother said that to me / once," / she said. "She was at
"엄마가 말했어요 예전에," 그녀가 말했다. "엄마는 빨래 중이었고

her wash-tub / an' I was in a bad temper / an' talkin' ill
  저는 화가 나서 사람들을 욕하고 있었는데,

of folk, / an' she turns round on me / an' says: / 'Tha'
  엄마가 저를 돌아보더니 말씀하셨어요: '이런 꼬마 심술

young vixen, tha'! There tha' stands sayin' / tha' doesn't
쟁이! 서서 말하는 것 봐 이 사람도 싫다

like this one / an' tha' doesn't like that one. How does tha'
저 사람도 싫다. 그러는 넌 어떤데?'

like thysel'?' It made me laugh / an' it brought me to my
  그 말에 웃음이 터져서 제정신이 들었죠

senses / in a minute."
  순식간에."

She went away in high spirits / as soon as she had given
그녀는 들뜬 기분으로 가버렸다 메리에게 주자 마자

Mary / her breakfast. She was going to walk five miles /
  아침 식사를. 그녀는 5마일을 걸을 것이었다

> ### Key Expression
>
> **~as well as… : …뿐만 아니라 A도**
>
> A as well as B는 '…뿐만 아니라 ~도'라는 의미로 뒤부터 해석하는 것에 유의하세요. 비슷한 뜻으로 not only~ but also… 구문이 있는데, 이때는 ~와 …의 위치가 반대가 됩니다.
>
> ex) The high, deep, blue sky arched over Missethwaite as well as over the moor.
> 높고 깊고 푸른 하늘이 황무지뿐 아니라 미셀스와이트에도 드리워졌다.

recollection 회상 | folk 사람 | vixen 심술궂은 여자 | bring someone to senses ~를 정신차리게 하다 |
thoroughly 완전히 | fountain 분수대 | of one's own accord 자진해서

across the moor to the cottage, / and she was going to help her mother / with the washing / and do the week's baking / and enjoy herself thoroughly.

Mary felt lonelier than ever / when she knew / she was no longer in the house. She went out into the garden / as quickly as possible, / and the first thing she did / was to run round and round / the fountain flower garden / ten times. She counted the times carefully / and when she had finished / she felt in better spirits. The sunshine made the whole place look different. The high, deep, blue sky arched / over Misselthwaite / as well as over the moor, / and she kept lifting her face / and looking up into it, / trying to imagine / what it would be like / to lie down on one of the little snow-white clouds / and float about. She went into the first kitchen-garden / and found Ben Weatherstaff working there / with two other gardeners. The change in the weather / seemed to have done him good. He spoke to her / of his own accord.

"Springtime's comin,'" / he said. "Cannot tha' smell it?"
"봄이 오고 있네요," 그가 말했다. "봄의 향기를 맡을 수 있지 않나요?"

Mary sniffed / and thought she could.
메리가 코를 킁킁대자 맡을 수 있는 것 같았다.

"I smell something / nice and fresh and damp," / she said.
"뭔가 냄새가 나네 향긋하고 신선하고 촉촉한," 그녀가 말했다.

"That's th' good rich earth," / he answered, / digging away.
"그게 기름진 땅의 냄새예요," 그가 대답했다, 땅을 파면서.

"It's in a good humor / makin' ready to grow things. It's
"땅이 기분이 좋은 거죠 키워 낼 준비를 하고 있는 게 . 기뻐하는

glad / when plantin' time comes. It's dull in th' winter /
거예요 씨뿌리는 때가 오니까. 따분한 겨울에는

when it's got nowt to do. In th' flower gardens out there /
할 일도 없으니까. 저쪽 꽃밭에는

things will be stirrin' down below in th' dark. Th' sun's
컴컴한 땅 밑에서 꿈틀거리고 있을 거예요. 햇빛이 따뜻하게 비추

warmin' 'em. You'll see bits o' green spikes / stickin' out o'
고 있으니까. 초록빛 새싹을 볼 수 있을 거예요 검은 흙을 뚫고 나오는

th' black earth / after a bit."
조금 있으면."

"What will they be?" / asked Mary.
"그 싹들이 자라서 뭐가 되는데?" 메리가 물었다.

"Crocuses an' snowdrops an' daffydowndillys. Has tha'
"크로커스랑 아네모네랑 수선화가 되지요.

never seen them?"
아가씨는 한 번도 본 적이 없나요?"

"No. Everything is hot, and wet, and green / after the rains
"없어. 온통 뜨겁고, 축축하고, 초록으로 무성해지니까 비가 내린 후

in India," / said Mary. "And I think things grow up / in a
인도에서는," 메리가 말했다. "그리고 자라버리지

night."
하룻밤 사이에."

sniff 냄새를 맡다 | damp 축축한 | stirring 꿈틀거리는 | spike 새싹 | stick out 튀어나오다 | crocuses 크로커스 (이른 봄에 작은 튤립 같은 꽃이 피는 식물) | snowdrops 스노드롭, 아네모네 | daffydowndilys (→daffodil) 수선화

"These won't grow up in a night," / said Weatherstaff.
"이것들은 하룻밤 사이에 자라지는 않을 거예요," 웨더스태프가 말했다.

"Tha'll have to wait for 'em. They'll poke up a bit higher
"기다려야 하지요. 이쪽에서 더 많이 돋아나나 싶으면,

here, / an' push out a spike more there, / an' uncurl a leaf
저쪽에서 쑤욱 올라오고, 하루는 잎이 활짝 펴지는가

this day / an' another that. You watch 'em."
하면 다음 날은 저쪽의 잎이 활짝 펴지고. 한 번 보세요."

"I am going to," / answered Mary.
"그럴게," 메리가 대답했다.

Very soon / she heard the soft rustling flight of wings /
곧 날개가 부드럽게 파닥거리는 소리를 들었다

again / and she knew at once / that the robin had come
또 다시 / 그리고 바로 알아챘다 그 붉은가슴울새가 다시 왔다는 것을.

again. He was very pert and lively, / and hopped about /
새는 매우 활기차고 생기가 넘쳐서, 깡총거렸다

so close to her feet, / and put his head on one side / and
메리의 발치까지 다가와서, 그리고 고개를 갸우뚱하며

looked at her so slyly / that she asked Ben Weatherstaff a
장난기 넘치는 표정으로 쳐다보았다 그녀는 벤 웨더스태프에게 한 가지 질문을 했다.

question.

"Do you think he remembers me?" / she said.
"이 새가 나를 기억한다고 생각해?" 그녀가 말했다.

> ### Key Expression
>
> **관계부사 where**
>
> 관계부사 where는 '전치사 + 관계대명사'의 의미로, 명사인 선행사를 수식하는 형용사절을 이끕니다. 선행사에는 장소를 나타내는 명사가 오며 '~하는 곳[명사]'이라고 해석합니다.
>
> ex) The one where the old rose-trees are.
>   (= in which)
>   오래된 장미나무들이 있는 곳이요.

"Remembers thee!" / said Weatherstaff indignantly. "He
"기억하다마다요!" 웨더스태프가 화가 난 듯 말했다.
knows every cabbage stump / in th' gardens, / let alone th'
"저 새는 모든 양배추를 알고 있지요 밭에 있는, 사람들은 말할 것도
people. He's never seen a little wench / here before, / an'
없죠. 자그마한 아가씨를 본 적이 없으니까 여기에서 전에는,
he's bent on findin' out / all about thee. Tha's no need to
알아내려고 애를 쓰고 있는 거예요 아가씨에 대해 모든 것을. 아무것도 숨기려 할 필요가
try to hide anything / from him."
없어요 저 놈한테서."
"Are things stirring down below / in the dark / in that
"뭔가 꿈틀거리고 있을까 어두운 땅 속에서 저 화원에도
garden / where he lives?" / Mary inquired.
새가 살고 있는?" 메리가 물었다.
"What garden?" / grunted Weatherstaff, / becoming surly
"무슨 화원이요?" 웨더스태프가 퉁명스레 말했다, 다시 무뚝뚝해져서는.
again.

"The one / where the old rose-trees are." She could not
"그곳 말야 오래된 장미 덩굴이 있는." 메리는 물어 보지 않을 수 없
help asking, / because she wanted so much to know. "Are
었다, 무척 알고 싶었기 때문에.
all the flowers dead, / or do some of them come again / in
"모든 꽃들이 다 죽은 걸까, 아니면 몇 가지는 다시 피어날까
the summer? Are there ever any roses?"
이번 여름에? 장미가 있기는 할까?"
"Ask him," / said Ben Weatherstaff, / hunching his
"저 새한테 물어 보세요," 벤 웨더스태프가 말했다, 붉은가슴울새 쪽으로 어깻짓을 하
shoulders toward the robin. "He's the only one / as knows.
면서. "저 새 밖에 없으니까 아는 건.
No one else has seen inside it / for ten year'."
아무도 그 안을 본 사람이 없으니 십 년 동안."

poke up 돋아나다, 위로 솟다 | pert 활기찬 | hop 깡총깡총 뛰다 | slyly 익살맞게 | indignantly 분개해서 |
stump 뿌리 | wench 계집아이 | bend on 마음과 노력을 기울이다 | grunt 툴툴거리다 | surly 퉁명스러운 |
hunching 활모양으로 구부리다

77

Ten years was a long time, / Mary thought. She had been
십 년이면 긴 세월이라고, 메리는 생각했다. 그녀가 십 년 전에 태

born ten years ago.
어났으니.

She walked away, / slowly thinking. She had begun to like
메리는 걸어갔다. 천천히 생각하며. 그녀는 화원이 좋아지기 시작했다

the garden / just as she had begun to like / the robin and
좋아지기 시작했던 것처럼 붉은가슴울새와 디콘과

Dickon and Martha's mother.
마사의 어머니가.

She was beginning to like Martha, too. That seemed a
그녀는 마사도 좋아지기 시작했다. 좋아할 사람들이 너무도

good many people to like / —— when you were not used
많은 것 같았다 — 좋아하는 일이 익숙하지 않았기에.

to liking. She thought of the robin / as one of the people.
그녀는 붉은가슴울새를 생각했다 좋아하는 사람들 가운데 하나라고.

She went to her walk outside / the long, ivy-covered wall
그녀는 산책을 나섰다 긴, 담쟁이덩굴 담장 밖으로

/ over which she could see the tree-tops; / and the second
그 너머로 나무 꼭대기를 볼 수 있는; 그리고 두 번째로

time / she walked up and down / the most interesting and
그 길을 왔다갔다 했을 때 정말 흥미롭고 신나는 일이

exciting thing / happened to her, / and it was all through /
그녀에게 일어났다. 그리고 전적으로

Ben Weatherstaff's robin.
벤 웨더스태프의 붉은가슴울새 덕분이었다.

She heard a chirp and a twitter, / and when she looked at
메리가 새가 지저귀고 짹짹거리는 소리를 듣고서, 황량한 꽃밭을 바라 보았을 때

the bare flower-bed / at her left side / there he was hopping
왼쪽 편에서 새가 깡충거리고 있었다

about / and pretending to peck things / out of the earth / to
쪼는 시늉을 하면서 무언가를 꺼내려고

persuade her / that he had not followed her. But she knew
그녀에게 주장하는 듯이 자신이 메리를 따라온 게 아니라고. 하지만 그녀는 알아챘다

/ he had followed her / and the surprise so filled her / with
새가 자신을 따라 왔음을 그리고 놀라움으로 가득 찼다

delight / that she almost trembled a little.
기쁨과 함께 몸이 살짝 떨릴 정도의.

"You do remember me!" / she cried out. "You do! You are
"정말 나를 기억하는구나!" 그녀가 소리쳤다. "그래 맞아!

prettier than anything else in the world!"
넌 이 세상에서 가장 예쁜 새야!"

She chirped, and talked, and coaxed / and he hopped, /
그녀는 재잘거리며, 말을 걸고, 달랬다 그리고 새는 깡충거리며,

and flirted his tail / and twittered. It was as if he were
꼬리를 흔들고 짹짹 울어댔다. 그것은 마치 새가 말을 하고 있는 듯 했다.

talking. His red waistcoat was like satin / and he puffed
새의 빨간 가슴은 공단 같았는데 그 작은 가슴을 부풀리자

his tiny breast out / and was so fine / and so grand / and
너무나 멋지고 환상적이고

so pretty / that it was really as if he were showing her /
예뻐 보여서 마치 정말로 그녀에게 보여 주는 듯했다

how important / and like a human person / a robin could
얼마나 중요한지 그리고 사람처럼 붉은가슴울새도 될 수 있는

be. Mistress Mary forgot / that she had ever been contrary
지를. 메리는 잊어버렸다 자신이 심술궂은 아이였다는 것을

/ in her life / when he allowed her to draw closer and
지금껏 살아오는 동안 새가 점점 더 가까이 다가오도록 했을 때,

closer to him, / and bend down and talk / and try to make
몸을 구부려서 말을 걸고, 붉은가슴울새와 같은 소리

something like robin sounds.
를 내면서.

Key Expression

be used to ~ing : ~ 하는데 익숙하다

be used to ~ing는 '~하는데 익숙하다'라는 뜻을 가진 숙어입니다. used 대신 accustomed를 써도 같은 의미가 됩니다. to 다음에 ~ing 형태의 동사가 온다는 점에 주의하세요.

ex) That seemed a good many people to like — when you were not used to liking.
좋아할 많은 사람들이 있는 듯 했다 — 좋아하는 데에 익숙하지 않을 때라도.

tree-tops 나무 꼭대기 | bare 황량한 | peck 쪼다 | coax 달래다 | flirt 쫑긋쫑긋 움직이다 | puff 부풀리다 |
draw closer 가까이 다가가다 | bend down 몸을 구부리다

Oh! To think / that he should actually let her come / as
아! 생각해 보면 정말은 새가 메리에게 허락한 것일 게다

near to him as that! He knew / nothing in the world /
자신에게 그렇게 다가오도록! 새는 알고 있었다 이 세상의 그 어떤 것도

would make her put out her hand toward him / or startle
그녀에게 손을 내밀라고 시킬 수 없으리란 것을 또는 조금도 자신

him in the least tiniest way. He knew it / because he was
을 놀라게 하지 않으리란 것을. 새는 알고 있었다 왜냐하면 정말 사람이었으

a real person / —— only nicer than / any other person / in
니까 — 착하기만 한 어느 누구보다도

the world. She was so happy / that she scarcely dared to
이 세상에서. 그녀는 너무 행복해서 숨을 쉴 수 없을 정도였다.

breathe.

The flower-bed was not quite bare. It was bare of flowers
꽃밭이 그렇게 휑한 것은 아니었다. 꽃이 없었던 것 뿐

/ because the perennial plants had been cut down / for
다년생살이 식물들이 베어져 있었기 때문에

their winter rest, / but there were tall shrubs and low ones
겨울 동안 휴식을 위해, 그러나 키 큰 덤불과 작은 덤불이 있었다

/ which grew together / at the back of the bed, / and as
함께 자라난 꽃밭 뒤쪽에는, 그리고 붉은가

the robin hopped about under them / she saw him hop /
슴울새가 덤불 아래에서 뛰어다니고 있을 때 메리는 새가 폴짝 뛰는 것을 보았다

over a small pile / of freshly turned up earth. He stopped
작은 흙더미 위에서 새로 갈아엎은. 새는 그 위에 멈춰

on it / to look for a worm. The earth had been turned up
섰다 벌레를 찾으려고. 그 흙더미는 갈아엎은 것이었다

/ because a dog had been trying to dig up a mole / and he
왜냐하면 개가 두더쥐 구멍을 파려고 해서

had scratched quite a deep hole.
꽤 깊숙한 구멍을 긁어냈기 때문에.

perennial plant 다년생/사철 식물 | shrub 덤불 | worm 벌레 | mole 두더지 | rusty 녹슨 | brass 동 | hung (hang의 과거분사) 걸려 있다

Mary looked at it, / not really knowing / why the hole was
there, / and as she looked / she saw something / almost
buried in the newly-turned soil. It was something / like
a ring of rusty iron or brass / and when the robin flew up
into a tree nearby / she put out her hand / and picked the
ring up. It was more than a ring, / however; / it was an old
key / which looked / as if it had been buried a long time.
Mistress Mary stood up / and looked at it / with an almost
frightened face / as it hung from her finger.
"Perhaps it has been buried / for ten years," / she said in a
whisper. "Perhaps it is the key to the garden!"

Key Expression

however : 그러나

however는 '그러나'라는 의미를 갖는 접속부사입니다. 이때 however는 문장의 앞이나 중간, 뒤 등 쓰이는 위치가 자유로우며 ,와 함께 쓰입니다.
특히 문장 중간에 ,를 앞뒤에 두고 삽입되는 경우에 해석을 하다가 갑자기 끊기게 되는 경우가 많은데요. 글을 읽다가 '~, however, ~'가 보이면 however를 문장 맨 앞에 놓고 '그러나~'로 해석해 보세요.

ex) It was more than a ring, however; it was an old key.
그러나, 그것은 고리 이상의 것으로 오래된 열쇠였다.

mini test 3

A. 다음 문장을 해석해 보세요.

(1) She was thinking / that the small plain face / did not look quite as sour / at this moment / as it had done / the first morning she saw.
→

(2) Mary felt lonelier than ever / when she knew / she was no longer in the house.
→

(3) It was really as if he were showing her / how important and like a human person / a robin could be.
→

(4) It was more than a ring, / however; / it was an old key / which looked / as if it had been buried a long time.
→

B. 다음 주어진 문구가 알맞은 문장이 되도록 순서를 맞춰 보세요.

(1) 절대로 메리는 하늘이 그렇게 푸르다고 상상한 적이 없었다.
(a sky / dreamed of / so / Mary / blue / had)
→

(2) 그것을 말하는 데에는 시간이 너무 오래 걸린다.
(to / so / say / takes / long / it / It)
→

(3) 너는 세상에서 그 어떤 것보다 더 예뻐.
(anything else / You / prettier / are / in the world / than)
→

A. (1) 그녀는 그 작고 평범한 얼굴이 처음 보았던 날 아침에 그랬던 것처럼 심술궂어 보이진 않는다고 생각했다. (2) 메리는 집 안에 그녀가 더 이상 없다는 걸 알게 되자 전보다 더 외로움을 느꼈다. (3) 그것은 정말로 그가 그녀에게 붉은가슴울새가 얼마나 중요하며 사람처럼 될 수 있는지를 보여 주려는 듯 했다. (4)

The Secret Garden

(4) 메리는 그 구멍이 왜 거기 있는지 정말 알지 못한 채 그것을 바라보았다.
(really / why / the hole / knowing / was / not / there)
→

C. 다음 주어진 문장이 본문의 내용과 맞으면 T, 틀리면 F에 동그라미 하세요.

(1) Mary began to like to play outside.
 (T / F)

(2) Martha thought that Mary was getting uglier and uglier.
 (T / F)

(3) In Yorkshire, it is always rainy or dark.
 (T / F)

(4) It was robin that help Mary to find the old key.
 (T / F)

D. 의미가 비슷한 것끼리 서로 연결해 보세요.

(1) blazing   ▶   ◀ ① smile
(2) puzzled   ▶   ◀ ② twitter
(3) grin   ▶   ◀ ③ burning
(4) chirp   ▶   ◀ ④ confused

Answer

그러나, 그것은 고리 이상의 것으로, 오랫동안 묻혀 있었던 것처럼 보이는 낡은 열쇠였다. | B. (1) Never had Mary dreamed of a sky so blue. (2) It takes so long to say it. (3) You are prettier than anything else in the world. (4) Mary looked at it, not really knowing why the hole was there. | C. (1) T (2) F (3) F (4) T | D. (1) ③ (2) ④ (3) ① (4) ②

5

THE ROBIN WHO SHOWED THE WAY
길을 보여 준 붉은가슴울새

She looked at the key / quite a long time. She turned
메리는 열쇠를 바라보았다 꽤 오랫동안. 열쇠를 몇 번이나

it over and over, / and thought about it. As I have said
뒤집어 보고, 그것에 대해 생각했다. 전에도 말했듯이,

before, / she was not a child / who had been trained to
 메리는 아이가 아니었다 허락을 청하도록 훈련을 받은

ask permission / or consult her elders about things. All
 또는 여러 가지 일에 대해 어른들과 상의하도록. 열쇠에

she thought about the key / was that if it was the key to
대해 그녀가 생각할 수 있는 모든 것은 그 열쇠가 비밀의 화원열쇠라면,

the closed garden, / and she could find out where the door
 그리고 그 문이 어디에 있는지 찾아낼 수 있다면,

was, / she could perhaps open it / and see what was inside
 아마도 그 문을 열 수 있고 담장 안에 뭐가 있는지 살펴볼 수 있으리

the walls, / and what had happened to the old rose-trees. It
라는 것이었다. 그리고 오래된 장미 덩굴들에게는 무슨 일이 일어났는지.

was because it had been shut up / so long / that she wanted
화원이 잠겨져 있었기 때문에 너무 오랫동안 그녀는 그것이 보고 싶었다.

to see it. It seemed / as if it must be different from other
 그것은 보였다 다른 곳들과 다를 것 같이

places / and that something strange must have happened
 그리고 이상한 일이 일어났을 것 같이

to it / during ten years. Besides that, / if she liked it / she
 십 년 동안. 그 외에도, 만일 그녀가 그곳을 좋아한다면

could go into it every day / and shut the door behind her, /
매일 그 안에 들어갈 수 있을 것이었다 그리고 문을 잠그고,

and she could make up some play of her own / and play it
자신만의 놀이를 만들어 혼자서 놀 수 있을

quite alone, / because nobody would ever know where she
것이었다. 아무도 그녀가 어디에 있는지 모를 것이기 때문에,

over and over 다시 또다시 (반복되는 동작을 나타냄) | permission 허락 | elders 원로들, 어른들, 나이 많은 사람들 | besides 외에도

was, / but would think / the door was still locked / and the
key buried in the earth. The thought / of that pleased her
very much.

Living as it were, / all by herself / in a house / with a
살고 있다고 해도, 그녀 혼자서 집에

hundred mysteriously closed rooms / and having nothing
신비하게 닫혀 있는 100개의 방이 있는 아무것도 할 것이 없는

whatever to do / to amuse herself, / had set her inactive
자신을 즐겁게 해 줄, 그녀의 잠자던 머리를 작동하게 했고

brain to working / and was actually awakening her
실제로 그녀의 상상력을 깨우고 있었다.

imagination. There is no doubt / that the fresh, strong, pure
의심의 여지가 없었다 신선하고, 강하고, 맑은 공기가

air / from the moor / had a great deal to do with it. Just as
황무지로부터의 이것과 깊은 관계가 있다는 것은.

it had given her an appetite, / and fighting with the wind /
그녀에게 식욕을 돋구게 해 준 것처럼, 그리고 바람과 싸우는 일이

had stirred her blood, / so the same things had stirred her
메리의 피를 요동치게 했듯이, 그와 똑같은 일들이 메리의 마음도 뒤흔들어 놓았다.

mind. In India / she had always been too hot / and languid
인도에서 메리는 늘 너무 더웠고 나른하고 약했다

and weak / to care much about anything, / but in this place
무언가에 관심을 갖기에는, 그러나 이곳에서

/ she was beginning / to care / and to want to do new
그녀는 시작했다 관심을 갖고 새로운 일을 하고 싶어 하기를.

things. Already she felt less "contrary," / though she did
이미 그녀는 덜 "심술쟁이"처럼 느껴졌다, 왜 그런지는 알지 못했지만.

not know why.

She put the key in her pocket / and walked up and down
그녀는 열쇠를 주머니에 넣고 길을 따라 왔다 갔다 했다.

her walk. No one but herself / ever seemed to come there, /
자기 말고는 아무도 그곳에 온 적이 없는 듯 했다.

so she could walk slowly / and look at the wall, / or, rather,
그래서 천천히 걸을 수 있었다 담장을 보면서, 아니, 그보다는,

---

inactive 활동하지 않는 | a great deal 아주 많은 양 | baffling 당황케 하는 | glossy 광택이 있는, 번들번들한 | pace 걷다 | get in 들어가다 | in the best of spirits 기분이 최고다

/ at the ivy growing on it. The ivy was the baffling thing.
그 위에 자라고 있는 담쟁이덩굴을 보면서. 담쟁이덩굴은 알쏭달쏭한 것이었다.

Howsoever carefully she looked / she could see nothing
아무리 주의 깊게 살펴보아도   아무것도 볼 수 없었다

/ but thickly growing, glossy, dark green leaves. She was
무성하게 자라난, 윤기 있고, 진독색을 띤 이파리밖에.   그녀는 아주 많이

very much disappointed. Something of her contrariness /
실망했다.   그녀의 심술궂은 마음이

came back to her / as she paced the walk / and looked over
다시 돌아왔다   길을 걸으며   올려다보니

it / at the tree-tops inside. It seemed so silly, / she said to
안에 있는 나무 꼭대기를.   너무 바보같다고,   혼잣말을 했다,

herself, / to be near it / and not be able to get in. She took
           그곳에 가까이 있으면서 들어가 볼 수 없다는 것이.

the key in her pocket / when she went back to the house, /
열쇠를 호주머니에 넣고   집에 돌아가면서,

and she made up her mind / that she would always carry
마음먹었다   언제나 들고 다녀야겠다고

it with her / when she went out, / so that if she ever should
             밖에 나올 때는,   만일 숨겨진 문을 발견하기라도 한다면

find the hidden door / she would be ready.
                       준비가 되어있도록.

Mrs. Medlock had allowed Martha to sleep / all night / at
메들록 부인은 마사가 잘 수 있도록 허락했다   하룻밤을

the cottage, / but she was back at her work / in the morning
오두막집에서,   그러나 그녀는 일터로 돌아왔다   아침에

/ with cheeks redder than ever / and in the best of spirits.
그 여느 때보다 볼이 발그레해져서는   최고의 기분으로.

Key Expression

형용사 + as + 주어 + 동사 : ~라고 하더라도

형용사 + as + 주어 + 동사는 '~라고 하더라도, ~했지만'라는 의미의 양보구문이에요. 형용사 자리에 부사, 명사, 동사원형이 들어가기도 해요. 이 구문은 뒤에 ,를 동반하며 문장 중간에 들어갈 때에는 앞뒤에 쉼표를 넣어 삽입구로 사용합니다.

ex) Living as it were, all by herself in a house with a hundred mysteriously closed rooms ~.
살아 있다고는 해도, 100개의 신비하게 닫겨진 방이 있는 집에서 홀로 ~.

"I got up at four o'clock," she said. "Eh! It was pretty on th' moor with th' birds gettin' up an' th' rabbits scamperin' about an' th' sun risin'. I didn't walk all th' way. A man gave me a ride in his cart an' I did enjoy myself."

She was full of stories of the delights of her day out. Her mother had been glad to see her and they had got the baking and washing all out of the way. She had even made each of the children a doughcake with a bit of brown sugar in it.

"I had 'em all pipin' hot when they came in from playin' on th' moor. An' th' cottage all smelt o' nice, clean hot bakin' an' there was a good fire, an' they just shouted for joy. Our Dickon he said our cottage was good enough for a king."

In the evening they had all sat round the fire, and Martha and her mother had sewed patches on torn clothes and mended stockings and Martha had told them about the

little girl / who had come from India / and who had been
인도에서 왔고 시중을 받아온
waited on / all her life / by what Martha called "blacks" /
평생동안 마사가 "검둥이"라고 부르는 사람들에 의해
until she didn't know / how to put on her own stockings.
모를 정도로 자기 양말을 신는 법도.
"Eh! They did like to hear / about you," / said Martha.
"세상에! 아이들은 정말로 듣고 싶어 했지요 아가씨에 대해서," 마사가 말했다.
"They wanted to know / all about th' blacks / an' about th'
"이들은 알고 싶어 했어요 검둥이에 대한 모든 것을 그리고 배에 대해서
ship / you came in. I couldn't tell 'em enough."
아가씨가 타고 온. 충분히 얘기해 줄 수가 없었지만요."
Mary reflected a little.
메리는 잠시 생각에 잠겼다.
"I'll tell you a great deal more / before your next day out,"
"한참 더 많이 얘기해 줄게 다음 쉬는 날이 오기 전에,"
she said, "so that you will have more / to talk about. I dare
그녀가 말했다, "네가 더 많이 가질 수 있도록 이야기 할 거리가. 분명히
say / they would like to hear / about riding on elephants
그들은 듣고 싶어 할 거야 코끼리와 낙타 타는 것에 대해,
and camels, / and about the officers / going to hunt tigers."
장교들에 대해 호랑이 사냥을 하러 다니는."
"My word!" / cried delighted Martha. "It would set 'em
"세상에!" 마사는 기뻐서 소리쳤다. "그렇게 하면 애들 정신을 쏙 빼
clean off their heads. Would tha' really do that, / Miss? It
놓을 거예요. 정말 그래 주시겠시요, 아가씨?
would be same / as a wild beast show / like we heard they
같겠네요 야생 동물쇼랑 한 번 열렸다고 들은
had / in York once."
요크셔에서."

get (sth) out of the way ~을 방해가 안 되는 곳에 치우다 | brown sugar 흑설탕 | patch 헝겊 조각 | stockings 양말 | reflect 비춰지다, 반사되다, 심사숙고 하다

"India is quite different from Yorkshire," / Mary said slowly, / as she thought the matter over. "I never thought of that. Did Dickon and your mother like to hear you / talk about me?"

"Why, / our Dickon's eyes nearly started out o' his head, / they got that round," / answered Martha. "But mother, / she was put out / about your seemin' to be all by yourself like. She said, / 'Hasn't Mr. Craven got no governess for her, / nor no nurse?' / and I said, / 'No, / he hasn't, / though Mrs. Medlock says he will / when he thinks of it, / but she says / he mayn't think of it / for two or three years.'"

Key Expression

양보의 접속사 though

though는 '~이지만, ~일지라도'라는 의미를 가진 양보의 부사절을 이끄는 접속사입니다. though 대신 although를 쓰기도 하죠.
비슷한 의미를 가진 전치사로 '~에도 불구하고'라는 의미의 in spite of(despite)가 있어요.

ex) Though Mrs. Medlock says he will when he thinks of it, ~.
메들록 부인은 그가 그것에 대해 생각하면 그렇게 할 거라고 하지만, ~.

"I don't want a governess," / said Mary sharply.
"나는 가정교사를 두고 싶지 않아," 메리는 날카롭게 말했다.

"But mother says / you ought to be learnin' your book
"하지만 어머니가 말했지요 아가씨는 공부를 해야 한다고

/ by this time / an' you ought to have a woman / to look
지금쯤이면 그리고 여자가 있어야 한다고

after you, / an' she says: / 'Now, Martha, / you just think
아가씨를 돌봐줄, 그리고 어머니가 말했지요: '자, 마사야, 너도 생각해 보렴

/ how you'd feel yourself, / in a big place like that, /
어떻게 느낄지, 그렇게 넓은 집에서,

wanderin' about all alone, / an' no mother. You do your
홀로 돌아다니며, 엄마도 없이. 너는 최선을 다하거라

best / to cheer her up,' / she says, / an' I said I would."
아가씨가 힘을 낼 수 있게.' 어머니가 말했지요. 그래서 제가 그럴 거라고 말했어요."

Mary gave her a long, steady look.
메리는 그녀를 오랫동안 응시했다.

"You do cheer me up," / she said. "I like to hear you
"넌 정말로 내게 힘을 주고 있어," 그녀는 말했다. "나는 네 이야기를 듣는 것이 좋아."

talk."

Presently Martha went out of the room / and came back
이내 마사는 방을 나갔다가

with something held in her hands / under her apron.
손에 무언가를 들고 돌아왔다 앞치마 속에.

"What does tha' think," / she said, / with a cheerful grin.
"뭐라고 생각하세요," 그녀는 말했다, 활기찬 미소를 띠며.

"I've brought thee a present."
"아가씨한테 선물을 가져왔어요."

"A present!" / exclaimed Mistress Mary. How could a
"선물이라고!" 메리가 소리쳤다. 어떻게 오두막집에서

cottage / full of fourteen hungry people / give any one a
열 네 명의 배고픈 사람들로 가득한 그 누구에게 선물을 줄 수

present!
있단 말인가!

put out 화가 나다, 잠잠케 하다, 폐를 끼치다 | look after 돌보다 | apron 앞치마

"A man was drivin' across the moor peddlin'," / Martha
"한 장사꾼이 황무지를 지나가고 있었어요," 마사가 설명했다.

explained. "An' he stopped his cart / at our door. He had
"그가 마차를 세웠어요 우리 집 문 앞에. 그에게는 냄비

pots an' pans an' odds an' ends, / but mother had no
랑 프라이팬이랑 이런 저런 것들이 있었는데요, 어머니는 돈이 없었어요

money / to buy anythin'. Just as he was goin' away / our
뭔가를 사기엔. 그가 가려구 했는데

'Lizabeth Ellen called out, / 'Mother, / he's got skippin'-
우리 엘리자베스 엘렌이 소리쳤어요, '어머니, 아저씨가 줄넘기를 가지고 있어요

ropes / with red an' blue handles.' An' mother she calls
빨간색과 파란색 손잡이가 달린.' 그리고 어머니는 갑자기 소리쳤어요,

out quite sudden, / 'Here, / stop, / mister! How much are
'여기요, 멈춰 보세요, 아저씨! 이것이 얼마지요?'

they?' An' he says / 'Tuppence', / an' mother she began
그리고 아저씨가 말했어요 '2펜스구먼요,' 어머니는 주머니를 뒤지기 시작했어요

fumblin' in her pocket / an' she says to me, / 'Martha,
그리고 저한테 말했어요, '마사야, 네가 월급을

tha's brought me thy wages / like a good lass, / an' I've
나한테 가져왔지 착한 아이답게, 그리고 나는 네 군

got four places / to put every penny, / but I'm just goin' to
데가 있다 1펜스씩 넣어야 할, 하지만 2펜스를 꺼내야겠구나

take tuppence out of it / to buy that child a skippin'-rope,'
그 아이에게 줄넘기를 사 주기 위해,'

/ an' she bought one / an' here it is."
그리고 어머니는 샀어요 그리고 여기 그게 있지요."

She brought it out / from under her apron / and exhibited it
마사는 그것을 꺼냈다 앞치마 아래에서 그리고 아주 자랑스레 그

quite proudly. It was a strong, slender rope / with a striped
것을 보여 줬다. 튼튼하고, 가느다란 줄이었다 빨간색과 파란색 줄무

red and blue handle / at each end, / but Mary Lennox had
늬가 있는 양 끝에, 하지만 메리 레녹스는 한 번도 본 적이

never seen / a skipping-rope before. She gazed at it / with
없다 지금껏 줄넘기를. 그녀는 그것을 눈여겨 보았다

---

peddlin' (→peddling) 행상하는, 시시한 | skipping-rope 줄넘기 줄 | tuppence (→two pence) 2펜스 | fumble 더듬다 | wage 급여 | slender 날씬한, 호리호리한 | striped 줄무늬의 | gaze at 지켜보다, 응시하다

The Secret Garden

a mystified expression.
어리둥절한 표정으로.

"What is it for?" / she asked curiously.
"이건 무엇을 위한 거지?" 그녀가 호기심을 갖고 물었다.

"For!" / cried out Martha. "Does tha' mean / that they've
"무엇을 위한 거냐구요!" 마사가 소리쳤다. "그 말은

not got skippin'-ropes / in India, / for all they've got /
줄넘기가 없다는 거네요 인도에는, 가지고 있으면서도

elephants and tigers and camels! No wonder / most of
코끼리랑 호랑이랑 낙타는! 당연하네요 그들의 대부분이

'em's black. This is what it's for; / just watch me."
검둥이인 것이. 이게 뭘 위한 거냐 하면요; 그저 저를 보세요."

And she ran into the middle of the room / and, / taking
그리고 마사는 방 한가운데로 달려갔다 그리고,

a handle in each hand, / began to skip, and skip, and
양손에 각각 손잡이를 하나씩 잡고, 깡충, 깡충, 깡충, 뛰기 시작했다,

skip, / while Mary turned in her chair / to stare at her, /
메리가 의자에서 돌아앉았다 그녀를 지켜보려고,

and the queer faces in the old portraits / seemed to stare
그리고 오래된 초상화 속의 괴상한 얼굴들도 그녀를 쳐다보는 것 같았다,

at her, too, / and wonder / what on earth / this common
그리고 궁금해하는 듯했다 도대체 이렇게 천한 오두막집 딸이

little cottager / had the impudence to be doing / under
뻔뻔스럽게 무엇을 하고 있는지

their very noses. But Martha did not even see them. The
자기들 코 앞에서. 그러나 마사는 쳐다보지도 않았다.

interest and curiosity in Mistress Mary's face / delighted
메리 아가씨의 얼굴의 흥미와 호기심이 그녀를 기쁘게 했다,

her, / and she went on skipping / and counted as she
그래서 계속해서 뛰었다 그리고 뛰면서 수를 세었다

skipped / until she had reached a hundred.
백 번을 뛸 때까지.

mystify 어리둥절하게 하다 | skip 깡충깡충 뛰다, 건너다 | common 천한

"I could skip longer than that," / she said when she stopped. "I've skipped as much as five hundred / when I was twelve, / but I wasn't as fat then / as I am now, / an' I was in practice." Mary got up from her chair / beginning to feel excited herself.

"It looks nice," / she said. "Your mother is a kind woman. Do you think / I could ever skip like that?"

"You just try it," / urged Martha, / handing her the skipping-rope. "You can't skip a hundred at first, / but if you practice / you'll mount up. That's what mother said. She says, / 'Nothin' will do her more good / than skippin' rope. It's th' sensiblest toy / a child can have. Let her play out / in th' fresh air skippin' / an' it'll stretch her legs an' arms / an' give her some strength in 'em.'"

It was plain / that there was not a great deal of strength / in Mistress Mary's arms and legs / when she first began to skip. She was not very clever at it, / but she liked it so much / that she did not want to stop.

"Put on tha' things / and run an' skip out o' doors," / said Martha. "Mother said / I must tell you / to keep out o' doors / as much as you could, / even when it rains a bit, / so as tha' wrap up warm."

Mary put on her coat and hat / and took her skipping-rope over her arm. She opened the door to go out, / and then suddenly thought of something / and turned back rather slowly.

"Martha," / she said, / "they were your wages. It was your two-pence really. Thank you." She said it stiffly / because she was not used to / thanking people / or noticing that they did things for her. "Thank you," / she said, / and held out her hand / because she did not know / what else to do.

Key Expression

as much as you could : 가능한 한 많이

as ~(형용사/부사) as + 주어 + can는 '가능한 ~하게'라는 의미를 가진 구문으로 주어 + can 대신에 간단하게 possible를 써도 됩니다.

ex) Mother said I must tell you to keep out of doors as much as you could.
엄마가 말하기를 네게 가능한 한 많이 밖에 있으라고 말해야 한대.

---

in practice 숙련하고 있다 | urge 재촉하다, 충고하다 | mount up 늘어나다, 증가하다, 등단하다 | stretch one's legs 다리의 근육을 당기다 (stretch the body 기지개를 켜다) | clever 영리한 | wrap up 둘둘 싸매다 | notice 알아채다

Martha gave her hand / a clumsy little shake, / as if she
was not accustomed / to this sort of thing either. Then she
laughed.

"Eh! Th' art a queer, old-womanish thing," / she said. "If
tha'd been our 'Lizabeth Ellen / tha'd have given me a
kiss."

Mary looked stiffer than ever.

"Do you want me to kiss you?"

Martha laughed again.

"Nay, / not me," / she answered. "If tha' was different, /
p'raps tha'd want to thysel'. But tha' isn't. Run off outside
/ an' play with thy rope."

Mistress Mary felt a little awkward / as she went out of
the room. Yorkshire people seemed strange, / and Martha
was always rather a puzzle to her. At first / she had
disliked her very much, / but now she did not.

---

clumsy 서툰 | accustomed 익숙한 | awkward 어색하다 | gust 갑자기 센 바람 | upon one's word 맹세코, 꼭 | buttermilk 버터밀크 (버터를 만들고 남은 밀크)

The skipping-rope was a wonderful thing. She counted and skipped, and skipped and counted, until her cheeks were quite red, and she was more interested than she had ever been since she was born. The sun was shining and a little wind was blowing —— not a rough wind, but one which came in delightful little gusts and brought a fresh scent of newly turned earth with it. She skipped round the fountain garden, and up one walk and down another. She skipped at last into the kitchen-garden and saw Ben Weatherstaff digging and talking to his robin, which was hopping about him. She skipped down the walk toward him and he lifted his head and looked at her with a curious expression. She had wondered if he would notice her. She wanted him to see her skip.

"Well!" he exclaimed. "Upon my word. P'raps tha' art a young 'un, after all, an' p'raps tha's got child's blood in thy veins instead of sour buttermilk. Tha's skipped red into thy cheeks as sure as my name's Ben Weatherstaff. I wouldn't have believed tha' could do it."

97

"I never skipped before," / Mary said. "I'm just beginning. I can only go up to twenty."

"Tha' keep on," / said Ben. "Tha' shapes well enough at it / for a young 'un / that's lived with heathen. Just see / how he's watchin' thee," / jerking his head toward the robin. "He followed after thee yesterday. He'll be at it again / today. He'll be bound to find out / what th' skippin'-rope is. He's never seen one. Eh!" shaking his head at the bird, / "tha' curiosity will be th' death of thee sometime / if tha' doesn't look sharp."

Mary skipped round / all the gardens / and round the orchard, / resting every few minutes. At length / she went to her own special walk / and made up her mind / to try / if she could skip the whole length of it. It was a good long skip / and she began slowly, / but before she had gone halfway down the path / she was so hot and breathless / that she was obliged to stop. She did not mind much, / because

---

jerking 홱 움직이는 | be obliged to ~ 하지 않으면 안 되다 | lo and behold 어찌된 영문인지, 이것 보시라

she had already counted up to thirty. She stopped / with
이미 서른 번까지 세었기 때문에.   그녀는 멈췄다

a little laugh of pleasure, / and there, / lo and behold, /
작은 기쁨의 웃음을 터뜨리며,   그리고 거기에,   어찌된 영문인지,

was the robin swaying / on a long branch of ivy. He had
붉은가슴울새가 흔들거리고 있었다   긴 담쟁이덩굴 줄기 위에.   새는 그녀를 쫓

followed her / and he greeted her / with a chirp. As Mary
아왔던 것이다   그리고 그녀에게 인사를 했다   짹짹거리면서.   메리가 새를 향

had skipped toward him / she felt something heavy in her
해 줄넘기를 넘으며 나아갔을 때   그녀는 주머니 속에 무언가 묵직한 것을 느꼈다

pocket / strike against her at each jump, / and when she
매번 뛸 때마다 그녀에게 부딪히는 것을,   그리고 붉은가슴울새를 보

saw the robin / she laughed again.
았을 때   그녀는 다시 한 번 웃었다.

"You showed me / where the key was / yesterday," / she
"네가 내게 보여 줬지   열쇠가 어디 있는지   어제,"

said."
그녀는 말했다.

"You ought to show / me the door / today; / but I don't
"보여 줘야 해   내게 그 문을   오늘은;   하지만 생각하진 않아

believe / you know!"
네가 알고 있을 거라고는!"

Key Expression

so~that… : 너무 ~해서 …하다

so + 형용사/부사 + that…는 '너무 ~해서 …하다'라는 의미로 결과를 나타내는 구문이에요. so 대신 much를 사용기도 하며, ~ 자리에 형용사나 부사가 아닌 명사를 넣을 경우에는 so 대신 such + (a)를 사용합니다.

ex) She was so hot and breathless that she was obliged to stop.
그녀는 너무 덥고 숨이 차서 멈출 수밖에 없었다.

The robin flew / from his swinging spray of ivy / on to
the top of the wall / and he opened his beak / and sang
a loud, lovely trill, / merely to show off. Nothing in the
world / is quite as adorably lovely as a robin / when he
shows off / —— and they are nearly always doing it.
Mary Lennox had heard a great deal / about Magic /
in her Ayah's stories, / and she always said / that what
happened almost at that moment / was Magic.
One of the nice little gusts of wind / rushed down the
walk, / and it was a stronger one / than the rest. It was
strong enough / to wave the branches of the trees, / and
it was more than strong / enough to sway / the trailing
sprays of untrimmed ivy / hanging from the wall. Mary
had stepped close to the robin, / and suddenly / the
gust of wind swung aside / some loose ivy trails, / and
more suddenly still / she jumped toward it / and caught
it in her hand. This she did / because she had seen /

something under it / —— a round knob / which had been
그 아래 무언가를   — 동그란 손잡이를   나뭇잎들에 가려진 채
covered by the leaves / hanging over it. It was the knob
                        그 위에 매달려 있는.   문의 손잡이였다.
of a door.

She put her hands under the leaves / and began to pull /
그녀는 손을 나뭇잎들 밑으로 집어 넣어   당기기 시작했다
and push them aside. Thick as the ivy hung, / it nearly
그리고 옆으로 밀어냈다.   담쟁이덩굴이 무성하게 들어져 있었지만,
all was a loose / and swinging curtain, / though some
거의 모든 덩굴이 느슨하고   흔들거리는 커튼 같았다,   몇몇은 뻗어 있었지만
had crept / over wood and iron. Mary's heart began to
                나무와 철 위에.   메리의 가슴은 두근거리기 시작했다
thump / and her hands to shake a little / in her delight
        그리고 손은 약간 떨리기 시작했다   기쁨과 흥분으로 인해.
and excitement. The robin kept singing / and twittering
                  붉은가슴울새는 계속해서 노래하고   지저귀었다
away / and tilting his head on one side, / as if he were
        고개를 한쪽으로 갸우뚱거리면서,
as excited as she was. What was this / under her hands
그녀만큼 신이 났다는 듯이.   이것은 무엇이었을까   그녀의 손 밑에 있는
/ which was square / and made of iron / and which her
  네모지고   철로 만들어지고   그녀의 손가락이 찾아낸 구
fingers found a hole in?
멍이 달려 있는?

---

swing (전후, 좌우로) 흔들리다 | spray 줄기 | untrimmed 다듬지 않은 | loose 축 늘어진 | knob (문의) 손잡이, 꼭지 | thump (주먹으로) 치다, 두드리다, 쿵쾅거리다 | tilt 기울이다

It was the lock of the door / which had been closed ten
그것은 문의 자물쇠였다   십 년 동안 잠겨 있던

years / and she put her hand in her pocket, / drew out the
            그리고 그녀는 손을 주머니에 집어 넣어,   열쇠를 꺼내서

key / and found it fitted the keyhole. She put the key in /
        열쇠구멍에 딱 맞아 들어가는 것을 발견했다.   그녀는 열쇠를 넣어서

and turned it. It took two hands to do it, / but it did turn.
돌렸다.   그 일에는 두 손이 필요했다,   하지만 정말로 돌아갔다.

And then / she took a long breath / and looked behind her
그리고나서   그녀는 깊은 숨을 들이마시고   뒤를 돌아다 보았다

/ up the long walk / to see if any one was coming. No one
   긴 산책로 끝을   누가 오고 있는지 보기 위해.   아무도 오고

was coming. No one ever did come, / it seemed, / and she
있지 않았다.   아무도 온 적이 없었다,   그렇게 보였다,   그리고 그녀는

took another long breath, / because she could not help it,
다시 한 번 깊은 숨을 들이마셨다,   그럴 수밖에 없었기 때문에,

/ and she held back / the swinging curtain of ivy / and
     그리고 잡아서 들었다   흔들거리는 담쟁이덩굴 커튼을

pushed back the door / which opened slowly — slowly.
그리고 문을 밀었다   천천히 열렸다 — 천천히.

Then she slipped through it, / and shut it behind her, / and
그리고는 그녀는 그 사이로 살그머니 들어가서,   문을 닫고,

stood / with her back against it, / looking about her / and
서 있었다   문에 등을 기댄 채,   주위를 살펴보면서

breathing quite fast / with excitement, and wonder, and
그리고 아주 가쁜 숨을 쉬었다   흥분과, 경이로움과, 기쁨으로.

delight.

She was standing / inside the secret garden.
그녀는 서 있었다   비밀의 화원 안에.

can not help it 어쩔 수 없다

mini test 4

A. 다음 문장을 해석해 보세요.

(1) All she thought about the key / was that if it was the key to the closed garden, / and she could find out where the door was, / she could perhaps open it.
→

(2) It was / because it had been shut up so long / that she wanted to see it.
→

(3) There is no doubt / that the fresh, strong, pure air / from the moor / had a great deal to do with it.
→

(4) It was plain / that there was not a great deal of strength / in Mistress Mary's arms and legs / when she first began to skip.
→

B. 다음 주어진 문장이 되도록 빈칸에 써 넣으세요.

(1) 그녀 자신 외에는 누구도 그 곳에 들어간 적이 없는 것 같았다.
_____ ever seemed to come there.

(2) 아무리 주의 깊게 보아도 그녀는 굵게 자란 반짝이는 진 녹색의 잎사귀들밖에는 볼 수 없었다.
_____ she could see nothing but thickly growing, glossy, dark green leaves.

(3) 네게 가능한 한 많이 야외에 머무르라고 말해야겠어.
I must tell you to keep out of doors _____ .

(4) 그녀는 너무 덥고 숨이 차서 멈출 수밖에 없었다.
She was _____ she was obliged to stop.

A. (1) 그 열쇠에 대해 그녀가 생각했던 전부는 만약 그것이 닫힌 정원의 열쇠이고 그녀가 문이 어디있는지 찾을 수 있다면, 아마도 그 문을 열 수 있으리라 것이었다. (2) 그건 왜냐하면 그것이 그렇게 오랫동안 닫혀있었고 그녀가 보기를 원하기 때문이었다. (3) 의심할 여지가 없이 황무지로부터의 신선하고 강하고 깨

The Secret Garden

C. 다음 주어진 문구가 알맞은 문장이 되도록 순서를 맞춰 보세요.

(1) 나는 당신이 말하는 것을 듣고 싶어요.
   (to / talk / hear / I / like / you)
   →

(2) 그게 엄마가 말씀하신 거야.
   (mother / what / That's / said)
   →

(3) 어제 너는 내게 열쇠가 어딨는지 보여 줬지.
   (where / me / showed / was / the key / You)
   →

(4) 그것은 나뭇가지를 흔들 만큼 강했다.
   (to wave / the branches / strong / It was / enough / of / the trees)
   →

D. 의미가 서로 비슷한 것끼리 연결해 보세요.

(1) languid   ▶   ◀ ① not relaxed or comfortable
(2) impudence   ▶   ◀ ② a sudden strong wind
(3) awkward   ▶   ◀ ③ very slow and with little energy
(4) gusts   ▶   ◀ ④ rude to other people

꿋꿋한 공기가 많은 관계가 있다. (4) 처음 줄넘기를 시작했을 때에는 메리의 팔 다리에 그리 힘이 없었다는 사실은 명백했다. | B. (1) No one but herself (2) However carefully she looked (3) as much as you could (4) so hot and breathless that | C. (1) I like to hear you talk. (2) That's what mother said. (3) You showed me where the key was yesterday. (4) It was strong enough to wave the branches of the trees. | D. (1) ③ (2) ④ (3) ① (4) ②

6

DICKON
디콘

The sun shone down / for nearly a week / on the secret garden. The Secret Garden was / what Mary called it / when she was thinking of it. She liked the name, / and she liked still more the feeling / that when its beautiful old walls shut her in / no one knew / where she was. It seemed almost like / being shut out of the world / in some fairy place. The few books / she had read and liked / had been fairy-story books, / and she had read / of secret gardens / in some of the stories. Sometimes / people went to sleep in them / for a hundred years, / which she had thought / must be rather stupid. She had no intention of going to sleep, / and, in fact, / she was becoming wider awake every day / which passed at Misselthwaite. She was beginning to like / to be out of doors; / she no longer hated the wind, / but enjoyed it. She could run / faster, / and longer, / and she could skip up to a

---

fairy 요정, 요정의, 상상의 | rather 꽤, 약간, 상당히 | intention 의도, 작정 | awake 깨어 있는

hundred. The bulbs in the secret garden / must have been
비밀의 화원의 구근들은   많이 놀랐을 것이다.

much astonished. Such nice clear places / were made round
          그렇게 좋은 깨끗한 곳들이   주위에 만들어져서

them / that they had all the breathing space / they wanted,
     구근들은 실컷 숨쉴 수 있는 공간을 가질 수 있었다   그들이 원했던,

/ and really, / if Mistress Mary had known it, / they began /
  그리고 정말로, 메리가 그 사실을 알았다면,   그것들은 기운을 내

to cheer up / under the dark earth / and work tremendously.
기 시작했을 것이다 어두운 땅 아래서   활발하게 움직이기 시작했을 것이다.

The sun could get at them / and warm them, / and when
햇빛이 그것들에 닿아서   따뜻하게 데워 주었다,

the rain came down / it could reach them at once, / so they
그리고 비가 왔을 때도   바로 그것들에게 닿을 수 있었다,   그래서 구근

began to feel / very much alive.
들은 느끼기 시작했다 정말로 살아있음을.

Key Expression

must have p.p : ~ 했음에 틀림없다

must는 의무(~해야 한다)와 강한 추측(~임에 틀림없다)의 두 가지 뜻을 가진 조동사입니다.
의무의 must인 경우 과거형으로는 비슷한 뜻을 가진 동사 had to를 사용하는 것이 보편적입니다. 반면에 과거에 대한 강한 추측을 나타낼 경우에는 must have p.p를 사용하며 '~했음에 틀림없다'라고 해석합니다.
must보다 약한 추측을 나타내는 조동사 may와 might의 경우도 같은 방법으로 과거를 표현하는데요. may have p.p는 '~였을 것 같다', might have p.p는 '~였을지도 모른다'의 뜻을 가집니다.

ex) The bulbs in the secret garden must have been much astonished.
비밀의 화원 안에 있는 구근들도 많이 놀랐음에 틀림없다.

bulb 구근, 알뿌리 | astonished 놀란 | cheer up 기운을 차리다 | tremendously 엄청나게 | alive 살아있는

Mary was an odd, determined little person, / and now
메리는 별나고, 단호한 성격의 아이였는데,

she had something interesting / to be determined about, /
이제 그녀에게는 재미있는 일이 있었다   결정해야 할,

she was very much absorbed, / indeed. She worked / and
그녀는 폭 빠졌다,   정말로.   그녀는 일했다   땅을 파고

dug and pulled up weeds steadily, / only becoming more
구준히 잡초를 뽑으며,   즐겁기만 했다

pleased / with her work every hour / instead of tiring of it.
    매 시간 자신의 일이   지겨워지기보다.

It seemed to her like / a fascinating sort of play. She found
그것은 그녀에게 마치 ~같았다   매력적인 놀이인 것.   그녀는 발견했다

/ many more of the sprouting pale green points / than she
더 많이 삐죽 솟은 연두빛 싹들을

had ever hoped to find. They seemed to be starting up /
찾기 바랐던 것보다.   그것들은 움트는 것 같았다

everywhere and each day / she was sure / she found tiny
어디에서나 매일   그녀가 확신했기에   자신이 작고 새로운 싹을

new ones, / some so tiny / that they barely peeped / above
발견했다고,   어떤 것들은 너무 작아서   겨우 볼 수 있었지만   땅 위로

the earth. There were so many / that she remembered
올라온 것을.   정말 많았다   기억하고 있는 것들이

/ what Martha had said / about the "snowdrops by the
마사가 말했던 것들   "수천 개의 아네모네"에 대해,

thousands," / and about bulbs / spreading and making
    그리고 구근들에 대해   퍼져서 새로운 싹을 틔워 내는.

new ones. These had been left to themselves / for ten
    이것들은 홀로 남겨졌다   10년 동안

years / and perhaps they had spread, / like the snowdrops,
    그리고 아마 퍼졌을 것이다,   아네모네처럼,

/ into thousands. She wondered / how long it would be /
수천 개로.   그녀는 궁금했다   얼마나 오랫동안 그것들이 있었는지

before they showed / that they were flowers. Sometimes
보여 주기 전까지   자신들이 꽃이라는 사실을.   때때로

determined 단호한 | absorb 빠져들다 | weed 잡초 | instead of ~대신에 | fascinating 흥미로운, 매력적인 | sprout 싹트다 | peep 고개를 내밀고 보다 | snowdrop 아네모네 | bloom 꽃, 개화기 | intimate 친밀한 | spring 솟아오르다 | flatter 알랑거리다, 아첨하다 | evident 명백한 | civil 정중한, 예의 바른 | salaam 살람(이슬람교도의 인사말), 이마에 손바닥을 대고 절하다

/ she stopped digging / to look at the garden / and try to imagine / what it would be like / when it was covered / with thousands of lovely things / in bloom.

During that week of sunshine, / she became more intimate / with Ben Weatherstaff. She surprised him / several times / by seeming to start up / beside him / as if she sprang out of the earth. The truth / was that she was afraid / that he would pick up his tools / and go away / if he saw her coming, / so she always walked toward him / as silently as possible. But, in fact, / he did not object to her / as strongly as he had at first. Perhaps / he was secretly rather flattered / by her evident desire / for his elderly company. Then, also, / she was more civil / than she had been. He did not know / that when she first saw him / she spoke to him / as she would have spoken to a native, / and had not known / that a cross, sturdy old Yorkshire man / was not accustomed / to salaam to his masters, / and be merely commanded / by them / to do things.

"Tha'rt like th' robin," / he said to her / one morning / when
"아가씨는 그 붉은가슴울새 같네요." 그가 그녀에게 말했다 어느 날 아침

he lifted his head / and saw her standing by him. "I never
고개를 들었을 때 옆에 서 있는 그녀를 보고는. "저는 모르겠어요

knows / when I shall see thee / or which side tha'll come
언제 아가씨를 보게 될 지 어느 쪽에서 아가씨가 올 지."

from."

"He's friends with me now," / said Mary.
"그 새는 이제 나랑 친구야," 메리가 말했다.

"That's like him," / snapped Ben Weatherstaff. "Makin' up
"그 놈이 항상 그렇죠," 벤 웨더스태프가 끼어들었다. "여자들한테 알랑거

to th' women folk / just for vanity an' flightiness. There's
리는 거예요 허영심이나 변덕으로.

nothin' he wouldn't do / for th' sake o' showin' off / an'
안 하는 짓이 없어요 자기를 자랑할 수만 있으면

flirtin' his tail-feathers. He's as full o' pride / as an egg's
꼬리 깃을 실랑살랑 흔드는 걸요. 자만이 가득 찼지요

full o' meat."
고기로 가득 찬 달걀처럼."

He very seldom talked much / and sometimes did not even
그는 거의 말을 하지 않았고 때로는 대답조차 하지 않았다

answer / Mary's questions / except by a grunt, / but this
메리의 질문에 툴툴거리는 걸 빼면, 그러나 오늘

morning / he said more than usual. He stood up / and rested
아침에는 그가 평소보다 말을 많이 했다. 그는 일어서더니

one hobnailed boot / on the top of his spade / while he
징이 박힌 부츠 한 짝을 벗어서 그의 삽 위에 놓았다

looked her over.
그녀를 쳐다보면서.

"How long has tha' been here?" / he jerked out.
"여기 얼마나 있었지요?", 그가 불쑥 물었다.

"I think / it's about a month," / she answered.
"내 생각엔 약 한 달 정도," 그녀가 대답했다.

vanity 허영심 | show off 자랑하다 | flirt 추파를 던지다 | pluck (털 등을) 뽑다 | sour 시큼한, 톡 쏘는 | wrinkle 주름이 지다

"Tha's beginnin' / to do Misselthwaite credit," / he said.
"아가씨가 시작하네요. 미셀스와이트의 면목을 세우기," 그가 말했다.

"Tha's a bit fatter / than tha' was / an' tha's not quite so
"아가씨는 약간 더 살이 쪘네요 예전보다 그리고 그렇게 얼굴이 노랗지도 않고,

yeller. Tha' looked like a young plucked crow / when tha'
아가씨는 털 뽑힌 새끼 까마귀 같았어요 아가씨가 이 화원

first came into this garden. Thinks I to myself / I never set
에 처음 들어 왔을 때. 혼자 생각했지요 나는 본 적이

eyes on / an uglier, sourer faced young 'un."
없다고 더 못생기고 톡 쏘게 생긴 어린애는."

Mary was not vain / and as she had never thought / much
메리는 허영심이 없었다 그리고 그녀는 생각하지도 않았기에 자신의 외모

of her looks / she was not greatly disturbed.
가 잘났다고 그녀는 별로 속상하지 않았다.

"I know / I'm fatter," / she said. "My stockings are getting
"나도 알아 난 살찌고 있어," 그녀가 말했다. "스타킹이 점점 끼는 걸

tighter. They used to make wrinkles. There's the robin,
예전에는 주름이 졌었는데. 저기 붉은가슴울새가 있어,

Ben Weatherstaff."
벤 웨더스태프."

Key Expression

빈도부사

빈도부사는 '얼마나 자주'를 표현하는 부사입니다. 빈도부사를 사용할 때에는 특히 위치에 주의해야 하는데요. 일반 부사와는 달리 be동사/조동사의 뒤, 일반동사 앞에 위치하며 때로는 문장의 맨 앞이나 맨 뒤에 쓰이기도 합니다. 의문문의 경우에는 be동사/조동사/do동사 + 주어 + 빈도부사 + 일반동사의 순입니다.
빈도가 높은 순서부터 대표적인 빈도부사를 열거하면 다음과 같습니다.

always 항상(100%)
usually, generally 보통, 대체로
often, frequently 자주, 종종
sometimes, occasionally 때때로 가끔(50%)
seldom, rarely, hardly, scarcely 거의 ~하지 않는
never 결코 ~하지 않는(0%)

특히 never와 seldom 류의 빈도부사는 부정(not)의 의미를 포함한 것으로 해석하며 부정문에 사용할 수 없어요.

There, indeed, was the robin, / and she thought / he looked
거기엔, 진짜, 붉은가슴울새가 있었다. 그리고 그녀는 생각했다 그것이 전보다

nicer than ever. His red waistcoat was as glossy as satin /
더 예뻐 보인다고. 그것의 빨간 조끼는 공단처럼 빛났고

and he flirted his wings and tail / and tilted his head / and
날개와 꼬리를 살랑댔다 그리고 머리를 갸우뚱거리며

hopped about with all sorts of lively graces. He seemed
기운차고 우아하게 폴짝 뛰어다녔다. 그것은 마치 결정한 것

determined / to make Ben Weatherstaff admire him. But
같았다 벤 웨더스태프가 자신을 존경하도록 만들기로.

Ben was sarcastic.
그러나 벤은 비꼬았다.

"Aye, there tha' art!" / he said. "Tha' can put up with
"그래, 네가 있구나!" 그가 말했다. "네가 나를 참아낼 수 있겠지

me / for a bit sometimes / when tha's got no one better.
잠깐 동안은 더 좋은 사람을 얻지 못한다면.

Tha's been reddenin' up thy waistcoat / an' polishin' thy
네 조끼를 더 빨갛게 했고 깃털을 더 반질반질하게 하고

feathers / this two weeks. I know / what tha's up to. Tha's
있구나 요 2주 간. 나는 알고 있지 네가 뭘 했는지. 너는 구애

courtin' / some bold young madam / somewhere tellin'
를 했지 어떤 대담한 아가씨에게 어딘가에서 그녀에게 거짓말을 하며

thy lies to her / about bein' th' finest cock robin / on
네가 가장 멋진 수놈 붉은가슴울새이며

Missel Moor / an' ready to fight / all th' rest of 'em."
미셀 황무지에서 싸울 준비가 되었다고 모든 수놈들과."

"Oh! Look at him!" / exclaimed Mary.
"오! 쟤를 보세요!" 메리가 소리쳤다.

The robin was evidently / in a fascinating, bold mood. He
그 새는 확실히 황홀하고, 대담한 기분에 있었다.

hopped closer and closer / and looked at Ben Weatherstaff
그는 더 가까이 폴짝폴짝 뛰어 와서 벤 웨더스테프를 바라보았다

---

waistcoat 조끼 | tilt 고개를 갸우뚱하다 | put up with 참다 | satin 공단(비단의 종류) | sarcastic 비꼬는 |
polish 광내다 | bold 대담한

The Secret Garden

/ more and more engagingly. He flew on / to the nearest
점점 더 애교스럽게.　　　　　　　　　　　　새는 날아 올랐다　　가장 가까운 까치밥 나무

currant bush / and tilted his head / and sang a little song /
덤불 위로　　　　그리고 머리를 갸우뚱하며　　　작게 노래를 불렀다

right at him.
그 앞에서.

"Tha' thinks / tha'll get over me / by doin' that," / said
"네가 생각하고 있구나   네가 나를 이길 거라고   그렇게 해서,"   벤이 말했다.

Ben, / wrinkling his face up / in such a way that Mary felt
   얼굴을 찡그리면서   메리가 확실히 느낀 방법으로

sure / he was trying / not to look pleased. "Tha' thinks /
   그는 노력하고 있다고   기쁘게 보이지 않으려고.   "너는 생각하는구나

no one can stand out / against thee —— that's / what tha'
아무도 눈에 띄지 않는다고   너 말고는 — 그게

thinks."
네가 생각하는 거지."

The robin spread his wings / —— Mary could scarcely
그 새가 날개를 폈다   — 메리는 거의 믿을 수 없었다

believe / her eyes. He flew / right up to the handle of Ben
   그녀의 눈을.   새는 날았다   벤 웨더스태프의 삽의 손잡이 위로

Weatherstaff's spade / and alighted on the top of it. Then
   그리고 그 꼭대기에 내려앉았다.

the old man's face / wrinkled itself slowly / into a new
그러자 그 노인의 얼굴도   천천히 주름이 잡혔다   새로운 표정으로.

expression. He stood still / as if he were afraid to breathe /
   그는 여전히 서 있었다   마치 숨쉬기 두려워하는 것처럼

—— as if he would not have stirred for the world, / lest his
— 그가 세상을 휘젓지 않을 것처럼,

robin should start away. He spoke quite / in a whisper.
그의 새가 날아갈까 봐.   그는 조용히 말했다   속삭임으로.

"Well, I'm danged!" / he said as softly / as if he were
"당했구나!"   그가 부드럽게 말했다   마치 그가 말하고 있는 것처럼

saying / something quite different. "Tha' does know / how
   꽤 다른 것을.   "너는 알고 있구나

to get at a chap / —— tha' does! Tha's fair unearthly, / tha's
어떻게 환심을 사는지   — 너는 아는 거야!   진짜 터무니 없지,

so knowin'."
잘도 아는구나."

And he stood without stirring —— almost without drawing
그리고 그는 움직이지 않고 서 있었다   — 거의 숨도 쉬지 않고

expression 표정 | whisper 속삭이다 | grin 활짝 웃다 | bachelder 홀아비, 독신자(= bachelor) | lodge 오두막, 수위실 | tater 감자의 사투리 | persist 집요하게 계속하다

his breath —— until the robin gave another flirt to his wings
— 그 새가 날개에 다시 파닥거림을 주고

/ and flew away. Then he stood / looking at the handle of
그리고 날아갈 때까지. 그러자 서 있었다 삽의 손잡이를 바라보며

the spade / as if there might be Magic in it, / and then he
그것에 마법이 있었던 것처럼, 그리고 나서 그는 다시

began to dig again / and said nothing for several minutes.
땅을 파기 시작했다 그리고 몇 분간을 말하지 않았다.

But because he kept breaking into a slow grin / now and
그러나 그가 계속 웃음을 지었기 때문에 때때로,

then, / Mary was not afraid / to talk to him.
메리는 두렵지 않았다 그에게 말하기가.

"Have you a garden of your own?" / she asked.
"당신만의 화원을 가지고 있나요?" 그녀가 물었다.

"No. I'm bachelder / an' lodge with Martin at th' gate."
"아니요. 나는 홀아비이고 저 문의 마틴하고 같이 지내요."

"If you had one," / said Mary, / "what would you plant?"
"만약 하나 가지고 있다면," 메리가 말했다. "뭘 심을 건가요?"

"Cabbages an' 'taters an' onions."
"양배추하고 감자하고 양파요."

"But if you wanted to make / a flower garden," / persisted
"그렇지만 만약 당신이 원한다면 화원을," 메리가 계속했다.

Mary, / "what would you plant?"
"뭘 심을 건가요?"

Key Expression

lest~should… : ~할까 봐

lest + 주어 + (should) + 동사원형
= for feat that + 주어 + (should) + 동사원형
= so that + 주어 + may not + 동사원형

lest는 '~할까 봐' 또는 '~하지 않도록'이라는 의미를 가진 접속사로, should를 동반하여 쓰입니다. '~할까 봐'라는 의미가 될 때는 afraid 등 두려움을 뜻하는 단어와 함께 쓰이는 경우가 많아요. 여기서 should는 생략 가능하며 이럴 때는 바로 동사원형이 오게 됩니다.
또한 lest가 부정의 의미를 포함하고 있기 때문에 should 다음에 not이 쓰이지 않는다는 점에 주의하세요.

ex) He stood still as if he were afraid to breathe lest his robin should start away.
그는 붉은가슴울새가 날아가 버릴까봐 두려운 듯 가만히 서 있었다.

"Bulbs an' sweet-smellin' things / —— but mostly roses."

Mary's face lighted up.

"Do you like roses?" / she said.

Ben Weatherstaff rooted up / a weed / and threw it aside / before he answered.

"Well, yes, I do. I was learned / that by a young lady / I was gardener to. She had a lot / in a place / she was fond of, / an' she loved 'em / like they was children / —— or robins. I've seen / her bend over / an' kiss 'em.'" / He dragged out / another weed / and scowled at it. "That were as much as ten year' ago."

"Where is she now?" / asked Mary, / much interested.

"Heaven," / he answered, / and drove his spade / deep into the soil, / "'cording to what parson says."

"What happened / to the roses?" / Mary asked again, / more interested than ever.

"They was left to themselves."

---

scowl 찡그리다 | reluctantly 마지못해 | prune 가지를 치다 | inquire 질문하다

Mary was becoming quite excited.

"Did they quite die? Do roses quite die / when they are left to themselves?" / she ventured.

"Well, I'd got to like 'em / —— an' I liked her —— / an' she liked 'em," Ben Weatherstaff admitted reluctantly. "Once or twice a year / I'd go an' work at 'em a bit —— prune 'em / an' dig about th' roots. They run wild, / but they was in rich soil, / so some of 'em lived."

"When they have no leaves / and look gray and brown and dry, / how can you tell / whether they are dead or alive?" / inquired Mary.

"Wait / till th' spring gets at 'em —— wait / till th' sun shines on th' rain / and th' rain falls on th' sunshine / an' then / tha'll find out."

Key Expression

명사절을 이끄는 접속사 if & whether

whether가 접속사로서 명사절을 이끌 때에는 '~인지 아닌지'라는 의미로 쓰입니다. 명사절의 whether는 if로 바꿔 쓸 수 있지만 주어나 전치사의 목적으로 쓰일 경우에는 if를 사용할 수 없어요.

ex) How can you tell whether they are dead or alive?
그것들이 죽었는지 살았는지 어떻게 알아볼 수 있나요?

"How —— how?" / cried Mary, / forgetting to be careful.
"어떻게 — 어떻게?" 메리가 소리쳤다, 조심하는 것도 잊고.

"Look along th' twigs an' branches / an' if tha' see a bit of
"큰 가지와 작은 가지를 따라 살펴보세요 작은 갈색 혹이 보이는지

a brown lump / swelling here an' there, / watch it / after th'
여기저기 부풀어 오른, 그걸 지켜보다가 따뜻한

warm rain / an' see / what happens." He stopped suddenly
비가 온 후에 살펴보세요 무슨 일이 일어났는지." 그는 갑자기 멈추고

/ and looked curiously at / her eager face. "Why does tha'
그리고 호기심 어린 표정으로 바라보았다 그녀의 열중한 얼굴을. "아가씨는 신경 쓰는 건가요

care / so much about roses / an' such, all of a sudden?" / he
장미에 그토록 그렇게 갑자기?"

demanded.
그가 물었다.

Mistress Mary felt / her face grow red. She was almost
메리는 느꼈다 얼굴이 빨개지는 걸. 그녀는 겁이 났다

afraid / to answer.
대답하기.

"I —— I want to play that —— / that I have a garden of my
"난 — 난 상상한 것뿐이야 — 내 소유의 화원을 갖고 있다고,"

own," / she stammered. "I —— / there is nothing for me to
그녀는 더듬거렸다. "난 — 할 일이 하나도 없어

do. I have nothing —— / and no one."
난 가진 게 없고 — 그리고 아무도 없어."

"Well," / said Ben Weatherstaff slowly, / as he watched her,
"글쎄요," 벤 웨더스태프가 천천히 말했다, 그녀를 바라보면서,

/ "that's true. Tha' hasn't."
"그건 사실이네요. 아가씨는 가진 게 없죠."

He said it / in such an odd way / that Mary wondered / if he
그가 말해서 이상한 말투로 메리는 궁금해졌다

was actually a little sorry for her. She had never felt sorry
그가 진짜로 자기를 동정하는 건지. 그녀는 자신이 불쌍하다고 느낀 적이 없었다;

for herself; / she had only felt tired and cross, / because she
그녀는 다만 피곤하고 짜증이 났을 뿐이었다.

---

lump 솟아 오른 곳, 혹 | swell 부어 오르다 | curiously 호기심 어리게 | stammer 말을 더듬다 | odd 이상한 | cross 짜증난

118 The Secret Garden

disliked people and things so much. But now / the world
왜냐하면 그녀는 사람들과 일들을 매우 싫어했기 때문에.   그러나 이제는

seemed to be changing / and getting nicer. If no one found
세상이 변하는 것 같았다   그리고 더 좋아지는 것 같았다. 만약 아무도 발견하지 못한

out / about the secret garden, / she should enjoy herself /
다면   그 비밀의 화원에 대해서.   그녀는 즐길 수 있을 것이다

always.
언제까지나.

She stayed with him / for ten or fifteen minutes longer / and
그녀는 그와 함께 있었다   10분이나 15분 이상   그리고

asked him as many questions / as she dared. He answered /
그에게 많은 질문을 했다   용기를 내서.   그는 대답했다

every one of them / in his queer grunting way / and he did
모든 질문에   이상한 툴툴거리는 말투로   하지만 정말로 짜증

not seem really cross / and did not pick up his spade / and
을 내는 것 같지는 않았고   삽을 집어 들지도 않았으며

leave her.
그녀를 떠나지도 않았다.

He said / something about roses / just as she was going
그는 이야기했다   장미에 대해   그녀가 막 가려고 할 때

away / and it reminded her of the ones / he had said he had
그리고 그 이야기는 그 꽃들을 생각나게 했다   그가 좋아했었다고 말했던.

been fond of.

"Do you go and see those other roses now?" / she asked.
"요즘도 장미를 보러 가?"   그녀가 물었다.

"Not been this year. My rheumatics has made / me too stiff
"올해는 안 갔지요.   류머티즘 때문에   몸이 뻣뻣해서요."

in th' joints."

---

remind 상기시키다 | rheumatics 류마티스 | stiff 뻣뻣한 | joint 관절

He said it / in his grumbling voice, / and then quite suddenly / he seemed to get angry with her, / though she did not see / why he should.

"Now look here!" / he said sharply. "Don't tha' ask so many questions. Tha'rt th' worst wench / for askin' questions / I've ever come a cross. Get thee gone an' play thee. I've done talkin' for today."

And he said it so crossly / that she knew / there was not the least use / in staying another minute. She went skipping slowly down / the outside walk, / thinking him over / and saying to herself that, / queer as it was, / here was another person / whom she liked / in spite of his crossness. She liked old Ben Weatherstaff. Yes, she did like him. She always wanted / to try to make him talk / to her. Also she began to believe / that he knew everything / in the world about flowers.

---

grumble 툴툴거리다 | crossly 심통이 나서 | wench 아가씨, 젊은 처녀

There was a laurel-hedged walk / which curved round the
월계수 울타리의 산책로가 있었다   비밀의 화원 둘레를 에두르고

secret garden / and ended at a gate / which opened into a
문 앞에서 끝나는   어떤 숲으로 통하는,

wood, / in the park. She thought / she would skip round
공원에서.   그녀는 생각했다   산책로 주위를 줄넘기를 하면서

this walk / and look into the wood / and see if there were
숲을 조사해 봐야겠다고   토끼가 있는지 봐야겠다고

any rabbits / hopping about. She enjoyed the skipping very
뛰어다니는.   그녀는 줄넘기를 아주 재미있어 했다

much / and when she reached the little gate / she opened
그리고 작은 문에 도착했을 때   그녀는 그것을 열고

it / and went through / because she heard / a low, peculiar
안으로 들어갔다   들었기 때문에   낮은 이상한 휘파람 소리를

whistling sound / and wanted to find out / what it was.
그녀는 알아내고 싶었다   그게 뭔지.

It was a very strange thing / indeed. She quite caught her
그것은 아주 이상한 일이었다   정말로.   그녀는 숨을 죽이고

breath / as she stopped / to look at it. A boy was sitting
멈췄다   그것을 보기 위해.   한 소년이 앉아 있었다

/ under a tree, / with his back against it, / playing on a
나무 아래,   나무에 등을 기대고,   거친 나무 피리를 불면서.

rough wooden pipe. He was a funny looking boy / about
그는 재미있게 생긴 소년이었다   12살 정도 된.

twelve. He looked very clean / and his nose turned up /
그는 깔끔해 보였고   코는 들창코였으며

and his cheeks were as red as poppies / and never had
볼은 양귀비만큼 붉었는데   메리는 전혀 본 적이 없었다 /

Mistress Mary seen / such round and such blue eyes / in
그런 둥글고 푸른 눈을

any boy's face. And on the trunk of the tree / he leaned
어떤 소년의 얼굴에서도.   그리고 그 나무의 몸통 위에   그가 기대어 있는,

against, / a brown squirrel was clinging / and watching
갈색 다람쥐 한 마리가 앉아서   그를 바라보았고,

---

laurel 월계수 | peculiar 이상한 | breath 숨 | whistle 휘파람을 불다 | trunk 큰 줄기 | squirrel 다람쥐 |
cling 꼭 붙잡다, 매달리다

him, / and from behind a bush nearby / a cock pheasant
근처 덤불 뒤에서는   수꿩 한 마리가 우아하게

was delicately stretching his neck / to peep out, / and quite
목을 뻗고 있었다   망을 보기 위해,   그리고 그의 옆

near him / were two rabbits / sitting up / and sniffing with
에는   두 마리의 토끼가 있었다   똑바로 앉아서   코를 떨며 냄새를 맡고 있는

tremulous noses / —— and actually it appeared / as if they
— 정말로 그것은 보였다

were all drawing near / to watch him / and listen to the
마치 동물들이 주위로 몰려든 것처럼   그를 보기 위해   그리고 그 이상한 낮은 소리를 듣

strange low little call / his pipe seemed to make.
기 위해   그의 피리가 내는 것 같은.

When he saw Mary / he held up his hand / and spoke to her
그가 메리를 보고는   손을 들고   말을 걸었다

/ in a voice / almost as low as and rather like his piping.
목소리로   그의 피리만큼이나 낮은.

"Don't tha' move," / he said. / "It'd flight 'em."
"움직이지 마,"   그가 말했다.   "동물들이 도망가버릴 거야."

Mary remained motionless. He stopped / playing his pipe
메리는 꼼짝 않고 있었다.   그는 멈추고   피리 부는 것을

/ and began to rise / from the ground. He moved so slowly
일어나기 시작했다   땅에서.   그가 너무 천천히 움직여서

/ that it scarcely seemed / as though he were moving at all,
거의 보이지 않았다   움직이는 것처럼,

/ but at last / he stood on his feet / and then the squirrel
그러나 결국   그가 발을 딛고 일어서자   다람쥐가 쪼르르 달아나서

scampered / back up into the branches of his tree, / the
나무가지 위로 돌아갔고,

pheasant withdrew his head / and the rabbits dropped on all
수꿩은 머리를 움츠렸으며   토끼들은 네 발로 디디고

fours / and began to hop away, / though not at all as if they
뛰어가기 시작했다,   전혀 놀란 것 같지 않았지만.

were frightened.

pheasant 꿩 | delicately 우아하게 | tremulous 떨리는 | at last 결국, 마침내 | scamper 날쌔게 움직이다 | branch (나무)가지 | withdraw 물러나다

"I'm Dickon," / the boy said. / "I know / tha'rt Miss Mary."
"나는 디콘이에요," 소년이 말했다. "알겠어요 당신은 메리 아가씨라는 걸."

Then Mary realized / that somehow / she had known
그러자 메리는 깨달았다 어쩐지 그녀가 처음에 알고 있었다는 것을

at first / that he was Dickon. Who else could have been
그가 디콘이라는 걸. 다른 누가 홀릴 수 있겠는가

charming / rabbits and pheasants / as the natives charm
토끼와 수꿩들을 원주민들이 뱀을 홀리는 것처럼

snakes / in India? He had a wide, red, curving mouth / and
인도에서? 그는 넓고, 빨갛고, 휘어진 입을 가지고 있었고

his smile spread / all over his face.
그의 미소는 번졌다 얼굴 전체에.

"I got up slow," / he explained, / "because if tha' makes a
"저는 천천히 일어났지요," 그가 설명했다, "왜냐하면 빨리 움직이면

quick move / it startles 'em. A body 'as to move gentle /
동물들을 놀라게 하니까요. 살살 움직이고

an' speak low / when wild things is about."
말은 낮게 해야 되죠 야생 짐승들이 곁에 있을 땐."

He did not speak to her / as if they had never seen each
그는 얘기하지 않았다 그들이 전에 서로 본 적이 없는 사이인 듯

other before / but as if he knew her quite well. Mary knew
오히려 서로 잘 알고 있는 사이인 것처럼 말했다. 메리는 남자 아이들

nothing about boys / and she spoke to him a little stiffly /
에 대해 잘 몰랐다 그래서 그에게 약간 뻣뻣하게 말했다

because she felt rather shy.
약간 부끄러웠기 때문에.

"Did you get Martha's letter?" / she asked.
"마사의 편지를 받았니?" 그녀가 물었다.

He nodded / his curly, rust-colored head.
그는 끄덕였다 곱슬거리고, 녹슨 것 같이 붉은 머리를.

"That's why I come."
"그래서 내가 왔지요."

realize 깨닫다 | curve 약간 굽은 | startle 깜짝 놀라다 | rust 녹슨 | rake 갈퀴 | fork 갈퀴 | hoe 괭이 | trowel 모종삽 | larkspur 미나리아재비

He stooped / to pick up something / which had been lying
그는 멈춰섰다   뭔가 집어 들기 위해   땅 위에 놓여져 있었던

on the ground / beside him / when he piped.
            그의 옆에   피리를 부는 동안.

"I've got th' garden tools. There's a little spade / an'
"화원 도구들을 갖고 왔어요.   작은 삽도 있고요

rake an' a fork an' hoe. Eh! They are good 'uns. There's
갈퀴랑 쇠스랑이랑 괭이도요. 어! 좋은 것들이에요.

a trowel, too. An' th' woman in th' shop / threw in / a
모종삽도 있어요.   그리고 가게 아줌마가   넣어 주었어요

packet o' white poppy an' one o' blue larkspur / when I
흰 양귀비와 파란 참제비고깔 씨앗 봉지를요

bought th' other seeds."
다른 씨앗들을 살 때."

"Will you show the seeds to me?" / Mary said.
"씨앗을 나에게 보여 줄래?"   메리가 말했다.

Key Expression

That's why~ : 그것이 바로 ~한 이유이다

That's why~는 why 앞에 'the reason'이라는 선행사가 생략된 관계부사 구문이에요. '그것이 바로 ~한 이유이다', 혹은 앞문장의 결과를 나타내는 의미로 '그래서 ~하는 것이다'로 해석할 수 있어요.
That's why는 That's because와 비교해서 알아두어야 합니다. '왜냐하면'이라는 뜻을 가진 because는 원인을 이야기하기 위한 접속사죠. 따라서 다음과 같이 쓰입니다.

▶ (원인). That's why ~(결과)
▶ (결과). That's because~(원인)

ex) A: Did you get Martha's letter? 마사의 편지 받았어?
    B: That's why I come. 그래서 내가 왔어.

She wished / she could talk / as he did. His speech was so
그녀는 바랐다   뭔가 말할 수 있기를   그가 그랬듯이.   그의 말은 아주 빠르고 쉬웠다.

quick and easy. It sounded / as if he liked her / and was not
            그것은 들렸다   그가 그녀를 좋아해서   전혀 두려워하지 않는

the least afraid / she would not like him, / though he was
것처럼,   메리가 그를 좋아하지 않더라도,   그는 단지 평범한 황무지

only a common moor boy, / in patched clothes / and with
소년이었지만,   기운 옷을 입고

a funny face / and a rough, rusty-red head. As she came
웃기게 생긴 얼굴에   뻣뻣하고, 붉그스레한 머리를 하고 있는.   그녀가 그에게 가까이 가자

closer to him / she noticed / that there was a clean fresh
        그녀는 알아챘다   깨끗하고 상쾌한 냄새가 난다는 것을

scent / of heather and grass and leaves / about him, / almost
    히스 꽃과 풀과 이파리들의   그에게서,

as if he were made of them. She liked it very much / and
거의 마치 그가 풀로 만들어진 것 같이.   그녀는 그 냄새가 아주 좋았고

when she looked into his funny face / with the red cheeks /
그의 재미있는 얼굴을 관찰하면서   붉은 볼이며

and round blue eyes / she forgot / that she had felt shy.
둥글고 파란 눈을   그녀는 잊어버렸다   부끄러워했던 것도.

"Let us sit down / on this log / and look at them," / she said.
"앉아서   이 통나무 위에   그것들 좀 보자,"   그녀가 말했다.

They sat down / and he took a clumsy little brown paper
그들은 앉아서   어설프게 싼 작은 갈색 포장을 꺼냈다

package / out of his coat pocket. He untied the string /
        코트 주머니에서.   그가 줄을 풀자

and inside / there were ever so many neater and smaller
그 안에는   더 말끔하게 싼 작은 포장들이 많이 있었다

packages / with a picture of a flower / on each one.
        꽃 그림이 그려져 있는   각각 .

"There's a lot o' mignonette an' poppies," / he said.
"목서초와 양귀비가 많네요."   그가 말했다.

---

patched 기운 | heather 히스 (꽃) | clumsy 어설픈 | neat 말끔한 | mignonette 목서초 (꽃) |
whistle 휘파람 불다 | chirp 짹짹거리다 | holly 호랑가시나무 | scarlet 진홍색, 다홍색

"Mignonette's th' sweetest smellin' thing / as grows, /
"목서초는 가장 좋은 향기가 나죠   자라면서.

an' it'll grow / wherever you cast it, / same as poppies
그리고 자랄 거예요   아가씨가 어디에다 뿌려도,   양귀비도 그럴 거고요.

will. Them as'll come up / an' bloom / if you just whistle
그것들은 나와서   꽃이 피죠   휘파람만 불어줘도,

to 'em, / them's th' nicest of all." He stopped / and turned
제일 좋은 꽃들이에요."   그는 멈추고

his head quickly, / his poppy-cheeked face / lighting up.
고개를 재빨리 돌렸다,   그의 양귀비같이 빨간 얼굴을   빛내며.

"Where's that robin / as is callin' us?" / he said.
"붉은가슴울새가 어디 있죠   우리를 부르는 것 같은데?"   그가 말했다.

The chirp came / from a thick holly bush, / bright with
그 짹짹거리는 소리는 들렸고 울창한 호랑가시나무에서,   빨간 열매로 반짝이는,

scarlet berries, / and Mary thought / she knew / whose it
                  메리는 생각했다   알겠다고

was.
무엇의 울음 소리인지.

"Is it really calling us?" / she asked.
"그게 정말 우리를 부르는 걸까?"   그녀가 물었다.

> ### Key Expression

> **복합관계부사 wherever : 어디에서 ~하더라도**
> 복합관계부사란 관계부사 where, when, how에 ever가 결합된 형태로, 이들은 각각 장소, 시간, 정도를 나타내는 부사절을 이끕니다. 이 뿐만 아니라 '아무리[어디서/언제] 하더라도'라는 양보의 의미로도 쓰일 수도 있어요.
>
> ▶ whenever : ~할 때는 언제든지(= at any time when),
>   언제 ~하더라도(no matter when)
> ▶ wherever : ~한 곳은 어디든지(= at any place where),
>   어디에서 ~하더라도(= no matter where)
> ▶ however : 얼마나 ~하든지 (= no matter how),
>   아무리 ~ 하더라도 (however + 형용사/부사 + 주어 + 동사)
>
> ex) It'll grow wherever you cast it.
>   네가 어디에 뿌리더라도 그것은 자라날 거야.

"Aye," said Dickon, / as if it was the most natural thing / in the world, / "he's callin' some one / he's friends with. That's same as sayin' / 'Here I am. Look at me. I wants a bit of a chat.' There he is in the bush. Whose is he?"

"He's Ben Weatherstaff's, but I think / he knows me a little," / answered Mary.

"Aye, he knows thee," said Dickon / in his low voice again. "An' he likes thee. He's took thee on. He'll tell me / all about thee / in a minute."

He moved / quite close to the bush / with the slow movement. Mary had noticed before, / and then he made a sound / almost like the robin's own twitter. The robin listened a few seconds, intently, / and then answered quite / as if he were replying / to a question.

"Aye, he's a friend o' yours," / chuckled Dickon.

"Do you think he is?" / cried Mary eagerly. She did so want to know. "Do you think / he really likes me?"

twitter 지저귀다 | chuckle 빙그레 웃다 | eagerly 열렬히

128　The Secret Garden

"He wouldn't come near thee / if he didn't," / answered Dickon. "Birds is rare choosers / an' a robin can flout a body worse / than a man. See, / he's making up to thee now. 'Cannot tha' see a chap?' / he's sayin'."

And it really seemed / as if it must be true. He so sidled / and twittered and tilted / as he hopped on his bush.

"Do you understand / everything birds say?" / said Mary.

Dickon's grin spread / until he seemed all wide, red, curving mouth, / and he rubbed his rough head.

"I think I do, / and they think I do," / he said. "I've lived on th' moor with 'em so long. I've watched 'em / break shell / an' come out an' fledge / an' learn to fly / an' begin to sing, / till I think / I'm one of 'em. Sometimes I think / p'raps I'm a bird, or a fox, or a rabbit, or a squirrel, or even a beetle, / an' I don't know it."

---

flout 어기다, 무시하다 | sidle 옆걸음질 하다, 가만히 다가가다 | fledge 깃털이 나다 | beetle 딱정벌레

He laughed / and came back to the log / and began to
그는 웃으며 통나무로 돌아와서 말하기 시작했다

talk / about the flower seeds again. He told her / what
다시 꽃 씨앗에 대해. 그는 그녀에게 말했다

they looked like / when they were flowers; / he told her
어떻게 보이는 지 그것들이 꽃이 되었을 때; 그리고 말했다

/ how to plant them, / and watch them, / and feed and
어떻게 심고, 지켜보고, 거름을 주고 물을 주는지

water them.
에 대해.

"See here," / he said suddenly, / turning round to look
"여기를 보세요," 그가 갑자기 말했다, 고개를 돌려 그녀를 보면서.

at her. "I'll plant them / for thee myself. Where is tha'
"내가 심을 게요 아가씨 대신. 화원은 어디에 있어요?"

garden?"

Mary's thin hands clutched each other / as they lay on
메리는 여윈 손을 깍지 끼어 무릎 위에 놓았다.

her lap. She did not know / what to say, / so for a whole
그녀는 몰랐다 뭐라고 말할지, 그래서 한참 동안

minute / she said nothing. She had never thought of this.
그녀는 아무 말도 하지 않았다. 이것에 대해 생각해 본적도 없었다.

She felt miserable. And she felt / as if she went red and
그녀는 속이 상했다. 그리고 느꼈다 얼굴이 빨개져서 창백해짐을.

then pale.

"Tha's got a bit o' garden, / hasn't tha'?" / Dickon said.
"아가씨는 화원이 있죠, 그렇지 않아요?" 디콘이 말했다.

It was true / that she had turned red and then pale.
사실이었다 그녀가 빨개졌다가 창백해진 것은.

Dickon saw / her do it, / and as she still said nothing, / he
디콘은 보았다 그녀의 얼굴이 그렇게 되는 것을, 그리고 그녀가 여전히 아무 말도 하지 않아서,

began to be puzzled.
그는 당황하기 시작했다.

---

lap 무릎 | miserable 비참한 | pale 창백한 | fiercely 사납게, 발끈해서, 격정적으로 | good-humoredly
서글서글하게, 상냥하게

"Wouldn't they give thee a bit?" / he asked. "Hasn't tha'
"아가씨한테 땅을 주지 않았어요?" 그가 물었다.

got any yet?"
"아직도 땅이 없어요?"

She held her hands tighter / and turned her eyes toward
그녀는 두 손을 꼭 잡고 눈을 돌려 그를 보았다.

him.

"I don't know anything about boys," / she said slowly.
"남자 애들에 대해선 잘 모르지만," 그녀가 천천히 말했다.

"Could you keep a secret, / if I told you one? It's a great
"비밀을 지킬 수 있니, 내가 네게 말해 준다면?

secret. I don't know / what I should do / if anyone found
이건 중대한 비밀이야. 나는 모르겠어 어떻게 해야 하는지 만약 누군가 알게 된다면.

it out. I believe I should die!" She said / the last sentence
난 죽어버릴 거야!" 그녀는 말했다 마지막 문장을 아주 험악

quite fiercely.
하게

Dickon looked more puzzled than ever / and even rubbed
디콘은 그 전보다 더 당황한듯 보였고 손으로 비볐다

his hand / over his rough head again, / but he answered /
거친 머리를 또 다시, 그러나 그는 대답했다

quite good-humoredly.
아주 서글서글하게.

Key Expression

what~like = how

what은 '무엇'이라는 뜻의 의문사이지만 like를 동반하여 사용하면 how와 같은 '어떻게'라는 의미로 해석합니다. 즉 '날씨가 어때?'라고 물을 때 How is the weather? 혹은 What is the weather like? 둘 다 사용할 수 있어요.

ex) He told her what they looked like.
  그는 그녀에게 그들이 어떻게 생겼는지 이야기했다.

"I'm keepin' secrets all th' time," / he said. "If I couldn't
"난 언제나 비밀을 지켜요." 그가 말했다. "만약 비밀을 지킬 수 없

keep secrets / from th' other lads, / secrets about foxes'
으면 다른 아이들에게서 들은, 여우 새끼나, 새 둥지나, 들짐승 둥지에

cubs, an' birds' nests, an' wild things' holes, / there'd be
대한 비밀이나 안전하지 못할 거예요.

naught safe / on th' moor. Aye, I can keep secrets."
이 황무지에서. 그래요, 나는 비밀을 지킬 수 있어요."

Mistress Mary did not mean / to put out her hand / and
메리는 의도한 것은 아니었다 손을 빼서

clutch his sleeve / but she did it.
그의 소매를 움켜쥐는 것을 그러나 그렇게 했다.

"I've stolen a garden," / she said very fast. "It isn't mine.
"나는 화원을 훔쳤어." 그녀가 아주 빨리 말했다. "그것은 내 것이 아니야.

It isn't anybody's. Nobody wants it, / nobody cares for it, /
누구의 것도 아니야. 아무도 원하지 않고, 아무도 돌보지 않아,

nobody ever goes into it. Perhaps everything is dead / in it
아무도 그곳에 가지 않아. 아마 모든 것이 죽어 있을 거야 그 안에선

already. I don't know."
이미. 나도 모르겠어."

She began to feel hot / and as contrary / as she had ever felt
그녀는 열이 나는 것을 느끼기 시작했고 고집을 부렸다 예전에 그랬던 것처럼

/ in her life.
자신의 인생에서.

"I don't care, / I don't care! Nobody has any right / to
"난 상관 안 해, 상관 안 할 거야! 누구도 권리를 가지고 있지 않아

take it from me / when I care about it / and they don't.
나에게서 빼앗아 갈 내가 그걸 돌볼 때 그들은 하지 않았으니까.

They're letting it die, / all shut in by itself," / she ended
화원을 죽게 내버려 뒀으니까, 홀로 가둬버렸으니까," 그녀는 흥분해서 말을

passionately, / and she threw her arms / over her face / and
끝내고, 팔을 뻗어 얼굴을 감싸고는

---

lad 사내 아이 | cub (동물의) 새끼 | naught 무가치한, 나쁜 | clutch 움켜잡다 | passionately 흥분해서 | burst out 터뜨리다

burst out crying / poor little Mistress Mary.
울음을 터뜨렸다 불쌍한 메리 아가씨.

Dickon's curious blue eyes / grew rounder and rounder.
디콘의 호기심 빛나는 파란 눈은 점점 더 동그래졌다.

"Eh-h-h!" he said, / drawing his exclamation out slowly, /
"어-어-어!" 그가 말했다, 천천히 감탄사를 내뱉으며,

and the way he did it meant / both wonder and sympathy.
그 방식은 의미하는 것이었다 놀라움과 불쌍하다는 느낌을.

"I've nothing to do," / said Mary. "Nothing belongs to
"나는 할 게 없어." 메리가 말했다. "가진 게 아무것도 없어.

me. I found it myself / and I got into it myself. I was only
혼자 찾았고 혼자 들어갔어. 나는 그 붉은가슴

just like the robin, / and they wouldn't take it / from the
울새와 같아, 사람들은 그 새한테서 화원을 빼앗지는 않았잖아."

robin."

"Where is it?" / asked Dickon / in a dropped voice.
"그게 어디 있는데요?" 디콘이 물었다 목소리를 낮추며.

Mistress Mary got up / from the log / at once. She knew
메리는 일어났다 통나무에서 즉시. 그녀는 알았다

/ she felt contrary again, and obstinate, / and she did not
다시 버릇없이 고집 피우고 있다는 것을, 그래도 신경 쓰지 않았다.

care at all. She was imperious / and Indian, / and at the
그녀는 버릇없었지만 인도 사람들에게, 동시에

same time / hot and sorrowful.
열이 나고 슬펐다.

"Come with me / and I'll show you," / she said.
"나를 따라와 내가 보여 줄게," 그녀가 말했다.

Key Expression

재귀대명사 '~self'의 두 가지 용법

'~자신'을 뜻하는 ~self 형태의 대명사를 재귀대명사라고 부릅니다. 재귀대명사의 쓰임에는 두 가지가 있는데 '~자신'이란 의미로 쓰일 때에는 재귀용법, '직접'이란 의미로 쓰일 때에는 강조용법이라 합니다. 재귀용법은 주어와 목적어가 같음을 알리기 위해, 강조용법은 주어가 그 행동을 직접 했음을 강조하기 위한 것이죠.

재귀용법과 강조용법의 쓰임을 구분하려면 재귀대명사를 가린 채 문장을 읽어보세요. 강조용법의 경우에는 재귀대명사가 없어도 문장이 성립합니다.

ex) I found it myself and I got into it myself. (강조용법)
내가 그걸 직접 발견했고 그 안으로 직접 들어갔다.
She had never felt sorry for herself. (재귀용법)
그녀는 자신을 불쌍하게 여긴 적이 없었다.

The Secret Garden

She led him / round the laurel path / and to the walk /
그녀는 그를 데리고 갔다 월계수 산책로를 돌아 그리고 그 길까지

where the ivy grew / so thickly. Dickon followed her /
담쟁이덩굴이 자라난 매우 무성하게. 디콘은 그녀를 따라 갔다

with a queer, almost pitying, look on his face. He felt / as
의아해 하고, 불쌍해 하는, 표정을 지으며. 그는 느꼈다

if he were being led / to look at some strange bird's nest /
이끌려 가고 있는 것처럼 이상한 새의 둥지를 보기 위해

and must move softly. When she stepped to the wall / and
그래서 부드럽게 움직여야 한다고. 메리가 그 벽에 다가가서

lifted the hanging ivy / he startled. There was a door / and
담쟁이덩굴을 들어 올렸을 때 그는 놀랐다. 거기에는 문이 있었고

Mary pushed it slowly open / and they passed in together,
메리가 그것을 천천히 밀어 열자 같이 안으로 들어갔다,

/ and then / Mary stood / and waved her hand / round
그리고 나서 메리는 서서 손을 흔들었다

defiantly.
거만한 태도로.

"It's this," / she said. "It's a secret garden, / and I'm the
"이게 그거야," 그녀가 말했다. "이게 비밀의 화원이야, 그리고 나는 세상에서 유

only one in the world / who wants it to be alive."
일한 사람이야. 화원이 살아있기를 바라는."

Dickon looked round / and round about it, / and round and
디콘은 주변을 둘러 보고 또 둘러 보았다, 몇 번이고 다시 둘러보았다.

round again.

"Eh!" he almost whispered, / "it is a queer, pretty place!
"아!" 그가 거의 속삭이며 말했다, "묘하지만 예쁜 곳이네요!

It's like / as if a body was in a dream."
이건 마치 / 내 몸이 꿈속에 있는 것 같아요."

---

exclamation 탄성 | sympathy 동정심 | contrary 버릇없는, 엇나가는 | obstinate 고집센, 완강한 | imperious 고압적인 | startle 깜짝 놀라게 하다 | defiantly 반항적으로

mini test 5

A. 다음 문장을 해석해 보세요.

(1) There were so many / that she remembered / what Martha had said / about the "snowdrops by the thousands," / and about bulbs / spreading and making new ones.
→

(2) Sometimes / she stopped digging / to look at the garden / and try to imagine / what it would be like.
→

(3) He very seldom talked much / and sometimes did not even answer / Mary's questions / except by a grunt.
→

(4) Nobody has any right / to take it from me / when I care about it / and they don't.
→

B. 다음 주어진 문구가 알맞은 문장이 되도록 순서를 맞춰 보세요.

(1) 비밀의 화원의 구근들은 많이 놀랐음에 틀림없다.
(much / been / must / astonished / have)
→ The bulbs in the secret garden _____
_____ .

(2) 그는 처음에 그랬던 것처럼 강하게 반대하지는 않았다.
(had / at / as / as / he / first / strongly)
→ He did not object to her _____

(3) 그는 붉은가슴울새가 날아가버릴까 봐 가만히 서 있었다.
(should / start / his robin / away / lest)
→ He stood still _____ .

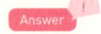

A. (1) 마사가 말했던 "수천 개의 아네모네", 그리고 퍼져서 새싹을 틔워가는 구근들에 대해 그녀가 기억하는 것들은 아주 많았다. (2) 때때로 그녀는 땅 파기를 멈추고 정원을 바라보며 그것이 어떻게 될지 상상하려 했다. (3) 그는 거의 말을 하지 않았고 때로는 메리의 질문에 툴툴거리기만 하고 대답조차 하지 않았다.

(4) 그것들이 죽었는지 살았는지를 어떻게 알 수 있어요?
(whether / dead / can / are / tell / or / how / they / alive? / you)
→

C. 다음 주어진 문장이 본문의 내용과 맞으면 T, 틀리면 F에 동그라미 하세요.

(1) Mary became absorbed in digging and pulling up weeds.
 (T / F)
(2) Ben Weatherstaff came to help Mary with gardening.
 (T / F)
(3) Dickon believed he could communicate with animals.
 (T / F)
(4) Mary introduced her secret garden to Dickon.
 (T / F)

D. 의미가 서로 비슷한 말끼리 연결해 보세요.

(1) obstinate ▶   ◀ ① grumble
(2) startle ▶   ◀ ② frighten
(3) grunt ▶   ◀ ③ determined
(4) clumsy ▶   ◀ ④ awkward

Answer

(4) 내가 그것을 좋아하고 그들은 그렇지 않을 때에는 아무도 내게서 그걸 빼앗아갈 권리는 없어요. | B. (1) must have been much astonished. (2) as strongly as he had at first. (3) lest his robin should start away. (4) How can you tell whether they are dead or alive? | C. (1) T (2) F (3) T (4) T | D. (1) ③ (2) ② (3) ① (4) ④

7

"I AM COLIN"
"난 콜린이야"

Mary took the picture back to the house when she went to her supper and she showed it to Martha.

"Eh!" said Martha with great pride. "I never knew our Dickon was as clever as that. That there's a picture of a missel thrush on her nest, as large as life an' twice as natural."

Then Mary knew Dickon had meant the picture to be a message. He had meant that she might be sure he would keep her secret. Her garden was her nest and she was like a missel thrush. Oh, how she did like that queer, common boy!

She hoped he would come back the very next day and she fell asleep looking forward to the morning.

But you never know what the weather will do in Yorkshire, particularly in the springtime. She was awakened in the

missel thrush 개똥지빠귀 | nest 둥지, 보금자리, 소굴 | particularly 특히, 특별히 | pour down 쏟아져 내리다 | torrent 마구 쏟아짐, 빗발침

138 The Secret Garden

night / by the sound of rain beating with heavy drops /
굵은 방울로 떨어지는 빗소리에

against her window. It was pouring down in torrents /
그녀의 창문에. 비는 빗발치며 쏟아져 내리고 있었다

and the wind was "wuthering" / round the corners / and
그리고 바람은 "쌩쌩 불어"대고 있었다 모퉁이 주변에서

in the chimneys of the huge old house. Mary sat up in
크고 오래된 집의 굴뚝과. 메리는 침대에 앉아서

bed / and felt miserable and angry.
우울하고 화가 났다.

"The rain is as contrary / as I ever was," she said. "It
"비도 심술궂구나 내가 그랬던 것처럼," 메리가 말했다. "비가 온

came / because it knew I did not want it."
거야. 오지 말라고 바랬던 것을 알기에."

She threw herself back on her pillow / and buried
그녀는 베개에 다시 몸을 내던지고는 얼굴을 묻었다.

her face. She did not cry, / but she lay / and hated the
메리는 울지 않았지만, 누워서 굵게 떨어지는 빗소리를 증오

sound of the heavily beating rain, / she hated the wind
하고 있었고, "쌩쌩 불어"대는 바람도 싫었다.

and its "wuthering." She could not go to sleep again.
메리는 다시 잠이 들 수가 없었다.

Key Expression

as~as… 원급비교 : …만큼 ~한

A = B 일 때 쓰는 비교급 표현을 원급비교 혹은 동등비교라고 부르며 as + 형용사/부사 원급 + as…의 형태로 사용합니다. 이때 '…만큼 ~한'이라고 해석하지요.
참고로 첫번째 as 앞에 not을 붙여 not as(so) + ~ + as…가 되면 '…만큼 ~하지 않은'이라 해석하여 두번째 as 뒤의 것이 더 우월하다는 비교의 의미를 가지게 됩니다.

ex) I never knew our Dickon was as clever as that.
난 우리 디콘이 그렇게나 영리할 줄은 몰랐네요.
The rain is as contrary as I ever was.
비는 내가 예전에 그랬던 것처럼 심술궂네요.

The mournful sound kept her awake / because she felt
애절한 소리가 그녀를 깨웠다   왜냐하면 애절하다고 느꼈기

mournful herself. If she had felt happy / it would probably
때문에.   만약 그녀가 행복을 느꼈더라면   그 소리가 어쩌면 자장가가

have lulled her to sleep. How it "wuthered" / and how the
되었을지도 모른다.   얼마나 "쌩쌩 불어대는"지,   얼마나 굵은 빗방울들

big raindrops poured down / and beat against the pane!
이 쏟아져 내려서   유리에 부딪치던지!

"It sounds just like / a person lost on the moor / and
"~처럼 들리네   누군가 황무지에서 길을 잃고

wandering on / and on crying," / she said.
헤매이면서   계속 울고 있는 것처럼,"   메리가 말했다.

She had been lying awake / turning from side to side / for
메리는 잠이 깬 채 누워 있었다   이쪽 저쪽으로 뒹굴면서

about an hour, / when suddenly / something made her sit
거의 한 시간 동안,   그때 갑자기   무언가에 그녀는 일어나 앉아서

up in bed / and turn her head / toward the door listening.
고개를 문 쪽으로 돌렸다   문 소리가 나는 쪽으로.

She listened and she listened.
그녀는 계속 귀를 기울였다.

"It isn't the wind now," / she said in a loud whisper. "That
"이 소리는 바람 소리가 아니야,"   메리는 소리를 내어 속삭였다.

isn't the wind. It is different. It is that crying / I heard
"저건 바람 소리가 아니야. 다른 소리야.   그 울음 소리야

before."
지난번에도 들은 적이 있는."

The door of her room was ajar / and the sound came down
메리의 방문은 약간 열려 있었고   소리는 복도 끝에서부터 들렸다.

the corridor, / a far-off faint sound / of fretful crying. She
              멀리서 희미하게 들리는 소리였다   짜증 섞인 울음 소리.

listened for a few minutes / and each minute / she became
메리는 몇 분 동안 귀를 기울였다   시간이 흐를 수록   메리는 점점 더 확신

more and more sure. She felt as if / she must find out /
하게 되었다.   메리는 느꼈다   밝혀내야겠다고

---

mournful 애절한 | ajar 문이 조금 열려 있는 | far-off 먼, 멀리 떨어진, 옛날의 | rebellious 저항하는

The Secret Garden

what it was. It seemed even stranger / than the secret garden / and the buried key. Perhaps / the fact that she was in a **rebellious** mood / made her bold. She put her foot out of bed / and stood on the floor.

"I am going to find out / what it is," / she said. "Everybody is in bed / and I don't care about Mrs. Medlock / —— I don't care!"

Key Expression

동격의 that

접속사 that 앞에 오는 명사를 that절이 설명할 때 이를 '동격의 that'이라고 부릅니다. 동격의 that은 주로 다음과 같은 명사와 함께 쓰여서 '~라는 (명사)'로 해석해요.

the fact that ~ : ~라는 사실
the news that ~ : ~라는 뉴스
the idea that ~ : ~라는 의견
the suggestion that ~ : ~라는 제안
the feeling that ~ : ~라는 감정
the possibility that ~ : ~라는 가능성

동격의 that은 해석할 때 관계대명사 that과 비슷하게 해석되기 때문에 헷갈리는 경우가 많은데요. 관계대명사 that이 이끄는 절은 주어나 목적어가 빠진 불완전한 문장인 반면 동격의 that절은 완전한 문장임을 기억하세요.

ex) Perhaps the fact that she was in a rebellious mood made her bold.
아마도 그녀가 반항적인 기분이었다는 사실이 그녀를 대담하게 만들었다.

There was a candle / by her bedside / and she took it up / and went softly out of the room. The corridor looked very long and dark, / but she was too excited / to mind that. She thought / she remembered the corners / she must turn / to find the short corridor / with the door covered with tapestry / —— the one Mrs. Medlock had come / through the day she lost herself. The sound had come up that passage. So she went on / with her dim light, / almost feeling her way, / her heart beating so loud / that she fancied she could hear it. The far-off faint crying / went on / and led her. Sometimes / it stopped for a moment or so / and then began again. Was this the right / corner to turn? She stopped and thought. / Yes it was. Down this passage / and then to the left, / and then up two broad steps, / and then to the right again. Yes, there was the tapestry door.

---

fancy 상상하다 | faint 희미한 | broad 폭이 넓은 | brocade 양단, 두껍게 짠 비단

She pushed it open very gently / and closed it behind
메리는 부드럽게 문을 열고 뒤로 문을 닫았다,

her, / and she stood in the corridor / and could hear the
그리고 메리는 복도에 서 있었는데 그 울음 소리를 똑똑히 들을 수 있

crying quite plainly, / though it was not loud. It was on
었다, 큰 소리는 아니었지만. 그 소리는 반대편

the other side / of the wall at her left / and a few yards
에서 나오고 있었다 메리가 서 있는 왼쪽 벽의 그리고 몇 야드 더 지나서

farther on / there was a door. She could see a of light /
문이 있었다. 메리는 깜빡이는 불빛을 볼 수 있었다

coming from beneath it. The Someone was crying in that
그 아래에서 나오고 있는 것을. 그 누군가가 저 방 안에 있어,

room, / and it was quite a young Someone.
그리고 그건 어린 아이야.

So she walked to the door / and pushed it open, / and
그래서 문 앞으로 다가가서 문을 밀어서 열었다,

there she was standing / in the room!
그리고 메리는 서 있게 되었다 그 방 안에!

It was a big room / with ancient, handsome furniture in
큰 방이었다 오래되고 멋진 가구들이 있는.

it. There was a low fire / glowing faintly on the hearth /
낮은 불이 지펴져 있고 난로에서 희미하게 타는

and a night light burning / by the side of a carved four-
야간 등이 타고 있었다 네 개의 조각 기둥을 가진 침대 옆에서

posted bed / hung with brocade, / and on the bed / was
양단과 함께 매달린 채, 그리고 침대에는

lying a boy, / crying fretfully.
한 소년이 누워 있었다, 칭얼대며 울고 있는.

Mary wondered / if she was in a real place / or if she had
메리는 궁금했다　　　자신이 실존하는 곳에 있는 것인지

fallen asleep again / and was dreaming without knowing it.
아니면 다시 잠이 들어서　　자기도 모르게 꿈을 꾸고 있는 것은 아닌지.

The boy had a sharp, delicate face / the color of ivory / and
그 소년은 예리하고 섬세한 얼굴을 하고 있었다　　상아색의

he seemed to have / eyes too big for it. He had also a lot
그리고 갖고 있는 것처럼 보였다　얼굴에 걸맞지 않게 큰 눈을.　소년은 머리 숱도 많았다

of hair / which tumbled over his forehead in heavy locks /
굵은 곱슬머리의 머리카락이 이마에 흘러내려와 있어서

and made his thin face seem smaller. He looked like a boy
그의 작은 얼굴을 더 작아 보이게 했다.　　　그 소년은 보였다

/ who had been ill, / but he was crying / more as if he were
오랫동안 아파온 것처럼,　　그런데 그는 울고 있었다　　지치거나 화가 나서라기보다는

tired and cross / than as if he were in pain.
　　　　　　　　고통스러워서인 것처럼.

Mary stood near the door / with her candle in her hand, /
메리는 문 가까이에 서 있었다　　　손에 초를 든 채,

holding her breath. Then she crept / 'WHO ARE YOU? /
숨을 죽이고.　　　그러다가 살금살금 걸어가서 '넌 누구니?

── ARE YOU A GHOST?' / across the room, / and, / as
── 귀신이니?'라고 생각하며,　　　방을 가로질렀다,　　　그리고,

she drew nearer, / the light attracted the boy's attention
더 가까이 다가가자,　　촛불이 소년의 주의를 끌어

/ and he turned his head / on his pillow / and stared at
그가 고개를 돌렸다　　　　베개에서　　　그리고 메리를 빤히 보았다.

her, / his gray eyes opening so wide / that they seemed
　　　그의 잿빛 눈동자가 더 커져서　　　어마어마하게 보였다.

immense.

"Who are you?" / he said at last / in a half-frightened
"넌 누구니?"　　　소년도 드디어 말했다　　반쯤 놀란 속삭임으로.

whisper. "Are you a ghost?"
　　　　　　"귀신이니?"

tumble over 흘러 내려오다 | lock 머리채, (복수형으로) 머리털 | creep across 가로지르다 | immense 거대한 |
agate 마노 (보석의 일종)

144　The Secret Garden

"No, / I am not," / Mary answered, / her own whisper
"아니. 난 아니야." 메리가 대답했다. 메리의 속삭이는 목소리도

sounding half frightened. "Are you one?"
반쯤 놀란 듯 들렸다. "넌 귀신이니?"

He stared and stared and stared. Mary could not help
소년은 보고, 보고, 또 보았다. 메리는 알아차릴 수밖에 없었다

noticing / what strange eyes he had. They were agate gray
그의 눈동자가 얼마나 신기하게 생겼는지. 마노색이었는데

/ and they looked too big for his face / because they had
얼굴에 비해 너무 커 보였다 검은 속눈썹 때문에

black lashes / all round them.
눈동자 주변에 가득한.

"No," / he replied / after waiting a moment or so. "I am
"아니," 소년이 대답했다 잠시 동안 기다리더니.

Colin."
"난 콜린이야."

"Who is Colin?" / she faltered.
"콜린이 누구야?" 메리가 더듬거렸다.

"I am Colin Craven. Who are you?"
"내가 콜린 크레이븐이야. 넌 누구니?"

"I am Mary Lennox. Mr. Craven is my uncle."
"난 메리 레녹스라고 해. 크레이븐 씨는 내 고모부셔."

"He is my father," / said the boy.
"그 분은 내 아버지야," 소년이 말했다.

Key Expression

with를 사용한 부대상황

두 가지 일이 동시에 일어나는 상황을 부대상황이라고 합니다. with를 사용해 이를 간단하게 표현할 수 있는데 '~를 ~한 채로' 혹은 '~를 ~하면서'라고 해석합니다. with 부대상황 구문에는 다음과 같이 표현합니다.

- with + 목적어 + [형용사/전치사구/현재분사/과거분사]

ex) Mary stood near the door with her candle in her hand. (전치사구)
메리는 손에 초를 든 채 문 가까이에 섰다.

"Your father!" / gasped Mary. "No one ever told me / he had a boy! Why didn't they?"

"Come here," / he said, / still keeping his strange eyes fixed on her / with an anxious expression.

She came close to the bed / and he put out his hand / and touched her.

"You are real, / aren't you?" / he said. "I have such real dreams very often. You might be one of them."

Mary had slipped on a woolen wrapper / before she left her room / and she put a piece of it / between his fingers.

"Rub that / and see how thick and warm it is," / she said. "I will pinch you a little / if you like, / to show you / how real I am. For a minute / I thought you might be a dream too."

"Where did you come from?" / he asked.

"From my own room. The wind wuthered / so I couldn't go to sleep / and I heard someone crying / and wanted to find out who it was. What were you crying for?"

fix on ~에 고정하다 | real dreams 사실 같은 꿈 | wrapper 가운, 덮개

"Because / I couldn't go to sleep either / and my head
ached. Tell me your name again."

"Mary Lennox. Did no one ever tell you / I had come to live here?"

He was still fingering / the fold of her wrapper, / but he began to look / a little more / as if he believed / in her reality.

"No," / he answered. "They daren't."

"Why?" / asked Mary.

"Because / I should have been afraid / you would see me. I won't let people see me / and talk me over."

"Why? " / Mary asked again, / feeling more mystified / every moment.

"Because I am like this always, / ill and having to lie down. My father won't let / people talk me over either. The servants are not allowed / to speak about me. If I live

venture 모험하다, 조심스럽게 말하다, ~에 걸다

/ I may be a hunchback, / but I shan't live. My father hates to think / I may be like him."

"Oh, / what a queer house this is!" / Mary said. "What a queer house! Everything is a kind of secret. Rooms are locked up / and gardens are locked up / —— and you! Have you been locked up?"

"No. I stay in this room / because I don't want to be moved out of it. It tires me too much."

"Does your father come and see you?" / Mary ventured.

"Sometimes. Generally / when I am asleep. He doesn't want to see me."

"Why?" / Mary could not help asking again.

Key Expression

how/what으로 시작하는 감탄문

영어의 감탄문은 how와 what으로 시작하는 두 가지가 있어요. how는 형용사나 부사의 문장에 what은 명사가 있는 문장에 사용하는데 각각의 어순이 다르므로 잘 기억하세요.

▶ How + 형용사 / 부사 + (주어 + 동사)!
▶ What + (a / an) + 형용사 + 명사 + (주어 + 동사)!

ex) What a queer house this is!
　　이곳은 정말 이상한 집이야!
　　How queer (it is)!
　　정말 이상하구나!

A sort of angry shadow / passed over the boy's face.
약간의 화난 기색이 　　　　　소년의 얼굴에 스쳐 지나 갔다.

"My mother died / when I was born / and it makes him
"어머니가 돌아가셨어 　내가 태어났을 때　　　그래서 아버지를 비참하게

wretched / to look at me. He thinks / I don't know, / but
만드는 거야　　나를 보는 것이.　아버지는 생각하지 내가 모를 거라고,

I've heard people talking. He almost hates me."
하지만 사람들이 말하는 것을 들었어.　아버지가 나를 거의 싫어한다고."

"He hates the garden, / because she died," / said Mary half
"고모부는 화원을 싫어해,　　왜냐하면 고모가 죽었기 때문이지,"

speaking to herself.
메리는 반쯤 혼잣말로 말했다.

"What garden?" / the boy asked.
"무슨 화원?"　　소년이 물었다.

"Oh! Just —— just a garden she used to like," / Mary
"어!　그냥 — 그냥 고모가 좋아했던 화원이야,"　　　메리는 더듬거렸다.

stammered. "Have you been here always?"
"넌 항상 이곳에 있었니?"

"Nearly always. Sometimes / I have been taken to places at
"거의 항상.　　가끔씩　　　바닷가에 데려간 적은 있어,

the seaside, / but I won't stay / because people stare at me. I
　　　　　하지만 난 머물려 하지 않았지 왜냐하면 사람들이 나를 쳐다보니까.

used to wear an iron thing / to keep my back straight, / but
난 쇠로 된 무언가를 달고 있었어　　등을 펴게 만드는,

a grand doctor came from London / to see me / and said it
그런데 한 유명한 의사가 런던에서 오더니　　날 보러　　바보 같은 짓이라고

was stupid. He told them to take it off / and keep me / out
말했어.　　사람들에게 말해서 벗기라고 했지　그리고 나를 두라고

in the fresh air. I hate fresh air / and I don't want to go out."
신선한 공기가 있는 밖에. 난 신선한 공기를 싫어해서 밖에 나가는 게 싫어."

"I didn't / when first I came here," / said Mary. "Why do
"나도 그랬어　이곳에 처음 왔을 때는,"　메리가 말했다.　"왜 나를 계속 쳐

you keep looking at me / like that?"
다보는 거니　　　　그런 식으로?"

---

seaside 해변가 | take off 벗다 | wide awake 완전히 깨어 있다 | restlessly 가만히 못 있는, 들뜬

150　The Secret Garden

"Because of the dreams / that are so real," / he answered rather fretfully. "Sometimes / when I open my eyes / I don't believe I'm awake."

"We're both awake," / said Mary. She glanced round the room / with its high ceiling / and shadowy corners / and dim fire-light. "It looks quite like a dream, / and it's the middle of the night, / and everybody in the house is asleep / —— everybody but us. We are wide awake."

"I don't want it to be a dream," / the boy said restlessly. Mary thought of something / all at once.

"If you don't like people to see you," / she began, / "do you want me to go away?"

Key Expression

조동사 used to : ~하곤 했었다

used to는 '~하곤 했었다' 혹은 '~였었다'라는 의미로 과거의 습관이나 상태를 표현하며 '과거에는 했었지만 지금은 하지 않는다'는 의미가 함축되어 있어요. used to는 일종의 조동사처럼 굳어진 표현으로 뒤에는 동사원형이 오고 부정형은 used not to입니다.
숙어 표현인 be used to ~ing나 수동태형태의 be used 문장과의 구분에 주의하세요.

ex) I used to wear an iron thing to keep my back straight, but a grand doctor came from London to see me and said it was stupid.
(예전에는) 등을 똑바로 유지하기 위해 쇠로 된 물체를 달았어. 그런데 유명한 의사가 런던에서 날 보러 와서는 그건 어리석은 짓이라고 했지.

He still held the fold of / her wrapper / and he gave it a little pull.

"No," he said. "I should be sure / you were a dream / if you went. If you are real, / sit down on that big footstool / and talk. I want to hear about you."

Mary put down her candle / on the table near the bed / and sat down on the cushioned stool. She did not want to go away at all. She wanted to stay / in the mysterious hidden-away room / and talk to the mysterious boy.

"What do you want me to tell you?" / she said.

He wanted to know / how long she had been at Misselthwaite; / he wanted to know / which corridor her room was on; / he wanted to know / what she had been doing; / if she disliked the moor / as he disliked it; / where she had lived / before she came to Yorkshire. She answered all these questions / and many more / and he lay back on his pillow / and listened. He made her

footstool 발판 | hidden-away 숨어 있는 곳 | a great deal 다량, 상당량, 많이 | invalid 무효한, 병약자 | splendid book 그림책

tell him / a great deal about India / and about her voyage
고 했다 　　인도에 대한 많은 것들과 　　　그녀의 여행에 대해서

across the ocean. She found out / that because he had been
바다를 가로지른. 　　그녀는 알게 되었다 　　콜린이 환자였기 때문에

an invalid / he had not learned things / as other children
　　　　많은 것들을 배우지 못했다는 것을 　　다른 아이들이 배우는 것처럼.

had. One of his nurses / had taught him to read / when he
　　콜린의 보모 중 한 명이 　　읽는 법을 알려 줘서

was quite little / and he was always reading / and looking
콜린이 아직 어렸을 때 　그는 항상 책을 읽고 　　　　　　　그림책을 보았다.

at pictures in splendid books.

Though his father rarely saw him / when he was awake,
그의 아버지는 콜린을 거의 보지 않았지만 　　콜린이 깨어 있을 때에는,

/ he was given / all sorts of wonderful things / to amuse
　그는 받았다 　　여러 가지의 멋진 것들을 　　　　혼자서 가지고 놀

himself with. He never seemed to have been amused, /
수 있도록. 　　그는 즐긴 적은 없었던 듯 했다,

however. He could have anything he asked for / and was
하지만. 　콜린은 원하는 모든 것을 얻을 수 있었고

never made to do anything / he did not like to do.
강요 받지도 않았다 　　　　　하기 싫어하는 일을.

Key Expression

사역동사의 make의 수동태

make와 같은 사역동사는 목적보어로서 동사원형을 취하는 동사들입니다. 그러나 사역동사의 문장이 수동태로 전환되면 be + 사역동사의 p.p + to + 동사원형과 같은 형태로 to가 삽입됩니다.

ex) He made her tell him a great deal about India. (능동태)
　　그는 그녀에게 인도에 대한 많은 것들을 얘기하도록 했다.
　　He asked for and was never made to do anything he did not like to do. (수동태)
　　그는 자신이 하기 싫은 일은 요청하지도 강요 받지도 않았다.

또한 사역동사 중에서 have는 수동태가 되지 않으며 let은 be allowed to의 형태로 전환된다는 점도 함께 알아두세요.

"Everyone is obliged to / do what pleases me," / he said indifferently. "It makes me ill / to be angry. No one believes / I shall live to grow up."

He said it / as if he was so accustomed / to the idea / that it had ceased to matter to him / at all. He seemed to like / the sound of Mary's voice. As she went on talking / he listened in / a drowsy, interested way. Once or twice / she wondered / if he were not gradually falling into a doze. But at last / he asked a question / which opened up a new subject.

"How old are you?" / he asked.

"I am ten," / answered Mary, / forgetting herself for the moment, / "and so are you."

> ### Key Expression
>
> **so + 동사 + 주어 : ~도 역시 그래**
>
> 앞에 나온 말에 대한 동의를 표현할 때 '~도 그래'라는 뜻으로 so + 동사 + 주어 구문을 사용합니다. 이때 앞 문장에서 사용한 동사가 be 동사나 조동사일 때는 이를 그대로 받으며, 일반동사일 때는 do를 사용하여 받습니다. 시제와 인칭(주어)에 유의하여 사용하세요.
>
> ex) I am ten, and so are you.
> 나는 10살이야, 그리고 너 또한 그렇지.

"How do you know that?" / he demanded / in a surprised voice.
"네가 그걸 어떻게 알아?" 콜린이 요구했다 놀란 목소리로.

"Because when you were born / the garden door was locked / and the key was buried. And it has been locked for ten years."
"왜냐하면 네가 태어났을 때 화원이 잠겼고 열쇠가 묻혀버렸으니까. 그리고 그 화원은 십 년 동안 잠겨 있었어."

Colin half sat up, / turning toward her, / leaning on his elbows.
콜린은 반쯤 일어나 앉았다, 메리가 있는 쪽으로 몸을 돌리고, 자신의 팔꿈치로 기대며.

"What garden door was locked? Who did it? Where was the key buried?" he exclaimed / as if he were suddenly very much interested.
"어떤 화원의 문이 닫혔다고? 누가 닫은 거야? 어디에 열쇠가 묻혀 있다고?" 그가 소리쳤다 갑자기 매우 호기심이 생긴 듯.

"It —— it was the garden Mr. Craven hates," / said Mary nervously. "He locked the door. No one —— no one knew where he buried the key."
"그건 — 크레이븐 씨가 싫어하는 화원이야." 메리가 당황하며 말했다. "그 분이 문을 잠그셨대. 아무도 — 아무도 모른대 그 분이 어디에 열쇠를 묻었는지."

"What sort of a garden is it?" / Colin persisted eagerly.
"무슨 종류의 화원이지?" 콜린은 계속 물었다.

"No one has been allowed / to go into it / for ten years," / was Mary's careful answer.
"아무도 허락 받지 못했대 그 안에 들어갈 수 있도록 십 년 동안." 메리가 조심스럽게 대답했다.

---

indifferently 무관심한 | drowsy 졸리는, 나른하게 만드는 | doze 잠깐 잠, 낮잠 | nervously 신경질적으로, 초초하게

But it was too late / to be careful. He was too much like
하지만 이미 너무 늦었다   조심하기에는.   콜린은 메리와 너무도 비슷했다.

herself. He too had had nothing to think about / and the
그 역시 생각할 만한 것이 없어서   숨겨진 화원이라

idea of a hidden garden / attracted him / as it had attracted
는 주제가   그의 호기심을 끌었다   메리의 호기심을 끌었던 것처럼.

her. He asked question after question. Where was it? Had
그는 질문에 질문을 거듭했다.   어디에 있었는지?   문을 찾

she never looked for the door? Had she never asked the
아 본 적이 전혀 없는지?   화원사들에게 물어 본 적은 전혀 없는지?

gardeners?

"They won't talk about it," / said Mary. "I think / they
"그들은 말하려고 하지 않았어,"   메리가 말했다.   "내 생각에는

have been told / not to answer questions."
그들은 말을 들은 것 같아 질문들에 대답하지 말라고."

"I would make them," / said Colin.
"내가 대답하도록 만들 거야,"   콜린이 말했다.

"Could you?" / Mary faltered, / beginning to feel
"그렇게 할 수 있어?   메리가 더듬거렸다,   겁을 먹기 시작하면서.

frightened. If he could make people answer questions, /
만약 콜린이 사람들에게 대답하라고 강요한다면,

who knew / what might happen!
누가 알겠는가   무슨 일이 생길지!

"Everyone is obliged / to please me. I told you that," / he
"모두 의무가 있어   나를 기쁘게 할.   내가 말했잖아,"   그가

said. "If I were to live, / this place would sometime belong
말했다. "내가 계속 살아 있다면,   이곳은 언젠가 내 소유야.

to me. They all know that. I would make them tell me."
모두가 그것을 알아.   그들이 내게 말하도록 만들 거야."

Mary had not known / that she herself had been spoiled,
메리는 몰랐었다   그녀 자신도 버릇이 없었다는 것을.

/ but she could see quite plainly / that this mysterious boy
하지만 그녀는 꽤 분명히 알 수 있었다   이 신비한 소년이 버릇이 없다는 것을.

had been. He thought / that the whole world belonged to
그는 생각했다   모든 세상이 자신의 소유라고.

him. How peculiar he was / and how coolly he spoke of /
그가 얼마나 이상했던지   그렇게 덤덤하게 말을 하다니

not living.
살지 못한다는 말을.

falter 더듬거리다, 불안정해지다 | frighten 겁먹은, 무서워 하는

"Do you think / you won't live?" / she asked, / partly
"네 생각에는   오래 살지 못할 것 같아?" 메리가 물었다.

because she was curious / and partly / in hope of making
약간은 궁금했기 때문에   또 한편으로는   바람으로

him forget the garden.
화원에 대해서 잊었으면 하는.

"I don't suppose I shall," / he answered as indifferently / as
"못 살 것 같아,"   그가 무심하게 대답했다

he had spoken before. "Ever since I remember anything /
아까 말했던 것처럼.   "내가 기억하는 때로부터

I have heard people say / I shan't. At first / they thought / I
사람들이 말하는 것을 들었어   내가 살 수 없을 거라고. 처음에는   그들은 생각했지

was too little to understand / and now / they think / I don't
내가 너무 어려서 이해하지 못할 것이라고   그리고 지금   그들은 생각해   내가 듣지 못

hear. But I do. My doctor is my father's cousin. He is quite
할 거라고. 하지만 난 듣거든. 내 담당 의사는 아버지의 사촌이야.   그는 가난한 편이고

poor / and if I die / he will have all Misselthwaite / when
          만약 내가 죽으면   그가 미셀스와이트를 모두 갖게 되지

my father is dead. I should think / he wouldn't want / me
아버지가 돌아가실 때.   내가 생각할 수밖에 없어   그는 원치 않는다고

to live."
내가 살기를."

"Do you want to live?" / inquired Mary.
"넌 살고 싶니?"   메리가 질문했다.

"No," / he answered, / in a cross, tired fashion. "But I don't
"아니," 그가 대답했다.   성나고 피곤한 듯이.   "하지만 난 죽고 싶

want to die. When I feel ill / I lie here / and think about it /
지 않아.   내가 병들었다고 느낄 때   난 여기 누워서   죽음에 대해 생각해

until I cry and cry."
울고 또 울 때까지."

"I have heard you crying / three times," / Mary said, "but
"난 네가 우는 소리를 들었어   세 번,"   메리가 말했다.

I did not know / who it was. Were you crying about that?"
"하지만 몰랐지   그게 누구인지.   그것 때문에 울고 있었던 거야?"

---

in hope of ~ 하는 바람으로 | persistently 끈덕지게, 고집스럽게

She did so want him / to forget the garden.
메리는 정말로 원했다 그가 화원에 대해서 잊기를.

"I dare say," / he answered. "Let us talk about something
"감히 말하지만," 그가 대답했다. "다른 것에 대해 이야기 하자.

else. Talk about that garden. Don't you want to see it?"
그 화원에 대해서 말해 보자. 넌 보고 싶지 않아?"

"Yes," / answered Mary, / in quite a low voice.
"보고 싶어," 메리가 대답했다. 꽤 낮은 목소리로.

"I do," / he went on persistently. "I don't think I ever
"난 보고 싶어," 그는 고집스럽게 계속했다. "이렇게 정말 원했던 적이 없었던 것 같아

really wanted / to see anything / before, / but I want to
뭔가 보고 싶다고 예전에는, 하지만 난 그 화원이 보고

see that garden. I want the key dug up. I want the door
싶어. 난 그 열쇠를 파내고 싶어. 그 문을 열고 싶어.

unlocked. I would let them take me there / in my chair.
나를 그곳에 데려 가도록 할 거야 내 의자에 앉은 채.

That would be getting fresh air. I am going to make them
그게 신선한 공기를 주겠지. 내가 사람들에게 그 문을 열게 할 거야."

open the door."

Key Expression

간접의문문

의문문이 다른 문장 속에 명사절 형태로 들어갈 때 이를 간접의문문이라 합니다. 간접의문문은 명사절이므로 문장 속에서 주어, 목적어, 보어로 사용됩니다. 간접의문문은 어순과 시제에 주의해야 해요. 의문사 + 주어 + 동사의 형태로 어순이 바뀌며 동사의 시제도 주절의 시제에 맞추어야 한답니다.

ex) I did not know who it was.
 (= I did not know. + Who was it?)
 나는 그게 누구인지 몰랐다.

He had become quite excited / and his strange eyes
began to shine / like stars / and looked more immense than ever.

"They have to please me," / he said. "I will make them take me there / and I will let you go, too."

Mary's hands clutched each other. Everything would be spoiled / —— everything! Dickon would never come back. She would never again / feel like a missel thrush / with a safe-hidden nest.

"Oh, don't —— don't —— don't —— don't do that!" / she cried out.

He stared / as if he thought / she had gone crazy!

"Why?" / he exclaimed. "You said you wanted to see it."

"I do," / she answered / almost with a sob / in her throat, "but if you make them open the door / and take you in like that / it will never be a secret again."

He leaned still farther forward.

---

immense 어마어마한, 엄청난 | sob 흐느끼다, 울다 | tumble over one another 문맥상에서는 '횡설수설 하다'라는 의미로 쓰임 | pant 숨을 헐떡이다 | interrupt 끼어들다, 말을 끊다

"A secret," / he said. "What do you mean? Tell me."
"비밀이라니," 그가 말했다. "무슨 말이지? 나에게 말해 줘."

Mary's words / almost tumbled over one another.
메리의 말들은 거의 횡설수설 하는 듯 했다.

"You see / —— you see," / she panted, "if no one
"있잖아 — 있잖아," 그녀는 숨을 헐떡였다,

knows but ourselves / —— if there was a door, / hidden
"우리 말고는 아무도 모른다면 — 문이 하나 있는데,

somewhere / under the ivy / —— if there was / —— and we
어딘가에 숨겨진 담쟁이덩굴 아래 — 거기에 있다면 — 그리고 우리가

could find it; / and if we could slip through it / together
찾을 수 있다면; 우리는 그 안으로 들어가 같이

/ and shut it behind us, / and no one knew / any one was
문을 닫는다면, 아무도 모르게 되면 안에 사람이 있는 것을

inside / and we called it our garden / and pretended that
우리만의 화원이라고 하면 그리고 가정한다면

/ —— that we were missel thrushes / and it was our nest,
— 우리가 개똥지빠귀라고 그리고 그곳이 우리의 둥지라고,

/ and if we played there / almost every day / and dug and
그리고 그곳에서 논다면 거의 매일 흙을 파고 씨앗들을

planted seeds / and made it all come alive —— "
심고 모든 것들을 다시 살려내서 — "

"Is it dead?" he interrupted her.
"죽어 있는 거야?" 콜린이 메리의 말을 끊었다.

> ### Key Expression
>
> #### 접속사 that의 생략
> 접속사 that이 이끄는 절이 타동사의 목적어일 경우, that은 생략되는 경우가 많은데, 생략한 자리에 쉼표를 넣어 대신하기도 합니다.
> 접속사 that의 생략은 특히 that절의 문장이 간단하여 알아보기 쉬울 때 흔히 일어나며, that 전후에 부사구가 들어가 문장이 길어질 때는 생략하지 않습니다.
>
> ex) No one knew (that) any one was inside.
> 아무도 누군가가 안에 있다는 사실을 몰랐다.
> They don't know (that) I know that.
> 그들은 내가 그걸 알고 있다는 사실을 모른다.

"It soon will be / if no one cares for it," / she went on. "The
"곧 그렇게 될 거야   아무도 돌보지 않는다면,"   그녀는 계속 했다.

bulbs will live / but the roses ── "
"구근들은 살겠지   그렇지만 장미들은 ─ "

He stopped her again / as excited as she was herself.
그는 메리의 말을 또 끊었다   메리만큼이나 흥분을 해서

"What are bulbs?" / he put in quickly.
"구근들이 뭔데?"   그가 재빨리 끼어 들었다.

"They are daffodils and lilies and snowdrops. They are
"그건 수선화랑 백합이랑 아네모네들이야.   그것들은 움직이고

working / in the earth now / ── pushing up pale green
있어   지금 땅 속에서   ─ 연두빛 싹을 밀어 올리고 있어

points / because the spring is coming."
                왜냐하면 봄이 오고 있으니까."

"Is the spring coming?" / he said. "What is it like? You
"봄이 오고 있어?"   그가 말했다.   "봄은 어때?

don't see it in rooms / if you are ill."
방 안에서는 볼 수 없거든   병들어 있으면."

Key Expression

how to ~ : ~ 하는 방법

의문사가 이끄는 명사절은 '의문사 + to부정사'의 형태로 축약하여 사용하는 경우가 많은데, 문장 내에서 주어, 목적어, 보어의 기능을 합니다.
또한 이는 '의문사 + 주어 + should + 동사원형'의 절로 바꾸어 쓸 수 있습니다.

what to ~ : 무엇을 ~할지
which to ~ : 어느 것을 ~할지
where to ~ : 어디서 ~할지
who(m) to ~ : 누구를 ~할지
how to ~ : 어떻게 ~할지(=~하는 방법)

ex) I feel almost sure I can find out how to get in sometime.
(= how I should get~)
나는 언젠가 들어가는 방법을 알아낼 수 있을 것이라고 확신한다.

push up 솟아 오르다, 위로 밀어내다 | plead 애원하다

"It is the sun shining on the rain / and the rain falling on
"비가 온 뒤에 햇빛이 비추이고 햇빛 위로 비가 내리는 거야.

the sunshine, / and things pushing up / and working under
그리고 싹들이 솟아 오르는 거지 땅 속에서 움직이면서."

the earth," / said Mary. "If the garden was a secret / and
메리가 말했다. "만약 화원이 비밀이라면

we could get into it / we could watch / the things grow
그리고 우리가 안으로 들어갈 수 있다면 우리는 볼 수 있을 거야 그것들이 자라나는 것을

bigger / every day, / and see / how many roses are alive.
매일, 그리고 볼 수 있겠지 몇 송이의 장미들이 살아있는지.

Don't you. see? Oh, don't you see / how much nicer it
모르겠어? 모르겠니 얼마나 더 좋을지

would be / if it was a secret?"
만약 이것이 비밀이라면?"

He dropped back on his pillow / and lay there / with an
그는 다시 자신의 베개에 머리를 기대고 누웠다

odd expression on his face.
이상한 표정을 얼굴에 띄고는.

"I never had a secret," / he said, "except that one / about
"나는 비밀이라고는 없었어." 그가 말했다, "하나만 빼고는 어른이 될 때

not living to grow up. They don't know / I know that, / so
까지 살 수 없을 것이라는. 그들은 모르지 내가 알고 있다는 걸,

it is a sort of secret. But I like this kind better."
그러니까 비밀이라고 할 수 있지. 하지만 이런 종류의 비밀이 더 좋아."

"If you won't make them / take you to the garden," /
"그들에게 시키지 않는다면 화원으로 너를 대리고 가도록,"

pleaded Mary, "perhaps / —— I feel almost sure / I can
메리가 간청했다, "어쩌면 — 난 거의 확신할 수 있어 언젠가 찾을 수

find out / how to get in / sometime. And then / —— if the
있을 거라고 안으로 들어가는 방법을 언젠가는. 그리고 그 때 — 의사가 네게

doctor wants you / to go out in your chair, / and if you can
원한다면 의자를 타고 밖으로 나가라고, 그리고 네가 항상 할 수

always do / what you want to do, / perhaps / —— perhaps
있다면 원하는 것을, 어쩌면 — 어쩌면 한 아이를

we might find some boy / who would push you, / and we
찾을 수 있어서 너를 밀어줄 수 있는 우리끼리만

could go alone / and it would always be a secret garden."
갈 수 있을 것이고 그러면 그곳은 언제나 비밀의 화원이 될 거야."

163

"I should — like — that," / he said very slowly, / his
"난 — 그렇게 — 하고 싶어," 그는 아주 천천히 말했다.

eyes looking dreamy. "I should like that. I should not mind
그의 눈은 꿈을 꾸는 듯 했다. "난 그러고 싶어. 신선한 공기를 신경 쓰지 않을

fresh air / in a secret garden."
거야 비밀의 화원에서는."

Mary began to recover her breath / and feel safer / because
메리는 다시 숨을 고르게 쉬며 더 안전하다고 느끼기 시작했다

the idea of keeping the secret / seemed to please him. She
왜냐하면 비밀을 지킨다는 생각이 그의 기분을 풀어 준 것 같았기에. 그녀는

felt almost sure / that if she kept on talking / and could
거의 확신할 수 있었다 만약 계속 이야기를 한다면 그러면 만들 수 있을 것

make him / see the garden in his mind / as she had seen it /
이라고 그가 상상 속의 화원을 볼 수 있도록 자신이 보았던 것처럼

he would like it so much / that he could not bear to think /
그도 매우 좋아할 것이라고 참을 수 없을 것이라고

that everybody might tramp in to it / when they chose.
모든 사람이 그곳을 마음대로 밟는다는 생각이 자신들이 선택한 곳을.

"I'll tell you / what I think / it would be like, / if we could
"내가 말해 줄게 내 생각을 어떤 모습일지, 우리가 그곳에 들어

go into it," / she said. "It has been shut up so long / things
갈 수 있다면," 그녀가 말했다. "그곳은 아주 오랫동안 잠겨 있었어

have grown into a tangle perhaps."
온갖 것들이 서로 엉켜 있을 거야."

He lay quite still and listened / while she went on talking
그는 가만히 누워서 듣고 있었다 그녀가 계속 이야기 하는 동안

/ about the roses / which might have clambered / from
장미에 대해 엉켜서 기어오르는

tree to tree and hung down / — about the many birds /
나무에서 나무로 매달려 있는 — 그리고 많은 새들에 대해서

which might have built their nests / there / because it was
그들의 둥지를 틀었을지 모르는 그곳에 아주 안전한 곳이었기에.

so safe. And then / she told him about the robin and Ben
그리고 나서 그녀는 붉은가슴울새와 벤 웨더스태프에 대해서도 말했다.

---

dreamy 꿈을 꾸는 듯한, 공상적인 | recover 회복하다 | tangle 엉키다 | clamber 기어오르다, 기어 가다

Weatherstaff, / and there was so much to tell about the
그리고 붉은가슴울새는 말할 것이 많았고

robin / and it was so easy and safe / to talk about it / that
쉽고 안전한 주제였기에   말하기에도

she ceased to be afraid. The robin pleased him so much /
두려워 하는 것도 멈췄다.   붉은가슴울새 이야기는 그를 매우 즐겁게 해서

that he smiled / until he looked almost beautiful, / and at
그는 미소지었다   아름답게 보일 정도로,   처음에는

first / Mary had thought / that he was even plainer than
메리는 생각했었다   자기보다 그가 훨씬 못생겼다고,

herself, / with his big eyes and heavy locks of hair.
큰 눈과 무성한 머리 숱이.

"I did not know / birds could be like that," / he said. "But
"난 몰랐어   새들이 그럴 수 있는지,"   그가 말했다.

if you stay in a room / you never see things. What a lot
"하지만 네가 방안에 있다면   아무것도 볼 수 없겠지.   넌 정말 많은 것을 알

of things you know. I feel as if / you had been inside that
고 있구나.   생각이 들어   네가 그 화원 안에 들어갔던 것 같은."

garden."

> ### Key Expression ❗
>
> **삽입절 I think : 내가 ~라고 생각한 것**
> 문장 내에 주어 + think를 삽입해 '(주어)의 생각으로는' 혹은 '(주어)가 ~라고 생각하는 것'이라는 의미를 보충하는 경우가 있습니다.
> 이러한 삽입절은 think 외에도 believe, suppose, guess, imagine, know처럼 생각을 표현하는 동사에서 주로 사용됩니다.
>
> ex) I'll tell you what I think it would be like.
>   그것이 무엇이 될 지에 대해 내가 생각하는 것을 네게 말해 줄게.

She did not know what to say, / so she did not say anything. He evidently did not expect an answer / and the next moment / he gave her a surprise.

"I am going to let you look at something," / he said. "Do you see that rose-colored silk curtain / hanging on the wall / over the mantel-piece?"

Mary had not noticed it / before, / but she looked up and saw it. It was a curtain of soft silk / hanging over / what seemed to be some picture.

"Yes," / she answered.

"There is a cord hanging from it," / said Colin. "Go and pull it."

Mary got up, / much mystified, / and found the cord. When she pulled it / the silk curtain ran back on rings / and when it ran back / it uncovered a picture. It was the picture of a girl / with a laughing face. She had bright hair tied up with a blue ribbon / and her gay, lovely eyes

---

evidently 분명히, 눈에 띄게, 듣기로는 | run back 뒤로 가다, 돌아가다 | complainingly 불평하며, 투덜대며, 불만스레

were exactly like Colin's unhappy ones, / agate gray / and
looking twice as big as they really were / because of the
black lashes all round them.

"She is my mother," / said Colin complainingly. "I don't
see / why she died. Sometimes / I hate her for doing it."

"How queer!" / said Mary.

"If she had lived / I believe / I should not have been ill /
always," / he grumbled. "I dare say / I should have lived,
too. And my father would not have hated / to look at me.
I dare say / I should have had a strong back. Draw the
curtain again."

Key Expression

관계대명사 what : ~한 것

관계대명사 what은 선행사를 포함한 관계대명사로 '~한 것'이라 해석되며 명사절을 이끕니다.
여기에서 what은 the thing which[that]으로 바꾸어 생각할 수 있죠.
특히 '무엇'으로 해석되는 의문사 what 절과 구분에 주의하세요.

ex) It was a curtain of soft silk hanging over what seemed to be some picture.
(관계대명사 what)
그것은 어떤 그림처럼 보이는 것 위에 걸려 있는 부드러운 비단 커튼이었다.
What would Mrs. Medlock do if she found out that I had been here?
(의문사 what)
내가 여기 있었다는 것을 발견한다면 메들록 부인은 무엇을 할까요?

Mary did as she was told / and returned to her footstool.
메리는 시키는 대로 하고 / 의자로 다시 돌아갔다.

"She is much prettier than you," / she said, "but her eyes are
"어머니는 너보다 훨씬 아름다우시네," / 그녀가 말했다, / "하지만 눈은 너랑 꼭 닮

just like yours / —— at least / they are the same shape and
았어 / — 적어도 / 크기와 색이 똑같아.

color. Why is the curtain drawn over her?"
왜 그림 위에 커튼을 친 거지?"

He moved uncomfortably.
그는 불편한 듯이 움직였다.

"I made them do it," / he said. "Sometimes / I don't like to
"내가 그렇게 하라고 시켰어," / 그가 말했다. / "가끔씩 / 나는 보고 싶지 않아

see / her looking at me. She smiles too much / when I am
/ 어머니가 나를 쳐다보고 있는 것을. 어머니는 항상 웃고 있어 / 내가 병들어 있고 비참

ill and miserable. Besides, / she is mine / and I don't want /
할 때에도. / 또한, / 엄마는 내 것이야 / 그래서 원치 않아

everyone to see her."
다른 사람들이 어머니를 보는 것을."

There were a few moments of silence / and then Mary
잠시 동안의 침묵이 흐르고 / 메리가 말했다.

spoke.

"What would Mrs. Medlock do / if she found out that I had
"메들록 부인이 뭐라고 할까 / 내가 여기 있었단 것을 알게 되면?"

been here?" / she inquired.
/ 메리가 궁금했다.

Key Expression

비교급을 강조하는 부사들

비교급을 수식하여 '훨씬, 더욱'이란 의미로 강조하는 부사를 알아볼까요.

▶ even, much, far, a lot, still + 비교급
(*첫 글자를 따서 'emfas'로 외워보세요!)
▶ much, by far, the very + 최상급

ex) She is much prettier than you
그녀는 너보다 훨씬 예뻐.

The Secret Garden

"She would do as I told her to do," / he answered. "And I should tell her / that I wanted you to come here / and talk to me every day. I am glad you came."

"So am I," / said Mary. "I will come as often as I can, / but" / —— she hesitated —— / "I shall have to look / every day / for the garden door."

"Yes, / you must," / said Colin, "and you can tell me about it afterward."

He lay thinking a few minutes, / as he had done before, / and then he spoke again.

"I think / you shall be a secret, too," / he said. "I will not tell them / until they find out. I can always send the nurse out of the room / and say that I want to be by myself. Do you know Martha?"

"Yes, / I know her very well," said Mary. "She waits on me."

He nodded his head / toward the outer corridor.

uncomfortably 불편하게, 거북하게, 언짢게 | **hesitate** 망설이다

"She is the one / who is asleep in the other room. The nurse
"그녀가 바로 마사야   저 옆 방에서 자고 있는 사람이.

went away yesterday / to stay all night with her sister / and
보모가 어제 떠났거든   동생 집에서 밤을 지낸다고

she always makes Martha attend to me / when she wants to
그러면 항상 마사에게 시중을 들라고 하지   밖에 나가고 싶을 때면.

go out. Martha shall tell you / when to come here."
     마사가 네게 말해 줄 거야   언제 여기에 올 수 있을지."

Then / Mary understood / Martha's troubled look / when
그때   그녀는 이해할 수 있었다   마사가 지었던 난처한 표정을

she had asked questions / about the crying.
자신이 질문을 했을 때   그 울음소리에 대해.

"Martha knew about you / all the time?" / she said.
"마사는 널 알고 있었던 거야   항상?"   그녀가 말했다.

"Yes; / she often attends to me. The nurse likes to get away
"그래;   그녀는 종종 나의 시중을 들어줘. 보모는 나를 멀리하고 싶어 하거든

from me / and then Martha comes."
         그럴 때면 마사가 와."

"I have been here a long time," / said Mary. "Shall I go
"여기 너무 오래 있었던 것 같아,"   메리가 말했다. "이제 그만 갈까?

away now? Your eyes look sleepy."
              눈이 졸려 보여."

"I wish I could go to sleep / before you leave me," / he said
"자고 싶어   네가 떠나기 전에,"

rather shyly.
그가 약간 부끄러운 듯이 말했다.

"Shut your eyes," / said Mary, / drawing her footstool
"눈을 감아,"   메리가 말했다,   의자를 가까이 당기며,

closer, "and I will do / what my Ayah used to do / in India.
      "내가 해 줄게   내 보모가 해 줬던 것을   인도에서.

I will pat your hand and stroke it / and sing something quite
손을 토닥이고 쓸어 줄게   그리고 낮은 소리를 불러 줄게."

low."

stroke ~을 쓰다듬다, 어루만지다 | chant 구호, 성가, 짧은 반복적 노래 | Hindustani 힌두스탄 말(인도의 주요 공용어)

The Secret Garden

"I should like that perhaps," / he said drowsily.
"그럼 좋을 지도 모르겠다," 그가 졸린 듯 말했다.

Somehow / she was sorry for him / and did not want him
어쩐지 그가 불쌍해졌다 그리고 그가 깨어 있는 것을 원치 않

to lie awake, / so she leaned against the bed / and began
았다, 그래서 그녀는 침대에 기대어서

to stroke and pat his hand / and sing a very low little
그의 손을 토닥이고 쓸기 시작하며 낮고 작은 노래를 불렀다

chanting song / in Hindustani.
힌두어로 된.

"That is nice," / he said more drowsily still, / and she
"그거 좋은데," 그는 더욱 졸린 듯이 말했다,

went on chanting and stroking, / but when she looked at
그리고 그녀는 계속 노래를 부르며 쓰다듬었다. 하지만 그를 다시 보았을 때

him again / his black lashes were lying close against his
 짙은 눈썹이 볼에 닿아 있었고,

cheeks, / for his eyes were shut / and he was fast asleep.
 눈을 감고 있었고 그는 깊이 잠들어 있었다.

So she got up softly, / took her candle / and crept away
그래서 그녀는 조용히 일어나서, 그녀의 초를 들고 살금살금 나왔다

without making a sound.
아무 소리도 내지 않고.

Key Expression

without ~ ing : ~하지 않고

without은 '~없이'라는 의미의 전치사입니다. 전치사이므로 뒤에는 명사 혹은 명사에 상당하는 어구가 와야 합니다.

▶ without + 명사 : ~없이
▶ without + 동사~ing: ~하지 않고

ex) So she got up softly, took her candle and crept away without making a sound.
그래서 그녀는 조용히 일어나 초를 들고서 소리도 내지 않으면서 살금살금 나갔다.

mini test 6

A. 다음 문장을 해석해 보세요.

(1) It sounds / just like a person lost on the moor / and wandering on / and on crying.
→

(2) Perhaps / the fact that she was in a rebellious mood / made her bold.
→

(3) Mary wondered / if she was in a real place / or if she had fallen asleep again / and was dreaming without knowing it.
→

(4) If the garden was a secret / and we could get into it / we could watch the things grow bigger / every day, / and see how many roses are alive.
→

B. 다음 주어진 문장이 되도록 빈칸에 써 넣으세요.

(1) 우리 디콘이 그만큼 영리한 줄은 결코 몰랐어요.

I never knew _____.

(2) 나는 예전에는 등을 똑바로 유지하기 위해 쇠로 된 것을 차고 있었어.

_____ to keep my back straight,

(3) 나는 네가 우는 것을 세 번 들었어, 그런데 그게 무슨 소리인지는 몰랐어.

_____ but I did not know _____.

(4) 우리가 그곳에 들어갈 수 있다면 그곳이 어떨 거라고 내가 생각하는지를 들려줄게.

_____, if we could go into it.

A. (1) 그건 마치 황무지에서 길을 읽고 계속 헤매면서 울고 있는 사람의 소리처럼 들렸어요. (2) 아마도 그녀가 반항적인 기분이라는 사실이 그녀를 대담하게 만들었다. (3) 메리는 그녀가 현실의 장소에 있는 것인지 혹은 다시 잠이 들어서 모르는 사이에 꿈을 꾸고 있는 것인지 궁금했다. (4) 만약 그 화원이 비밀이고

C. 다음 주어진 문구가 알맞은 문장이 되도록 순서를 맞춰 보세요.

(1) 이곳은 정말 이상한 집이야!
(this / queer / house / a / What / is!)
→

(2) 그녀가 너보다 훨씬 더 예뻐.
(prettier / is / much / she / you / than)
→

(3) 할 수 있는 한 자주 올게.
(come / often / will / I / as / as / can / I)
→

(4) 내 유모가 인도에서 했던 것을 해 줄게.
(in India / used / what / my Ayah / to / do)
→ I will do _____.

D. 다음 단어에 대한 맞는 설명과 연결해 보세요.

(1) torrent ▶　　◀ ① confused by something very strange

(2) rebellious ▶　　◀ ② extremely large

(3) immense ▶　　◀ ③ a lot of water falling or flowing

(4) mystified ▶　　◀ ④ difficult to control

8

MAGIC
마법

Dr. Craven had been waiting some time / at the house /
크레이븐 박사는 잠시 기다리고 있었다   집에서

when they returned to it. He had indeed begun to wonder
메리와 콜린이 돌아오는 때를.   그는 정말로 궁금해지기 시작했다

/ if it might not be wise / to send someone out / to explore
  현명한 일이 아닐까라고   누군가를 보내는 것이

the garden paths. When Colin was brought back to his
화원의 길들을 찾아보도록.   콜린이 자기의 방으로 다시 되돌아 왔을 때

room / the poor man looked him over seriously.
       불쌍한 그는 콜린을 진지하게 살펴 보았다.

"You should not have stayed so long," / he said. "You must
"너무 오래 있지 않는 편이 좋았을 거야,"   그가 말했다.

not overexert yourself."
"지나치게 움직이지 않는 것이 좋을 거야."

"I am not tired at all," / said Colin. "It has made me well.
"난 전혀 피곤하지 않아,"   콜린이 말했다.   "밖에서 노는 것이 날 건강하게 했어요.

Tomorrow / I am going out in the morning / as well as in
내일은   아침에도 나갈 거예요   오후뿐만 아니라."

the afternoon."

"I am not sure / that I can allow it," / answered Dr. Craven.
"확신이 서질 않는구나 허락해도 될지,"   크레이븐 박사가 대답했다.

"I am afraid / it would not be wise."
"걱정이 되는구나   그것이 현명한 일이 아닐까 봐."

"It would not be wise / to try to stop me," / said Colin quite
"현명하지 못한 일이에요   나를 멈추려고 하는 게,"   콜린이 꽤 진지하게 말했다.

seriously. "I am going."
           "난 갈 거예요."

Even Mary had found out / that one of Colin's chief
메리 조차도 알게 되었다   콜린의 가장 큰 특이한 점 중 하나는

---

overexert 지나치게 쓰다 | little brute 의인화되어 악동이라는 의미로 쓰임 | desert island 무인도

peculiarities was / that he did not know / in the least / what a rude little brute he was / with his way of ordering / people about. He had lived / on a sort of desert island / all his life / and as he had been the king of it / he had made his own manners / and had had no one to compare / himself with. Mary had indeed been rather like him herself / and since she had been at Misselthwaite / had gradually discovered / that her own manners had not been of the kind / which is usual or popular. Having made this discovery / she naturally thought / it of enough interest / to communicate to Colin. So / she sat and looked at him / curiously / for a few minutes / after Dr. Craven had gone. She wanted to make him ask her / why she was doing it / and of course she did.

"What are you looking at me for?" / he said.

"I'm thinking / that I am rather sorry for Dr. Craven."

"So am I," / said Colin calmly, / but not without an air of some satisfaction. "He won't get Misselthwaite at all / now

I'm not going to die."
이제 난 죽지 않을 테니."

"I'm sorry for him because of that, / of course," / said Mary,
"그것 때문에도 안 됐지만, 물론," 메리가 말했다,

"but I was thinking / just then / that it must have been very
"하지만 생각하고 있었어 그때 끔찍했을 것이라고

horrid / to have had to be polite / for ten years / to a boy /
친절하게 대해야 했다니 십 년이나 한 소년에게

who was always rude. I would never have done it."
늘 버릇없이 구는. 나 같으면 그렇게 못했을 거야."

"Am I rude?" / Colin inquired undisturbedly.
"내가 버릇 없다고?" 콜린이 담담하게 물었다.

"If you had been his own boy / and he had been a slapping
"네가 크레이븐 박사의 아들이고 그가 폭력적인 사람이었다면,"

sort of man," / said Mary, "he would have slapped you."
메리가 말했다, "그는 너를 때리고 말았을 걸."

"But he daren't," / said Colin.
"하지만 감히 그렇게 할까," 콜린이 말했다.

"No, / he daren't," / answered Mistress Mary, / thinking the
"그래, 감히 그렇게는 못하겠지," 메리가 대답했다, 조용히 생각을 말했다.

thing out quite / without prejudice. "Nobody ever dared to
편견 없이 "아무도 감히 하지 못했겠지

do anything / you didn't like / —— because you were going
네가 싫어하는 것을 — 왜냐하면 너는 곧 죽을 아이였고

to die / and things like that. You were such a poor thing."
죽은 거나 마찬가지였으니까. 몹시 불쌍한 아이였구나."

"But," / announced Colin stubbornly, / "I am not going to
"하지만," 콜린이 고집스럽게 말했다, "난 불쌍한 아이가 되지 않을 거야.

be a poor thing. I won't let people think / I'm one. I stood on
사람들이 생각하지 못하도록 할 거야 날 불쌍한 아이라고.

my feet / this afternoon."
난 내 두 발로 섰다고 오늘 오후에."

"It is always having your own way / that has made you so
"언제나 제멋대로 구니까 그렇게 괴팍해질 수밖에 없었지,"

---

undisturbedly 차분히, 조용히 | slapping sort of a man 폭력적인 사람 | prejudice 편견을 갖다 | have one's own way 자기 멋대로 굴다 | impartially 공정하게

176　The Secret Garden

queer," Mary went on, / thinking aloud.
메리가 계속해서, 생각을 말했다.

Colin turned his head, / frowning.
콜린이 고개를 돌리며, 얼굴을 찌푸렸다.

"Am I queer?" / he demanded.
"내가 괴팍하다고?" 그가 되물었다.

"Yes," / answered Mary, "very. But you needn't be cross,"
"응," 메리가 대답했다, "아주. 하지만 화낼 필요는 없어,"

/ she added impartially, / "because so am I queer / ——
그녀가 공평하게 덧붙였다, "왜냐하면 나도 괴팍하니까

and so is Ben Weatherstaff. But I am not as queer / as I
—— 그리고 벤 웨더스패프도 그래. 하지만 난 괴팍하지는 않아 예전만큼

was / before I began to like people / and before I found
내가 사람들을 좋아하기 시작하기 전 아니 그 화원을 발견하기 전에."

the garden."

"I don't want to be queer," / said Colin. "I am not going
"난 괴팍해지고 싶지 않아," 콜린이 말했다. "나는 그런 사람이 안 될 거야,"

to be," / and he frowned again / with determination.
그리고 다시 한 번 찡그렸다 다짐하듯이.

He was a very proud boy. He lay thinking / for a while
그는 자존심이 강한 소년이었다. 그는 누워서 생각했고 잠시 동안

/ and then Mary saw / his beautiful smile begin / and
그때 메리는 보았다 그의 아름다운 미소가 다시 시작되어

gradually change / his whole face.
차츰 변하는 것을 그의 얼굴 전체가.

> ### Key Expression
>
> **as~as… 원급비교 : …만큼 ~한**
>
> A=B일 때 쓰이는 비교급 표현을 원급비교 혹은 동등비교라고 부르며 as + 형용사/부사 원급 + as…의 형태로 사용합니다. 이때 '…만큼 ~한'이라고 해석하지요.
> 참고로 첫 번째 as 앞에 not을 붙여 not as(so) + ~ + as…가 되면 '…만큼 ~하지 않은'이라 해석하여 두 번째 as 뒤의 것이 더 우월하다는 비교의 의미를 가지게 됩니다.
>
> ex) I never knew our Dickon was as clever as that.
> 난 우리 디콘이 그렇게나 영리할 줄은 몰랐네요.

"I shall stop being queer," he said, "if I go every day to the garden. There is Magic in there —— good Magic, you know, Mary. I am sure there is."

"So am I," said Mary.

"Even if it isn't real Magic," Colin said, "we can pretend it is. Something is there —— something!"

"It's Magic," said Mary, "but not black. It's as white as snow."

They always called it Magic and indeed it seemed like it in the months that followed —— the wonderful months —— the radiant months —— the amazing ones. Oh! The things which happened in that garden! If you have never had a garden you cannot understand, and if you have had a garden you will know that it would take a whole book to describe all that came to pass there. At first it seemed that green things would never cease pushing their way through the earth, in the grass, in the beds,

/ even in the crevices of the walls. Then / the green
담벼락의 갈라진 틈새에서조차. 그 뒤

things began to show buds / and the buds began to unfurl
파릇파릇한 것들이 꽃망울을 맺더니 망울들이 피어나기 시작하여

/ and show color, / every shade of blue, every shade of
색깔이 드러났다. 모든 파란색과 모든 보라색을,

purple, / every tint and hue of crimson. In its happy days
진홍색의 모든 색조와 빛깔을. 제철을 만나

/ flowers had been tucked away / into every inch and hole
꽃들이 들어찼다 구멍과 모퉁이에 빼곡하게.

and corner. Ben Weatherstaff had seen it done / and had
벤 웨더스태프는 그렇게 되는 것을 보았고

himself scraped out mortar / from between the bricks of
직접 모르타르를 제거했으며 담벼락의 벽돌들 사이에서

the wall / and made pockets of earth / for lovely clinging
땅에 구덩이를 만들었다 사랑스럽게 늘어진 식물들이 자라

things to grow on. Iris and white lilies / rose out of the
날 수 있도록. 붓꽃과 하얀 수선화들이 풀밭에 피어났고

grass / in sheaves, / and the green alcoves filled themselves
다발 지어서, 녹색의 구석진 곳을 채웠다

/ with amazing armies of the blue / and white flower lances
놀라운 파란색 군단으로 하얀 꽃이 줄지어 섰다

/ of tall delphiniums or columbines or campanulas.
키가 큰 참제비고깔이나 매발톱꽃 또는 초롱꽃들이.

> ### Key Expression 🔑
>
> **what ~ for : 왜(=why)**
> 의문사 what이 like를 동반하면 how의 의미가 되는데, what이 for를 동반하면 why, 즉 '왜, 무엇 때문에'라는 의미를 갖게 됩니다.
>
> ex) What are you looking at me for?
> 너는 왜 나를 쳐다보고 있니?

crevice 틈 | unfurl 펼쳐지다, 펴다 | tint 엷은 색, 색조 | hue 색상, 색조 | in one's happy days 제철을 만나다 | tuck away 메우다 또는 들어차다 | every inch 빼곡하게 | clinging 몸에 달라붙는, 사람에게 매달리는 | iris 붓꽃 | sheaf 다발, 묶음 | alcove (정원, 숲 등의) 우묵한 공간 | lance 긴 창 | delphinium 참제비고깔 꽃 | columbine 매발톱꽃 | campanula 초롱꽃돌이

"She was main fond o' them — she was," Ben Weatherstaff said. "She liked them things as was allus pointin' up to th' blue sky, she used to tell. Not as she was one o' them as looked down on th' earth — not her. She just loved it but she said as th' blue sky allus looked so joyful."

The seeds Dickon and Mary had planted grew as if fairies had tended them. Satiny poppies of all tints danced in the breeze by the score, gaily defying flowers which had lived in the garden for years and which it might be confessed seemed rather to wonder how such new people had got there. And the roses — the roses! Rising out of the grass, tangled round the sun-dial, wreathing the tree trunks and hanging from their branches, climbing up the walls and spreading over them with long garlands falling in cascades — they came alive day by day, hour by hour. Fair fresh leaves, and buds — and buds —

/ tiny at first but swelling / and working Magic / until they
처음에는 작았지만 점점 부풀어 올라   마법에 걸린 듯

burst and uncurled / into cups of scent / delicately spilling
마침내 터지고 피어나서는   향기 가득한 잔들로   섬세하게 향내가 넘쳐 흐르게

themselves / over their brims / and filling the garden air.
만들며   이파리의 끝에서   화원의 공기를 가득 채웠다.

Colin saw it all, / watching each change as it took place.
콜린은 그 모든 것을 보았다, 변화가 하나씩 일어날 때마다.

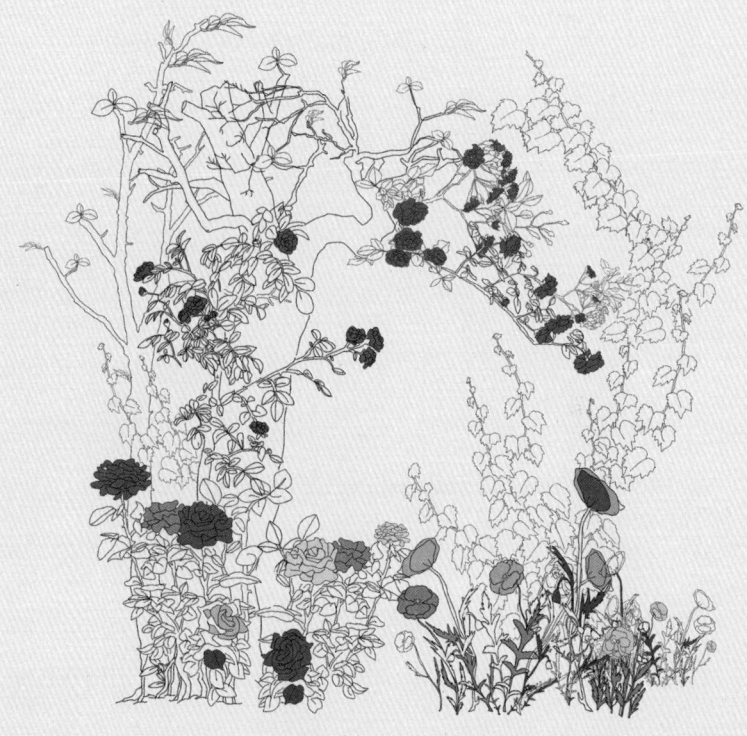

working magic 마법이 유효한, 마법에 걸린 | uncurled 동그랗게 말린 것을 풀다 | brims 위 끝부분, (모자의) 챙

Every morning / he was brought out / and every hour of
each day / when it didn't rain / he spent in the garden.
Even gray days pleased him. He would lie on the grass
/ "watching things growing," / he said. If you watched
long enough, / he declared, / you could see buds unsheath
themselves. Also / you could make the acquaintance /
of strange busy insect things / running about on various
unknown / but evidently serious errands, / sometimes
carrying tiny scraps of straw / or feather or food, / or
climbing blades of grass / as if they were trees / from whose
tops / one could look out / to explore the country. A mole
/ throwing up its mound / at the end of its burrow / and
making its way out / at last / with the long-nailed paws /
which looked so like elfish hands, / had absorbed him / one
whole morning. Ants' ways, beetles' ways, / bees' ways,
frogs' ways, / birds' ways, plants' ways, / gave him a new
world to explore / and when Dickon revealed them all / and
added foxes' ways, otters' ways, ferrets' ways, / squirrels'

ways, and trout' and water-rats' and badgers' ways, / there
오소리들의 사는 방법 등

was no end / to the things to talk about / and think over.
끝이 없었다.   이야기 거리나   생각할 거리가.

And this was not the half of the Magic. The fact that he
그리고 그것은 마법의 절반도 안 되었다.

had really once stood on his feet / had set Colin thinking
자신의 두 발로 설 수 있었다는 사실이   콜린을 엄청나게 생각하도록 만들었고

tremendously / and when Mary told him / of the spell she
             메리가 그에게 말했을 때   그녀가 일구어 낸 마법에 대해서

had worked / he was excited / and approved of it greatly. He
              그는 흥분했고   그것을 멋지게 인정했다.

talked of it constantly.
그는 그것에 대해 계속 이야기했다.

"Of course / there must be lots of Magic / in the world," /
"당연하지   여러 가지 마법이 있어   세상에는."

he said wisely / one day, "but people don't know / what it
그가 아는 체 하면서 말했다   하루는, "하지만 사람들은 모르지   그것이 어떤지

is like / or how to make it. Perhaps the beginning is just to
또는 어떻게 만들지.   어쩌면 그 시작은 그냥 말하는 것일 거야

say / nice things are going to happen / until you make them
     좋은 일이 일어날 거라고   정말로 일어나도록 만들 때까지.

happen. I am going to try and experiment"
      나는 실험하고 노력해 볼 거야."

> ### Key Expression
>
> #### even if : 비록 ~일지라도
> even if는 '비록 ~일지라도/하더라도'라는 뜻으로 양보구문을 이끄는 접속사입니다. 이와 비슷한 의미의 양보 접속사로 even though가 있습니다. 하지만 조건 접속사 if에서 출발한 even if와 양보 접속사 though의 의미를 강조한 even though는 그 쓰임에 차이가 있어요.
>
> even if I had a million dollars~ → 조건/가정의 문장
> even though I am a woman~ → 사실인 문장
>
> ex) Even if it isn't real Magic we can pretend it is.
>   그게 진짜 마술이 아니라 해도, 우리는 그렇다고 상상할 수 있어.

gray 잿빛의, 찌푸린 | unsheath 벗기다 | errand 사명 | ~ way ~ 하는 방법 | elfish 꼬마 요정 | otter 수달 |
ferret 흰 족제비 | trout 송어 | water-rat 물쥐 | badger 오소리

The next morning / when they went to the secret garden /
그 다음 날 아침 그들이 비밀의 화원에 갔을 때

he sent at once for Ben Weatherstaff. Ben came as quickly
즉시 벤 웨더스태프를 찾았다. 벤은 최대한 빨리 왔다

as he could / and found the Rajah standing on his feet
그리고 라자가 그의 발 앞에 서 있는 것을 보았다

/ under a tree / and looking very grand / but also very
나무 아래에서 굉장히 거대하게 보였지만 아주 예쁘게 웃으며.

beautifully smiling.

"Good morning, / Ben Weatherstaff," / he said. "I want
"좋은 아침이야, 벤 웨더스태프," 그가 말했다. "나는 원해

/ you and Dickon and Miss Mary to stand in a row / and
당신과 디콘과 메리가 일렬로 서서 내 이야기

listen to me / because I am going to tell you / something
를 들어주기를 여러분에게 말할 거니까

very important."
아주 중요한 것을."

"Aye, aye, sir!" / answered Ben Weatherstaff, / touching
"예, 예, 도련님!" 벤 웨더스태프가 대답했다. 이마를 만지며.

his forehead. (One of the long concealed charms / of Ben
(오랫동안 숨기고 있는 마법 중의 하나는

Weatherstaff / was that in his boyhood / he had once run
벤 웨더스태프가 어린 시절에 한 번은 집을 나가

away / to sea / and had made voyages. So he could reply
바다로 가서 항해를 했었다는 것이었다. 그래서 그는 선원처럼 대답할 줄

like a sailor.)
알았다.)

"I am going to try / a scientific experiment," / explained
"나는 시도해 볼 거야 과학적 실험을," 라자가 설명했다.

the Rajah. "When I grow up / I am going to make great
"내가 크면 위대한 과학적 발견을 이룰 거야

scientific discoveries / and I am going to begin now / with
그리고 지금 시작할 거야

this experiment"
이 실험으로."

184　The Secret Garden

"Aye, aye, sir!" / said Ben Weatherstaff promptly, / though this was the first time / he had heard of great scientific discoveries.

It was the first time / Mary had heard of them, / either, / but even at this stage / she had begun to realize that, / queer as he was, / Colin had read about a great many singular things / and was somehow / a very convincing sort of boy. When he held up his head / and fixed his strange eyes on you / it seemed as if you believed him / almost in spite of yourself / though he was only ten years old / —— going on eleven. At this moment / he was especially convincing / because he suddenly felt the fascination / of actually making a sort of speech / like a grown-up person.

Key Expression

once의 다양한 의미
- [부사] 한 번(현재완료와 함께 쓰이는 경우가 많음)
- [부사] (과거의) 언젠가, 한때
- [부사] (부정문/의문문에서) 한 번도, (if 뒤에서) 일단
- [접속사] 일단 ~하기만 하면, ~하자마자

Rajah 과거 인도의 국왕을 일컫는 말 | in a row 한줄로 나란히 | charm 마력, 마법 | run away 뛰쳐나가다 | voyages 여행, 항해 | promptly 즉각 | singular 특이한 | in spite of oneself 자기도 모르게, 무심코 | fascination 매력

"The great scientific discoveries / I am going to make," / he went on, / "will be about Magic. Magic is a great thing / and scarcely any one knows anything about it / except a few people in old books / —— and Mary a little, / because she was born in India / where there are fakirs. I believe Dickon knows some Magic, / but perhaps he doesn't know / he knows it. He charms animals and people. I would never have let him / come to see me / if he had not been an animal charmer / —— which is a boy charmer, too, / because a boy is an animal. I am sure / there is Magic in everything, / only we have not sense enough / to get hold of it / and make it do things for us / —— like electricity and horses and steam."

This sounded so imposing / that Ben Weatherstaff became quite excited / and really could not keep still.

"Aye, aye, sir," / he said / and he began to stand up quite straight.

---

fakir 파키르 (수피교 수도승으로 고행을 하거나 마술을 부리는 사람) | orator 연사 | keep ~ing 하면('계속 ~을 하다'라는 의미)

186　The Secret Garden

"When Mary found this garden / it looked quite dead," / the
"메리가 이 화원을 발견했을 때   거의 죽은 것처럼 보였어,"

orator proceeded. "Then / something began pushing things
연설자는 계속했다.   "그런 후   무언가가 여러 것들을 밀어 올리기 시작했어

up / out of the soil / and making things out of nothing. One
흙 밖으로   그리고 무에서 유를 창조했지.

day things weren't there / and another they were. I had
하루는 아무 것도 없다가   다른 날에는 있는 것이지.

never watched things before / and it made me feel very
나는 전에는 여러 가지 것들을 본 적이 없어   그래서 매우 호기심을 느꼈어.

curious. Scientific people are always curious / and I am
과학적인 사람들은 항상 호기심을 느끼는 법이고

going to be scientific. I keep saying to myself, / 'What is
나는 과학적인 사람이 될 거니까.   계속 나 자신에게 말하고 있어,   '무얼까?

it? What is it?' It's something. It can't be nothing! I don't
무얼까?'   무언가가 있어.   아무것도 아닐 리가 없어!

know its name / so I call it Magic. I have never seen the sun
그 이름은 모르겠어   그래서 나는 그것을 마법이라고 불러. 해가 뜨는 것을 본 적이 없지만

rise / but Mary and Dickon have / and from what they tell
메리와 디콘은 있으니까   그들이 내게 말해 주는 것에서

me / I am sure that is Magic too. Something pushes it up /
나는 그것 또한 마법이라고 확신해.   무언가가 그것을 밀어 올리고

and draws it. Sometimes / since I've been in the garden /
다시 그것을 끌어당겨. 가끔   내가 화원에 온 뒤로부터

I've looked up through the trees / at the sky / and I have had
나무들을 사이로 올려다 보았어   하늘을

a strange feeling / of being happy / as if something were
그리고 낯선 느낌을 가졌어   행복하다는   무언가가 밀어 올리고 끌어당기는 것처럼

pushing and drawing / in my chest / and making me breathe
내 가슴 속에서   그리고 숨을 가빠져.

fast. Magic is always pushing and drawing / and making
마법은 언제나 밀어 올리고 끌어당기고 있어

things out of nothing. Everything is made out of Magic, /
그리고 무에서 유를 창조해 내.   모든 것이 마법으로 이루어져 있어,

leaves and trees, / flowers and birds, / badgers and foxes and squirrels and people. So it must be all around us. In this garden / —— in all the places. The Magic in this garden / has made me stand up and know / I am going to live to be a man. I am going to make the scientific experiment / of trying to get some / and put it in myself / and make it push and draw me / and make me strong. I don't know how to do it / but I think / that if you keep thinking about it / and calling it / perhaps it will come. Perhaps that is the first baby way / to get it. When I was going to try to stand / that first time / Mary kept saying to herself / as fast as she could, / 'You can do it! You can do it!' / and I did. I had to try myself / at the same time, / of course, / but her Magic helped me / —— and so did Dickon's. Every morning and evening / and as often in the daytime / as I can remember / I am going to say, / 'Magic is in me! Magic is making me well! I am going to be as strong as Dickon, / as strong

daytime 낮 | drill 훈련

as Dickon!' And you must all do it, too. That is my
디콘처럼 튼튼하게!'라고. 그리고 여러분들도 모두 그렇게 해야 해. 그것이 나의 실험이야.

experiment. Will you help, / Ben Weatherstaff?"
도와줄 거지, 벤 웨더스태프?"

"Aye, aye, sir!" / said Ben Weatherstaff. "Aye, aye!"
"예, 예, 도련님!" 벤 웨더스태프가 말했다. "예, 예!"

"If you keep doing it / every day / as regularly / as
"계속해서 하게 되면 매일 규칙적으로

soldiers go through drill / we shall see / what will happen
군인들이 훈련을 받는 것처럼 보게 될 거야 어떤 일이 일어나는지

/ and find out / if the experiment succeeds. You learn
그리고 알게 될 거야 실험이 성공했는지. 우리는 여러 가지를

things / by saying them over and over / and thinking
배우지 그것들을 반복적으로 말하고 생각함으로써

about them / until they stay / in your mind forever / and I
그것들이 남아 있을 때까지 마음속에 영원토록 그리고

think / it will be the same with Magic. If you keep calling
내 생각에 마법도 마찬가지일 거야. 그것을 계속 부르면

it / to come to you / and help you / it will get to be part of
여러분에게 오라고 그리고 여러분을 도우라고 그것은 여러분의 일부가 될 거야

you / and it will stay / and do things."
그리고 남아 있으면서 여러 가지 일들을 할 거야."

Key Expression

keep ~ing : 계속해서 ~하다

'유지하다'의 뜻을 가진 동사 keep은 동명사를 목적어로 취합니다. keep ~ing는 '~하는 것을 계속하다', 즉 '계속해서 ~하다'의 뜻으로 계속의 의미를 강조하기 위해 이개를 넣기도 합니다.

ex) Mary kept saying to herself as fast as she could.
메리는 가능한 한 빨리 혼잣말을 계속했다.
Ben Weatherstaff became quite excited and really could not keep still.
벤 웨더스태프는 너무 흥분해서 가만히 있을 수가 없었다.

"I once heard an officer in India / tell my mother / that
"인도에 있을 때 한 번은 한 장교의 말을 들었어   우리 어머니에게 말하는 것을

there were fakirs / who said words over and over /
파키르가 있다고   말을 계속 반복하는

thousands of times," / said Mary.
수천 번."   메리가 말했다.

"I've heard Jem Fettleworth's wife say / th' same thing over
"저는 젬 페틀워즈의 부인이 말하는 것을 들었어요   똑같은 말을 계속해서

/ thousands o' times / —— callin' Jem a drunken brute," /
수천 번이나   — 젬을 술주정뱅이라고 부르면서."

said Ben Weatherstaff dryly. "Summat allus come o' that,
벤 웨더스태프가 담담하게 말했다.   "그 말대로 되지 뭡니까,

/ sure enough. He gave her a good hidin' / an' went to th'
아니나 다를까.   그는 그녀를 실컷 때리고   블루 라이언에 가서

Blue Lion / an' got as drunk as a lord."
     만신창이가 되도록 술을 마셨어요."

Colin drew his brows together / and thought a few minutes.
콜린은 눈살을 찌푸렸다   그리고 잠시 생각했다.

Then he cheered up.
그러고는 기운을 냈다.

Key Expression

강조의 do

동사의 의미를 강조하고 싶을 때 동사 앞에 조동사 do를 추가하여 '정말로 ~하다'라고 해석합니다. 이때 인칭과 시제에 맞춰 does, did 등으로 변화하며 그 뒤에는 동사원형이 옵니다.
강조의 do는 그 자체가 빠져도 문장에 영향을 주지 않으므로 다른 용법의 do와 구별할 수 있어요.

ex) You see something did come of it.
    너는 무언가가 정말로 일어났다는 것을 알고 있어.

---

brute 야수, 짐승, 또는 그와 같은 사람 | summat something 의 구어체를 글로 표현한 것 | brows 눈썹 | shrewd 기민한 | admiration 감탄, 존경

"Well," / he said, "you see something did come of it. She
"어쨌든," 그가 말했다, "무언가가 일어났다는 것은 알 수 있지.

used the wrong Magic / until she made him beat her. If
그녀는 잘못된 마법을 썼어 그가 자신을 때리도록 만드는.

she'd used the right Magic / and had said something nice
만일 그녀가 올바른 마법을 사용했다면 그리고 좋은 말을 했다면

/ perhaps he wouldn't have got as drunk as a lord / and
아마도 그는 만신창이처럼 술을 마시진 않았을 수도 있어 그리고 어쩌면

perhaps / —— perhaps he might have bought / her a new
—— 어쩌면 그가 사 왔을지도 몰라

bonnet."
그녀에게 새 모자를."

Ben Weatherstaff chuckled / and there was shrewd
벤 웨더스태프는 껄껄 웃었다 그리고 예민하게 존경심이 느껴졌다

admiration / in his little old eyes.
그의 작고 늙은 눈에서.

"Tha'rt a clever lad / as well as a straight-legged
"영리한 아이네요 꼿꼿한 다리를 가지기도 했고,

one, / Mester Colin," / he said. "Next time I see Bess
콜린 도련님은," 그가 말했다. "다음에 베스 페틀워스를 만날 때는

Fettleworth / I'll give her a bit of a hint / o' what Magic
약간의 힌트를 줘야겠네요 마법이 그녀에게 어떤 일을

will do for her. She'd be rare an' pleased / if th' sinetifik
할지. 그녀는 기뻐할 거예요

'speriment worked / —— an' so 'ud Jem."
그 과학적 실험이 성공한다면 —— 그리고 젬도요."

Dickon had stood / listening to the lecture, / his round
디콘은 서 있었다 강의를 들으며, 그의 동그란 눈을

eyes shining / with curious delight. Nut and Shell were on
빛내며 호기심 어린 기쁨으로. 넛과 쉘이 그의 어깨에 앉아 있었고

his shoulders / and he held a long-eared white rabbit / in
그는 귀가 긴 하얀 토끼를 안고 있었다

his arm / and stroked and stroked it softly / while it laid its
그의 품에 그리고 계속해서 부드럽게 쓰다듬었다 토끼는 귀를 등에 붙이고는

ears along its back / and enjoyed itself.
즐거워 했다.

"Do you think the experiment will work?" Colin asked him, wondering what he was thinking. He so often wondered what Dickon was thinking when he saw him looking at him or at one of his "creatures" with his happy wide smile.

He smiled now and his smile was wider than usual.

"Aye," he answered, "that I do. It'll work same as th' seeds do when th' sun shines on 'em. It'll work for sure. Shall us begin it now?"

Colin was delighted and so was Mary. Fired by recollections of fakirs and devotees in illustrations Colin suggested that they should all sit cross-legged under the tree which made a canopy.

"It will be like sitting in a sort of temple," said Colin. "I'm rather tired and I want to sit down."

"Eh!" said Dickon, "tha' mustn't begin by sayin' tha'rt tired. Tha' might spoil th' Magic."

Colin turned and looked at him —— into his innocent round eyes.

"That's true," he said slowly. "I must only think of the Magic."

It all seemed most majestic and mysterious when they sat down in their circle. Ben Weatherstaff felt as if he had somehow been led into appearing at a prayer-meeting. Ordinarily he was very fixed in being what he called "agen' prayer-meetin's" but this being the Rajah's affair he did not resent it and was indeed inclined to be gratified at being called upon to assist. Mistress Mary felt solemnly enraptured. Dickon held his rabbit in his arm, and perhaps he made some charmer's signal no one heard, for when he sat down, cross-legged like the rest, the crow, the fox, the squirrels and the lamb slowly drew near and made part of the circle, settling each into a place of rest as if of their own desire.

"The 'creatures' have come," said Colin gravely. "They want to help us."

Colin really looked quite beautiful, Mary thought. He held his head high as if he felt like a sort of priest and his strange eyes had a wonderful look in them. The light shone on him through the tree canopy.

"Now we will begin," he said. "Shall we sway backward and forward, Mary, as if we were dervishes?"

"I canna' do no swayin' back'ard and for'ard," said Ben Weatherstaff. "I've got th' rheumatics."

"The Magic will take them away," said Colin in a High Priest tone, "but we won't sway until it has done it. We will only chant."

"I canna' do no chantin'" said Ben Weatherstaff a trifle testily. "They turned me out o' th' church choir th' only time I ever tried it."

---

gravely 심각하게 | priest 성직자 | dervish 극도의 금욕 생활을 서약하는 수피교도. 의식을 행할 때 빠른 춤을 춘다

No one smiled. They were all too much in earnest.
아무도 웃지 않았다. 그들은 모두 너무도 진지했다.

Colin's face was not even crossed / by a shadow. He was
콜린의 얼굴엔 언짢은 빛이 없었다 조금도.

thinking only of the Magic.
오로지 마법만을 생각하고 있었다.

"Then I will chant," / he said. And he began, / looking
"그럼 내가 주문을 외울게," 그가 말했다. 그리고 그가 시작했다, 신비스러운 정령

like a strange boy spirit. "The sun is shining / ——
같은 모습으로. "해가 빛나고 있다

the sun is shining. That is the Magic. The flowers are
— 해가 빛나고 있다. 그것이 마법이다. 꽃들이 자라난다

growing / —— the roots are stirring. That is the Magic.
— 뿌리가 꿈틀댄다. 그것이 마법이다.

Being alive is the Magic / —— being strong is the Magic.
살아있는 것이 마법이다 — 튼튼한 것이 마법이다.

The Magic is in me / —— the Magic is in me. It is in
마법은 내 안에 있다 — 마법은 내 안에 있다. 그건 내 안에 있다

me / —— it is in me. It's in every one of us. It's in Ben
— 그건 내 안에 있다. 그건 우리 모두 안에 있다.

Weatherstaff's back. Magic! Magic! Come and help!"
벤 웨더스태프의 등에 있다. 마법이여! 마법이여! 와서 도우소서!"

Key Expression 🔑

look을 사용한 다양한 표현

흔히 '보다'라는 뜻으로 알고 있는 동사 look은 자동사이므로 뒤에 목적어를 취하려면 전치사 at을 써야 합니다. 뒤에 오는 전치사에 따라 다양한 의미로 쓰이는 look에 대해 알아볼까요.

look at ~을 보다 / look like ~처럼 보이다. ~한 것 같다 / look for 찾다, 찾아보다
look after 쫓다, 배웅하다, 보살펴 주다 / look over 검토하다, 조사하다 / look into
조사하다 / look 사물 up (정보를) 찾아보다 / look 사람 up (오랜만에) 방문하다
look up 올려다보다, 나아지다 / look down (on) 내려다 보다, 깔보다 / look back
되돌아 보다, 회상하다 / look about 주변을 둘러보다, 경계하다

ex) He began, looking like a strange boy spirit.
그가 신비한 정령 같은 모습으로 시작했다.
I've looked up through the trees at the sky.
나는 나무 사이로 하늘을 올려다 봤다.

He said it a great many times / —— not a thousand times / but quite a goodly number. Mary listened / entranced. She felt / as if it were at once queer and beautiful / and she wanted him to go on and on. Ben Weatherstaff began to feel soothed / into a sort of dream / which was quite agreeable. The humming of the bees / in the blossoms / mingled with the chanting voice / and drowsily melted into a doze. Dickon sat cross-legged / his rabbit asleep on his arm / and a hand resting on the lamb's back. Soot had pushed away a squirrel / and huddled close to him / on his shoulder, / the gray film dropped over his eyes. At last Colin stopped.

"Now / I am going to walk round the garden," / he announced.

Ben Weatherstaff's head had just dropped forward / and he lifted it / with a jerk.

"You have been asleep," / said Colin.

---

entranced 도취되다 | soothed 누그러지다 | humming 윙윙거리는, 콧노래 부르는 | soot 그을음, 검댕 | huddle 모이다 | film 얇은 껍질, 막 | mumble 중얼거리듯 말하다 | collection 헌금 걷기 | rheumatics 류마티즘

"Nowt o' th' sort," / mumbled Ben. "Th' sermon was good
enow / —— but I'm bound to get out / afore th' collection."

He was not quite awake yet.

"You're not in church," / said Colin.

"Not me," / said Ben, / straightening himself. "Who said I were? I heard every bit of it. You said / th' Magic was in my back. Th' doctor calls it rheumatics."

The Rajah waved his hand.

"That was the wrong Magic," / he said. "You will get better. You have my permission to go / to your work. But come back tomorrow."

Key Expression

긍정문과 부정문의 yet의 의미 차이

yet은 긍정문과 부정문에서 다음과 같이 의미에 차이가 있습니다.
▶ 부정문/의문문 : 아직
▶ 긍정문 : 이제, 앞으로(주로 미래형과 함께), / (그럴 것 같지 않지만) 그래도 (can/may 등과 함께)
또한 이 외에도 '그렇지만, 그래도'의 의미를 지닌 역접의 접속사로 쓰이기도 합니다.

ex) He was not quite awake yet.
그는 아직 완전히 깨어나지 않았다.

"I'd like to see thee walk round the garden," / grunted Ben.
"저는 도련님이 화원 주위를 걸어 다니는걸 보고 싶어요."   벤이 투덜거렸다.

It was not an unfriendly grunt, / but it was a grunt. In fact,
불친절한 투덜댐은 아니었지만,   투덜대는 것이었다.   실제로, 고집

being a stubborn old party / and not having entire faith
스럽고 나이 든 사람으로서   그리고 마법에 전적으로 믿음을 갖고 있지 않는

in Magic / he had made up his mind / that if he were sent
사람으로서   그는 마음을 먹었다   만일 여기에서 나간다면

away / he would climb his ladder / and look over the wall
   사다리를 타고 올라서   담장 너머로 바라볼 거라고

/ so that he might be ready / to hobble back / if there were
준비를 할 수 있도록   절뚝거리며 돌아오는 것에

any stumbling.
만일 넘어지는 일이 있다면.

The Rajah did not object to his staying / and so the
라자는 그가 머무는 것에 대해 반대하지 않았다

procession was formed. It really did look like a procession.
그리고 그렇게 행렬이 구성되었다.   정말로 행렬처럼 보였다.

Colin was at its head / with Dickon on one side / and Mary
콜린이 선두에 있었고   디콘이 한 쪽에   그리고 메리가

on the other. Ben Weatherstaff walked behind, / and the
다른 한 쪽에.   벤 웨더스태프는 뒤에서 걸었다.   그리고 "동물들"

"creatures" trailed after them, / the lamb and the fox cub
은 그들 뒤를 쫓았다.   양과 새끼 여우가 디콘에게 바짝 붙어 있었고,

keeping close to Dickon, / the white rabbit hopping along
   하얀 토끼는 깡충거리며 따라오거나

/ or stopping to nibble / and Soot following / with the
오물오물 씹기 위해 멈춰 섰고   숯검댕이는 따라왔다

solemnity of a person / who felt himself in charge.
사람처럼 근엄하게   자기가 책임자인 듯이.

---

grunted 불평하다 | hobble 다리를 절다, 절뚝거리다 | procession 행진, 행렬 | trailed 뒤를 쫓다 | nibble 잘근잘근 씹다 | solemnity 근엄함 | in charge 책임을 지다 | lookout 감시

198   The Secret Garden

It was a procession / which moved slowly / but with
그것은 행렬이었다   천천히 이동하는   하지만 위엄 있게.

dignity. Every few yards / it stopped to rest. Colin leaned
몇 야드 갈 때마다   행렬은 쉬기 위해 멈추었다.   콜린은 디콘의 팔에 기

on Dickon's arm / and privately Ben Weatherstaff kept a
대었고   벤 웨더스태프는 날카롭게 사방을 감시했다.

sharp lookout, / but now and then / Colin took his hand
   하지만 이따금   콜린은 자신을 지탱해 주는 손을 떼고

from its support / and walked a few steps alone. His head
   혼자서 몇 발자국을 걸었다.   그의 머리는 시종

was held up all the time / and he looked very grand.
일관 꼿꼿이 세우고 있었고   그는 매우 위엄 있어 보였다.

"The Magic is in me!" / he kept saying. "The Magic is
"마법이 내 안에 있어!"   그는 계속 말했다.   "마법이 나를 튼튼하게 만들

making me strong! I can feel it! I can feel it!"
고 있어!   난 느낄 수 있어!   난 느낄 수 있어!"

Key Expression

so that ~ : ~ 하도록, ~하기 위해서

'so that + 주어 + 동사'는 '~가 ~하도록'라는 의미를 가진 부사절로 'in order to + 동사원형'의 부사구로 바꾸어 쓸 수 있습니다.
'so ~ that' 구문과 헷갈리지 않도록 주의하세요.

ex) He would climb his ladder and look over the wall so that he might be ready
(=in order to be ready~)
to hobble back.
그는 절뚝거리며 돌아올 준비를 할 수 있도록 사다리에 올라가 벽을 살펴볼 것이다.

It seemed very certain / that something was upholding /
매우 확실해 보였다 무언가가 그를 붙들어 주고

and uplifting him. He sat on the seats / in the alcoves, /
세워 주고 있다는 것이. 그는 의자에 앉았고 화원의 정자 곁에.

and once or twice / he sat down on the grass / and several
그리고 한 번 또는 두 번 잔디밭에 앉았다 그리고 몇 번 길에서

times he paused in the path / and leaned on Dickon, / but
쉬거나 디콘에게 기댔다.

he would not give up / until he had gone all round the
하지만 그는 포기하지 않았다 화원을 모두 다 돌 때까지.

garden. When he returned to the canopy tree / his cheeks
나무 넝쿨로 돌아왔을 때 그의 볼은 발그레

were flushed / and he looked triumphant.
달아올라 있었고 승리감에 불타는 모습이었다.

"I did it! The Magic worked!" he cried. "That is my first
"내가 해냈어! 마법이 성공했어!" 그가 소리쳤다. "그것이 나의 첫 번째 과학적

scientific discovery."
발견이야."

"What will Dr. Craven say?" / broke out Mary.
"크레이븐 박사님이 뭐라고 하실까?" 메리가 외쳤다.

"He won't say anything," / Colin answered, "because he
"그는 아무 말도 안 할 거야." 콜린이 대답했다. "왜냐하면 그는 아무

will not be told. This is to be the biggest secret of all. No
것도 듣지 못할 거니까. 이건 가장 큰 비밀이 될 거야.

one is to know anything about it / until I have grown so
그 누구도 알아서는 안 돼 내가 아주 튼튼해 질 때까지

strong / that I can walk and run / like any other boy. I
내가 걷고 뛸 만큼 다른 여느 남자 아이들처럼.

shall come here every day / in my chair / and I shall be
나는 이곳에 매일 올 거야 휠체어를 타고 그리고 그것을 타고 집으로

taken back in it. I won't have people whispering / and
돌아갈 거야. 사람들이 숙덕거리게 하지 않을 거야

---

uphold 떠받치다 | uplift 북돋워주다 | triumphant 의기양양하다

asking questions / and I won't let my father hear about it /
질문을 받지도   그리고 아버지가 모르게 할 거야

until the experiment has quite succeeded. Then sometime /
실험이 아주 성공적일 때까지.   그런 후 언젠가

when he comes back to Misselthwaite / I shall just walk into
아버지가 미셀스와이트로 돌아오시면   그의 서재 안으로 걸어 들어가서

his study / and say / 'Here I am; / I am like any other boy. I
말할 거야   '내가 여기 있어요;   난 다른 남자 아이들과 같아요.

am quite well / and I shall live to be a man. It has been done
아주 건강해요   그리고 어른이 될 때까지 살 거예요.   과학적 실험 덕분이에요.'"

by a scientific experiment.'"
라고.

Key Expression

be to 부정사

'be to 부정사'는 to 부정사의 특수한 형태로 다음과 같이 다양한 의미를 지니고 있습니다. be 동사 뒤에 to 부정사가 나올 경우 명사적 용법으로 해석하는 것이 어색할 때 be to 부정사를 의심해 보세요.

▶ 예정 : ~할 예정이다(=will) → 미래를 나타내는 부사/부사구와 함께
▶ 의무 : ~해야 한다(=should)
▶ 가능 : ~할 수 있다(=can) → 주로 수동태로 쓰임
▶ 운명 : ~할 운명이다(=be destined to)
▶ 의도 : ~하고자 한다(=intend to)
▶ 가정 : ~한다면 → 가정법에서 were to 형태로 절대 불가능한 가정을 표현

ex) This is to be the biggest secret of all. No one is to know anything about it.
이건 가장 큰 비밀이 될 거야. (예정) 아무도 그것에 대해 알아서는 안 돼. (의무)
One of the things I am going to do is to be an athlete.
내가 하려는 일 중 하나는 운동선수가 되는 것이야. (명사적 용법)

"He will think / he is in a dream," / cried Mary. "He won't believe his eyes."

Colin flushed triumphantly. He had made himself believe / that he was going to get well, / which was really more than half the battle, / if he had been aware of it. And the thought which stimulated him / more than any other / was this imagining what his father would look like / when he saw that he had a son / who was as straight and strong as other fathers' sons. One of his darkest miseries / in the unhealthy morbid past days / had been his hatred / of being a sickly weak-backed boy / whose father was afraid to look at him.

"He'll be obliged to believe them," / he said. "One of the things / I am going to do, / after the Magic works / and before I begin to make scientific discoveries, / is to be an athlete."

"We shall have thee takin' to boxin' / in a week or so," /

half the battle 싸움의 절반, (절반은 해결된 것이다, 고비는 넘긴 것이다 등의 표현에 쓰임) | morbid 병이 있는

202　The Secret Garden

said Ben Weatherstaff. "Tha'lt end wi' winnin' th' Belt /
벤 웨더스태프가 말했다. "도련님은 벨트를 딸 거예요

an' bein' champion prize-fighter / of all England."
그리고 챔피언이 될 거예요 영국 전역에서."

Colin fixed his eyes on him sternly.
콜린은 근엄하게 그의 눈을 빤히 쳐다봤다.

"Weatherstaff," / he said, "that is disrespectful. You
"웨더스태프," 그가 말했다. "그건 무례한 거야.

must not take liberties / because you are in the secret.
제멋대로 행동해선 안 돼 당신이 비밀을 알고 있다고 해서.

However / much the Magic works / I shall not be a prize-
하지만 마법이 성공한다면 난 프로 권투선수가 되지 않을 거야.

fighter. I shall be a Scientific Discoverer."
과학적 발견자가 될 거야."

"Ax pardon / —— ax pardon, sir" / answered Ben, /
"죄송해요 — 죄송해요, 도련님" 벤이 대답했다.

touching his forehead / in salute. "I ought to have seed
그의 이마에 손을 올리며 경례의 표시로. "알았어야 했어요

/ it wasn't a jokin' matter," / but his eyes twinkled / and
농담이 아니라는 것을," 하지만 그의 눈은 반짝거렸고

secretly he was immensely pleased. He really did not
속으로는 말할 수 없이 기뻤다. 억박지름을 당하는 것에도 정말

mind being snubbed / since the snubbing meant / that the
개의치 않았다 억박지른다는 것은 의미했기에

lad was gaining strength and spirit.
아이가 힘과 활기를 되찾고 있다는 것을.

---

prize-fighter 프로 권투선수 | pardon 용서하다 | salute 경례 또는 인사(를 하다) | snubbed 억박지르다 | lad 소년, (친한 의미의) 녀석 | spirit 생기

mini test 7

A. 다음 문장을 해석해 보세요.

(1) Having made this discovery / she naturally thought it / of enough interest / to communicate to Colin.
→

(2) Nobody ever dared to do anything / you didn't like.
→

(3) If you keep doing it every day / as regularly as soldiers go through drill / we shall see what will happen / and find out / if the experiment succeeds.
→

(4) He had made up his mind / that if he were sent away / he would climb his ladder / and look over the wall / so that he might be ready / to hobble back / if there were any stumbling.
→

B. 다음 주어진 문구가 알맞은 문장이 되도록 순서를 맞추어 보세요.

(1) 그는 사람들에게 명령을 내리는 방식에 있어서 <u>그가 얼마나 버릇없는 아이인지</u> 전혀 알지 못했다.
(brute / he / rude / little / a / was / what)
→ He did not know in the least _____
_____ with his way of ordering people about.

(2) 왜 나를 쳐다보고 있는 거야?
(you / looking / are / me / What / for? / at)
→

(3) 사람들은 <u>그게 어떤지</u> 혹은 <u>어떻게 만들어야 하는지</u> 알지 못한다.
(like / is / what / it) (it / to / how / make)
→ People don't know _____ or _____.

A. (1) (1) 이러한 발견이 있은 후에 그녀는 자연스럽게 콜린과 이야기 하는 것이 충분히 재미있겠다고 생각했다. (2) 아무도 감히 네가 싫어하는 일을 하지 못하겠지, (3) 여러분이 그것을 군인들이 훈련받듯이 규칙적으로 매일 계속하면 우리는 무슨 일이 일어나는지 보고 실험이 성공했는지 알게 될 거야. (4) 그는 만약 나

(4) 그것은 느리지만 위엄있게 움직이는 행렬이었다.
(but / with / moved / which / dignity. / slowly)
→ It was a procession _____.

C. 다음 주어진 문장이 본문의 내용과 맞으면 T, 틀리면 F에 동그라미 하세요.

(1) Mary and Colin called the secret garden "the magic".
(T / F)
(2) The secret garden became the beautiful place full of a lot flowers.
(T / F)
(3) Dickon tried a new scientific experiment in his room.
(T / F)
(4) Dickon succeeded in skipping around the garden.
(T / F)

D. 의미가 비슷한 것끼리 서로 연결해 보세요.

(1) overexert   ▶   ◀ ① limp
(2) peculiarity   ▶   ◀ ② overuse
(3) hobble   ▶   ◀ ③ march
(4) procession   ▶   ◀ ④ characteristic

Answer

가게 되면 넘어지는 일이 있어도 절뚝거리며 다시 돌아올 준비를 할 수 있도록 사다리를 타고 올라가서 담장 너머를 조사해 보겠다고 결심했다. | B. (1) what a rude little brute he was (2) What are you looking at me for? (3) what it is like / how to make it (4) which moved slowly but with dignity | C. (1) T (2) T (3) F (4) F | D. (1) ② (2) ④ (3) ① (4) ③

205

9

IN THE GARDEN
화원에서

In each century / since the beginning of the world /
매 세기마다   이 세상이 시작된 이후로

wonderful things have been discovered. In the last
멋진 일들이 발견되어 왔다.   지난 세기에는

century / more amazing things were found out / than in
         더욱 놀라운 것들이 발견되었다

any century before. In this new century / hundreds of
그 이전 세기보다도.   이 새로운 세기에도

things still more astounding / will be brought to light. At
수백 가지의 훨씬 더 놀라운 일들이   빛을 보게 될 것이다.

first / people refuse to believe / that a strange new thing
처음에   사람들은 믿기를 거부했다   낯설고 새로운 것들이 이루어질 수 있다고,

can be done, / then they begin to hope / it can be done, /
              그리고 그들은 바라기 시작한다   그것이 이루어질 수 있기를

then they see / it can be done — then it is done / and all
그리고 나서 그들은 알게 된다 그것이 이루어질 수 있음을 — 그리고 이루어지면

the world wonders / why it was not done / centuries ago.
온 세계가 궁금해 한다   왜 그것이 이루어 지지 않았는지   몇 세기 전에는.

One of the new things / people began to find out / in the
새로운 일들 중 하나는   사람들이 알기 시작한   지난 세기에

last century / was that thoughts / —— just mere thoughts
              생각들이   — 단지 생각들이 —

—— / are as powerful as electric batteries / —— as good
     전기 배터리만큼 강력하다는 사실이었다   — 그리고 햇빛만큼

for one as sunlight is, / or as bad for one as poison. To
좋은 것이고,   또는 독만큼 나쁜 것이란 사실을.

let a sad thought or a bad one / get into your mind / is as
슬픈 생각이나 나쁜 것들을 두는 것은   네 마음으로 들어오도록

dangerous / as letting a scarlet fever germ / get into your
위험하다   성홍열 균을 놔두는 것만큼이나   당신의 몸 속으로 들어

---

discover 발견하다 | astound 충격을 주다 | refuse 거부하다 | electric 전기의 | poison 독 | scarlet fever 성홍열

body. If you let it stay there / after it has got in / you may
오도록. 만약 당신이 그것이 몸 속에 둔다면   들어온 이후에도

never get over it / as long as you live.
회복하지 못할 수도 있다   살아있는 한.

So long as Mistress Mary's mind was full / of disagreeable
메리의 마음이 가득 차 있는 동안

thoughts about her dislikes / and sour opinions of people /
싫어하는 것들을 증오하는 마음과   사람들에게 심술궂은 생각들과

and her determination / not to be pleased by / or interested
그녀의 결심으로   즐거워지지 않겠다는   또는 재미있어 하지

in anything, / she was a yellow-faced, sickly, bored / and
않겠다는.   그녀는 노란 얼굴에, 병약하며, 지루해 하고,

wretched child. Circumstances, / however, / were very
비참해 하는 어린애였다. 주변 환경은,   그러나,   그녀에게 매우 친절했다,

kind to her, / though she was not at all aware of it. They
그녀는 전혀 알아채지 못했지만.   그것들은

began to push her / about for her own good. When her
그녀를 밀어내기 시작했다   그녀에게 좋은 방향으로.

mind gradually filled itself / with robins, / and moorland
그녀의 마음이 점차 가득 차게 되었을 때   붉은가슴울새로,

cottages crowded with children, / with queer crabbed old
아이들로 붐비는 황무지 오두막으로,   별나고 심술궂은 늙은 화원사와

gardeners / and common little Yorkshire housemaids,
평범하고 어린 요크셔의 하녀들로,

/ with springtime / and with secret gardens / coming
봄과   비밀의 화원으로   매일매일 살아나는,

alive day by day, / and also with a moor boy and / his
그리고 황무지 소년과

"creatures," / there was no room left / for the disagreeable
그의 "동물들"로,   여유는 없었다   좋지 않은 생각들이 들어갈

thoughts / which affected her liver and her digestion / and
그녀의 간과 소화에 영향을 끼칠 만한

made her yellow and tired.
그리고 그녀를 누렇게 뜨고 피곤하게 할 만한.

as long as ~하는 한 = so long as | disagreeable 무례한, 무뚝뚝한 | determination 결정, 결심 | wretched 가여운, 불쌍한 | circumstance 환경, 상황 | gradually 점차 | crabbed 괴팍한 | affect 영향을 주다 | digestion 소화

So long as Colin shut himself up / in his room / and thought
콜린이 그 자신을 가두고 그의 방 안에 생각하는 동안

/ only of his fears / and weakness / and his detestation
그의 공포와 쇠약함과 혐오하는 마음만을 자신을 바라보는 사람들에 대해

of people who looked at him / and reflected hourly / on
그리고 매 시간 생각하는 동안

humps and early death, / he was a hysterical half-crazy
혹과 요절에 대해, 그는 신경질적인 반 미치광이 어린 우울증 환자가 되었다

little hypochondriac / who knew nothing of the sunshine
햇빛이나 봄에 대해서 모르는

and the spring / and also did not know / that he could get
그리고 역시 몰랐다 자신이 건강해질 수 있고

well / and could stand upon his feet / if he tried to do it.
자신의 두 발로 설 수 있다는 것도 만약 그렇게 하려고만 한다면.

When new beautiful thoughts / began to push out / the old
새롭고 아름다운 생각들이 밀어내기 시작했을 때

hideous ones, / life began to come back to him, / his blood
낡은 끔찍한 것들을, 삶은 그에게 다시 돌아오기 시작했고,

ran healthily through his veins / and strength poured /
그의 피는 그의 혈관을 건강하게 돌았고 힘은 그에게 넘쳐났다

into him like a flood. His scientific experiment / was quite
홍수처럼. 그의 과학적 실험은

practical and simple / and there was nothing weird about it
꽤 실제적이고 단순했으며 이상한 점이라곤 전혀 없었다.

at all. Much more surprising things / can happen to any one
더욱 더 놀라운 것은 누구에게나 일어날 수 있다는 것이다

/ who, / when a disagreeable or discouraged thought comes
~한 사람에게는, 기분 나쁘거나 낙담시키는 생각이 들어올 때

/ into his mind, / just has the sense to remember in time /
마음으로 때맞춰 기억해 내는 사람이라면

and push it out / by putting in an agreeable determinedly
또 밀어내는 사람이라면 마음에 들고 용기가 나는 생각들을 집어넣음으로써.

courageous one. Two things cannot be in one place.
그 두 가지는 한 곳에 있을 수 없는 것들이다.

"Where, you tend a rose, my lad,
"네가 장미를 가꾸는 곳에는, 아가야,

A thistle cannot grow."
엉겅퀴는 자랄 수 없단다."

detestation 혐오, 아주 싫어함 | reflect 반영하다 | hysterical 발작적인 | hypochondriac 심기증 환자 | hideous 흉측한, 끔직한 | vein 정맥 | experiment 실험 | weird 이상한 | discourage 낙담시키다 | courageous 용감한

While the secret garden was coming alive / and two
비밀의 화원이 살아나는 동안

children were coming alive with it, / there was a man /
그리고 두 아이도 그와 함께 살아나는 동안,   한 남자가 있었다

wandering about certain far-away beautiful places / in
멀리 떨어진 아름다운 곳들을 배회하고 있는

the Norwegian fiords and the valleys / and mountains of
노르웨이의 피오르드와 계곡들과   스위스의 산들을

Switzerland / and he was a man / who for ten years / had
          그리고 그는 사람이었다   10년 동안

kept his mind filled / with dark and heart-broken thinking.
마음을 채우고 있는   어둡고 가슴 아픈 생각들로.

He had not been courageous; / he had never tried / to put
그는 용기가 없었다;   그리고 그는 노력도 하지 않았다

any other thoughts / in the place of the dark ones. He had
뭔가 다른 생각을 그곳에 불어 넣으려고   어두운 생각들을 대신하는.

wandered by blue lakes / and thought them; / he had lain
그는 푸른 호수를 배회했고   그것들을 생각했다;   산기슭에 누워서도

on mountain-sides / with sheets of deep blue gentians /
                  짙푸른 용담꽃으로 둘러 싸인

blooming all about him / and flower breaths filling all the
그의 주위에서 꽃을 피우고 있는   그리고 꽃이 내뿜는 숨결이 공기를 채워도

air / and he had thought them. A terrible sorrow had fallen
그는 그것들을 생각했다.   그 끔찍한 슬픔은 그를 끌어내렸다

upon him / when he had been happy / and he had let his
          그가 행복했을 때

soul fill itself with blackness / and had refused obstinately
그리고 그의 영혼을 어둠으로 채웠고   고집스럽게 막았다

/ to allow any rift of light to pierce through. He had
어떤 빛이 뚫고 들어오는 것도.   그는 잊어버렸고

forgotten / and deserted / his home and his duties. When
            저버렸다   자신의 집과 의무를.

he traveled about, / darkness so brooded over him / that the
그가 여행을 하고 있을 때,   어둠이 그를 너무 잠식해 버려서

wander 배회하다 | fiord 피오르드(빙하작용으로 생긴 골짜기) | heart-broken 마음 아픈 | gentian 용담(종 모양 야생화) | rift 갈라진 틈 | pierce 관통하다,뚫다 | desert 저버리다 | duty 의무, 부담 | brood 곱씹다, (알을) 품다

sight of him was / a wrong done to other people / because it
그를 보는 것이 다른 사람들에게 나쁜 영향을 끼쳤다 왜냐하면 그것은

was / as if he poisoned the air about him / with gloom. Most
마치 그가 주변 공기를 중독시키는 것 같았으니까 우울함으로.

strangers thought / he must be either half mad / or a man
대부분의 낯선 이들은 생각했다 그가 반쯤 미쳤거나

with some hidden crime / on his soul. He was a tall man /
숨겨진 죄를 지은 사람이라고 영혼에. 그는 키가 크고

with a drawn face / and crooked shoulders / and the name
일그러진 얼굴에 굽은 어깨를 가진 사람이었다 그리고 이름은

/ he always entered on hotel registers was, / "Archibald
그가 항상 호텔 숙박부에 쓰는,

Craven, Misselthwaite Manor, Yorkshire, England."
"영국 요크셔의 미셀스와이트 장원의 아치볼드 크레이븐"이었다.

He had traveled / far and wide / since the day / he saw
그는 여행해 왔다 멀고 넓은 곳을 그 날 이후로

Mistress Mary in his study / and told her / she might have
서재에서 메리를 보았던 그리고 그녀에게 말했던 그녀에게 "조금의 땅"을

her "bit of earth." He had been / in the most beautiful places
가져도 된다고 말했던. 그는 살고 있었다 가장 아름다운 곳에,

/ in Europe, / though he had remained nowhere / more than
유럽에서, 아무 곳에도 머무르지 않았지만

a few days. He had chosen / the quietest and remotest spots.
며칠 이상. 그는 선택했다 가장 조용하고 외딴 곳을.

He had been on the tops of mountains / whose heads were
그는 산꼭대기에 있었다 봉우리가 구름 속에 있는

in the clouds / and had looked down on other mountains /
그리고 산들을 내려다 보았다

when the sun rose and touched them / with such light / as
태양이 떠올라 산들을 비출 때 그런 빛으로

made it seem as if the world were just being born.
마치 모든 세상이 막 태어난 것 같은.

gloom 우울 | crooked 비뚤어진 | register 등록 | remote 떨어진

But the light had never seemed to touch himself / until
그러나 그 빛은 결코 그를 감동시키는 것 같지 않았다

one day / when he realized / that for the first time in
그 날까지는   그가 깨달았던   십 년 만에 처음으로

ten years / a strange thing had happened. He was in a
이상한 일이 있어났다고.   그는 한 멋진 계곡에 있었다

wonderful valley / in the Austrian Tyrol / and he had
오스트리아 티롤 지방의

been walking alone / through such beauty / as might have
그리고 그는 홀로 걷고 있었다   그 아름다움 속을   구해 줄 지도 모르는,

lifted, / any man's soul / out of shadow. He had walked a
어떤 사람의 영혼이라도   어두운 그림자로부터.   그는 오래도록 계속 걸었지만

long way / and it had not lifted his. But at last / he had felt
그것이 그의 영혼을 구해주지는 못했다. 하지만 결국   그는 피곤함을 느

tired / and had thrown himself down / to rest / on a carpet
꼈고   주저앉았다   쉬기 위해

of moss / by a stream. It was a clear little stream / which
이끼로 된 카펫 위에   개울 옆의.   그것은 깨끗한 작은 개울이었다

ran quite merrily along on its narrow way / through the
좁은 길을 따라 신나게 흐르고 있는

luscious damp greenness. Sometimes / it made a sound
빽빽하고 축축한 이끼 사이로.   때때로   그것은 소리를 냈다

/ rather like very low laughter / as it bubbled over / and
나직한 웃음소리 같은   그것이 거품을 일으킬 때

round stones. He saw / birds come / and dip their heads
동그란 돌들 위에서.   그는 보았다   새가 와서   머리를 담그는 것을

/ to drink in it / and then flick their wings / and fly away.
물을 먹으려고   그리고 나서 날개를 푸드덕거리고   날아가는 것을.

It seemed like a thing alive / and yet its tiny voice / made
그것은 마치 살아있는 것 같았다   그러나 그 작은 소리는

the stillness seem deeper. The valley / was very, very still.
고요함을 더 깊게 만들었다.   그 계곡은   너무, 너무 고요했다.

valley 계곡 | moss 이끼 | stream 개울 | narrow 좁은 | luscious 감미로운, 부드러운 | bubble 거품이 일다 |
flick 휙 치다, 튀기다

212   The Secret Garden

As he sat gazing into / the clear running of the water, /
앉아서 들여다 보다가   맑게 흐르는 개울물을,

Archibald Craven gradually felt / his mind and body both /
아치볼드 크레이븐은 점차 느끼게 되었다   그의 마음과 몸 모두

grow quiet, / as quiet as the valley itself. He wondered / if
고요해지고 있다는 것을,   그 계곡만큼이나 고요하게.   그는 궁금했다

he were going to sleep, / but he was not. He sat and gazed
자신이 잠들려는 건지,   그러나 그건 아니었다.   그는 앉아서 바라보았다

at / the sunlit water / and his eyes began to see things /
햇빛에 빛나는 물을   그러다 그의 눈은 무언가를 발견했다

growing at its edge. There was one lovely mass of blue
가장자리에서 자라나고 있는 것을. 거기에는 사랑스러운 파란 물망초 한 무리가 있었다

forget-me-nots / growing so close to the stream / that its
    개울 아주 가까이에서 자라고 있어서

leaves were wet / and at these / he found himself looking
그 이파리들이 젖어 있는   그리고 이것들을   그는 자신이 바라보고 있다는 것을 알아챘다

/ as he remembered / he had looked at such things / years
그리고 기억해냈다   자신이 이런 것들을 바라봤다는 것을   수년 전에.

ago. He was actually thinking **tenderly** / how lovely it was
그는 실제로 감미롭게 생각했다   얼마나 그것들이 사랑스러운지

/ and what wonders of blue / its hundreds of little blossoms
그리고 얼마나 멋진 푸른 색인지   수백 송이의 작은 봉오리들이.

were.

Key Expression

as long as : ~하는 한

'as(so) long as'는 '~하는 동안'(=while) 혹은 '~하는 한'(=on condition that)이라는 의미를 가진 어구입니다. 뒤에는 주어+동사의 절이 오며 앞의 as 대신 so를 쓰기도 합니다.

ex) You may never get over it as long as you live.
   너는 살아있는 한 그것을 극복하지 못할 수도 있다.
   So long as Mistress Mary's mind was full of disagreeable thoughts ~
   메리의 마음이 유쾌하지 못한 생각으로 가득 차 있는 동안 ~

forget-me-not 물망초 | **tenderly** 부드럽게

He did not know / that just that simple thought / was
그는 알지 못했다 그 단순한 생각이

slowly filling his mind / —— filling and filling it / until
천천히 그의 마음을 채우고 있다는 것을 — 채우고 또 채우고 있다는 것을

other things were softly pushed aside. It was / as if a sweet
다른 것들이 부드럽게 밀려나게 될 때까지. 그것은 달콤하고 맑은 샘물

clear spring had begun to rise / in a stagnant pool / and
이 솟아나기 시작하는 것 같았다 구정물에서 그리고

had risen and risen / until at last it swept the dark water
계속 솟아나고 솟아나는 것과도 마침내 그것이 더러운 물을 밀어낼 때까지.

away. But of course / he did not think of this / himself.
그러나 물론 그가 이렇게 생각한 것은 아니었다 스스로.

He only knew / that the valley seemed to grow quieter
그는 단지 알았을 뿐이다 그 계곡이 점점 더 고요해지고 있다는 것을

and quieter / as he sat / and stared at the bright delicate
그가 앉아서 밝고 고귀한 푸른 것들을 바라보고 있는 동안.

blueness. He did not know / how long he sat there / or
그는 알지 못했다 얼마나 오랫동안 거기에 앉아 있었는지

what was happening to him, / but at last he moved / as if
또는 그에게 무슨 일이 일어나고 있었는지, 그러나 마침내 그는 움직였다

he were awakening / and he got up slowly / and stood on
마치 잠에서 깨어난 것처럼 그리고 천천히 일어나서 이끼 카펫 위에 섰다,

the moss carpet, / drawing a long, deep, soft breath / and
길고, 깊고 부드러운 숨을 내쉬고

wondering at himself. Something seemed to have been
그 자신에 놀라면서. 무언가가 풀어지고 해방된 듯 했다

unbound and released / in him, / very quietly.
그의 안에서, 아주 고요하게.

"What is it?" / he said, / almost in a whisper, / and he
"이게 뭐지?" 그가 말했다, 거의 속삭이듯,

passed his hand / over his forehead. "I almost feel as if
그리고 그는 손을 들어 이마를 짚었다. "거의 느꼈어 마치 — 내가 살아있

—— I were alive!"
는 것 같아!"

aside 한쪽으로 | spring 샘물 | stagnant 고여 있는 | sweep 쓸다, 휘몰아치다 | delicate 섬세하게 | unbound 속박이 풀린 | forehead 이마 | explain 설명하다 | by accident 우연히

I do not know enough / about the wonderfulness / of
나는 충분히 알 수 없다 / 경이로움이

undiscovered things / to be able to explain / how this had
발견되지 않은 것들에 대한 / 설명될 수 있는 지에 대해 / 어떻게 그 일이 그에게

happened to him. Neither does anyone else / yet. He did
일어났는지. / 다른 사람들도 마찬가지로 못한다 / 아직까지는.

not understand at all himself / —— but he remembered
그는 자신을 전혀 이해하지 못했다 / — 그러나 그는 이 이상한 시간을 기억했다

this strange hour / months afterward / when he was at
/ 몇 달 후 /

Misselthwaite again / and he found out / quite by accident
미셀스와이트에 다시 있었을 때 / 그리고 알아냈을 때 / 꽤 우연히

/ that on this very day / Colin had cried out / as he went
바로 그 날임을 / 콜린이 소리친 /

into the secret garden:
그가 비밀의 화원으로 들어 갔을 때:

"I am going to live forever / and ever and ever!"
"나는 영원히 살 거야, / 영원히 그리고 영원히!"

Key Expression

quieter and quieter : 점점 조용해지는

'비교급 + and + 비교급'은 '점점 더 ~한(하게)'이란 뜻을 가진 숙어입니다. 앞에 grow, become, get과 같은 상태 변화를 나타내는 2형식 동사와 함께 쓰여 '점점 더 ~해지다'라는 의미로 쓰이는 경우가 많아요.

ex) He only knew that the valley seemed to grow quieter and quieter.
그는 단지 계곡이 점점 더 조용해지는 듯 보인다는 것만 알았다.

The singular calmness remained with him / the rest of the evening / and he slept a new reposeful sleep; / but it was not with him very long. He did not know / that it could be kept. By the next night / he had opened the doors wide / to his dark thoughts / and they had come trooping / and rushing back. He left the valley / and went on his wandering way again. But, / strange as it seemed to him, / there were minutes / — sometimes half-hours — / when, without his knowing why, / the black burden seemed to lift itself again / and he knew / he was a living man / and not a dead one. Slowly — slowly / for no reason that he knew of — / he was "coming alive" / with the garden.

As the golden summer changed / into the deep golden autumn / he went to the Lake of Como. There he found / the loveliness of a dream. He spent his days / upon the crystal blueness of the lake / or he walked back into / the soft thick verdure of the hills / and tramped / until he was tired / so that he might sleep. But by this time / he had

begun to sleep better, / he knew, / and his dreams had
그는 잠을 더 잘 자기 시작했고,   그도 알았다,   그의 꿈이 멈췄다는 것을

ceased / to be a terror to him.
자신을 괴롭히는.

"Perhaps," / he thought, / "my body is growing stronger."
"아마도,"   그는 생각했다,   "내 몸이 더 튼튼해지는가 보군."

It was growing stronger but / —— because of the rare
그의 몸이 점점 더 튼튼해졌지만   —— 흔하지 않은 평화로운 시간들 때문에

peaceful hours / when his thoughts were changed / ——
그의 생각들이 바뀌었던 때의

his soul was slowly growing stronger, too. He began to
— 그의 영혼도 서서히 더욱 강해졌다.   그는 미셀스와이트를 생

think of Misselthwaite / and wonder / if he should not
각하기 시작했고   궁금해 했다   집에 가야 할 때가 아닌지.

go home. Now and then / he wondered vaguely / about
이따금   그는 살짝 궁금해졌다   그의 아들에 대해

his boy / and asked himself / what he should feel / when
그리고 자문해 봤다   그가 어떻게 느낄지를

he went / and stood by the carved four-posted bed again
그가 돌아가서   네 개의 조각기둥이 받치는 침대 옆에 다시 선다면

/ and looked down at / the sharply chiseled ivory-white
그리고 내려다 본다면   예리하게 조각한 듯한 상아빛의 얼굴을

face / while it slept / and, the black lashes / rimmed so
아이가 자고 있는 동안,   그리고 까만 속눈썹들을

startlingly the close-shut eyes. He shrank from it.
감은 두 눈을 빼빽이 둘러싸고 있는.   그는 그 생각으로 움츠러들었다.

---

singular 뛰어난 | reposeful 평온한 | troop 병력, 무리 | golden 빛나는, 소중한 | verdure 초목, 신록 | tramp 터벅터벅 걷다 | so that ~할 수 있도록 | terror 테러, 무서움, 공포 | vaguely 희미하게 | chiseled 조각된 | rim 테두리를 치다 | shrank 움찔하다, 줄어들다

One marvel of a day / he had walked so far / that when
어느 화창한 날　　　　　　그는 너무 멀리까지 걸어가서　　　　그가 돌아올 때는

he returned / the moon was high and full / and all the
　　　　　　　높고 둥근 달이 떠올라

world was purple shadow and silver. The stillness of lake
모든 세상이 자줏빛과 은빛으로 빛났다.　　　　　호수와 호숫가와 숲의 고요함은

and shore and wood / was so wonderful / that he did not
　　　　　　　　너무 멋져서　　　　　그는 별장 안으로 들어가

go into the villa / he lived in. He walked down to a little
지 않았다　　　　그가 살고 있던.　　그는 작은 그늘진 테라스로 걸어갔다

bowered terrace / at the water's edge / and sat upon a
　　　　　　　호수 가장자리에 있는　　　그리고 의자에 앉아

seat / and breathed in all the heavenly scents of the night.
　　　천상의 밤공기를 가득 들이 마셨다.

He felt the strange calmness / stealing over him / and it
그는 낯선 고요함을 느꼈다　　　　그의 마음을 빼앗는

grew deeper and deeper / until he fell asleep.
그리고 그것은 점점 더 깊어졌다　　그가 잠 들 때까지.

He did not know / when he fell asleep / and when he
그는 몰랐다　　　　그가 잠이 들고　　　꿈을 꾸기 시작했을 때;

began to dream; / his dream was so real / that he did not
　　　　　　　그의 꿈이 너무 현실적이어서　　그는 느끼지 못했다

feel / as if he were dreaming. He remembered afterward
　　　자신이 꿈을 꾸고 있다고.　　　그는 나중에 기억해냈다

/ how intensely wide awake and alert / he had thought
얼마나 완전하게 깨어서 정신차리고 있다고　　　자신이 생각했었는지.

he was. He thought / that as he sat / and breathed in the
그는 생각했다　　　자신이 앉아서

scent of the late roses / and listened to the lapping of the
철 늦은 장미의 향기를 들이 마시면서　물이 찰싹이는 소리를 들었을 때

water / at his feet / he heard a voice calling. It was sweet
　　　　발 밑에서　　　부르는 목소리를 들었다고.

and clear and happy / and far away. It seemed very far, /
그 소리는 달콤하고 맑고 행복하며　　멀리서 들려왔다.　　매우 멀었지만,

purple 자줏빛의 | bower 나무 그늘 | intensely 치열하게, 강렬하게 | alert 정신이 깨어 있는 | scent 냄새 |
distinctly 분명하게

but he heard it / as distinctly / as if it had been at his very
그는 그것을 들었다   분명하게   매우 가까이에 있었던 것처럼.

side.

"Archie! Archie! Archie!" / it said, / and then again, /
"아치! 아치! 아치!"   목소리가 말했다,   그리고 또 다시,

sweeter and clearer than before, / "Archie! Archie!"
전보다 더 달콤하고 더 맑게,   "아치! 아치!"

He thought / he sprang to his feet / not even startled. It
그는 생각했다   벌떡 일어났다고   심지어 놀라지도 않고.

was such a real voice / and it seemed so natural / that he
그것은 진짜 목소리였고   너무 당연해 보였다

should hear it.
그 목소리가 들리는 게.

"Lilias! Lilias!" he answered. "Lilias! Where are you?"
"릴리어스! 릴리어스!"   그가 대답했다.   "릴리어스! 어디에 있어?"

Key Expression

비교급을 사용한 필수 숙어들

비교급 + and + 비교급처럼 비교급 형용사/부사를 사용한 헷갈리기 쉬운 숙어들을 정리해 볼까요.

- no more than = only (단지)
- no less than = as many[much] as (~만큼)
- no better than = as good as (~와 다름없는)
- not more than = at most (기껏해야)
- not less than = at least (적어도)
- not better than = at best (기껏해야)

ex) He had remained nowhere more than a few days.
   그는 어떤 곳에서도 기껏해야 며칠밖에 머무르지 않았다.
   (* nowhere = not + anywhere)

"In the garden," it came back like a sound from a golden flute. "In the garden!"

And then the dream ended. But he did not awaken. He slept soundly and sweetly all through the lovely night. When he did awake at last it was brilliant morning and a servant was standing staring at him. He was an Italian servant and was accustomed, as all the servants of the villa were, to accepting without question any strange thing his foreign master might do. No one ever knew when he would go out or come in or where he would choose to sleep or if he would roam about the garden or lie in the boat on the lake all night. The man held a salver with some letters on it and he waited quietly until Mr. Craven took them. When he had gone away Mr. Craven sat a few moments holding them in his hand and looking at the lake. His strange calm was still upon him and something more —— a lightness as if the cruel thing which had been done had not happened

as he thought / —— as if something had changed. He was
생각되는 　— 뭔가가 달라진 것 같이.

remembering the dream / —— the real —— / real dream.
그는 그 꿈을 기억했다 　— 그 현실적인 — 현실적인 꿈을.

"In the garden!" / he said, / wondering at himself. "In
"화원에 있어!" 그가 말했다. 의아해 하며.

the garden! But the door is locked / and the key is buried
"화원에 있다니! 하지만 문은 잠겨 있고 그 열쇠는 깊이 묻혀 있는데."

deep."

When he glanced at the letters / a few minutes later / he
그가 그 편지들을 바라 보았을 때 몇 분 후 그는

saw / that the one / lying at the top of the rest / was an
알았다 한 통은 가장 위에 놓여 있는

English letter / and came from Yorkshire. It was directed
영국에서 온 것임을 그리고 요크셔에서 왔다는 것을. 그것은 글씨로

/ in a plain woman's hand / but it was not a hand / he
꾸밈없는 여자의 하지만 필체는 아니었다 그가 아는.

knew. He opened it, / scarcely thinking of the writer, /
그는 그것을 열었다, 발신인은 생각도 안 하고,

but the first words attracted his attention / at once.
그러나 처음 문장들이 그의 주의를 끌었다 즉시.

Key Expression

목적격 관계대명사의 생략

관계대명사 중에서 동사나 전치사의 목적어인 목적격 관계대명사는 흔히 생략되고 합니다.
명사 뒤에 연결어구 없이 주어+동사의 문장이 바로 이어지면 관계대명사의 생략을 염두에 두어야 합니다. 그 사이에 관계대명사를 넣어 관계대명사절이 앞의 명사(선행사)를 수식하는 것으로 해석해 보세요.

ex) But it was not a hand (that) he knew.
하지만 그것은 그가 알고 있는 손이 아니었다.
He had to make an effort to bring himself back to the place (that) he was standing in
그는 자신이 서 있던 장소로 돌아가기 위해 노력해야만 했다.

---

brilliant 반짝반짝 빛나는, 눈부신 | servant 하인 | stare 응시하다 | accustomed 익숙한 | roam 배회하다 |
salver 쟁반 | cruel 잔인한 | buried 묻힌 | glance 훑어 보다 | direct 향하다 | attract 마음을 끌다

"Dear Sir:

I am Susan Sowerby / that made bold to speak to you / once on the moor. It was about Miss Mary / I spoke. I will make bold to speak again. Please, sir, / I would come home / if I was you. I think you would be glad to come and / —— if you will excuse me, sir —— / I think your lady would ask you to come / if she was here.

Your obedient servant,

Susan Sowerby."

Mr. Craven read the letter twice / before he put it back / in its envelope. He kept thinking / about the dream.

"I will go back to Misselthwaite," / he said. "Yes, I'll go at once."

And he went through the garden to the villa / and ordered Pitcher to prepare / for his return to England.

In a few days / he was in Yorkshire again, / and on his long railroad journey / he found himself thinking of his boy /

---

obedient 순종적인 | envelope 봉투 | intend to ~할 작정이다 | drift 떠다니는 | rave 미친듯이 악을 쓰다 | take care of ~을 돌보다 | deform 기형이 되다 | cripple 불구가 되다

as he had never thought / in all the ten years past. During
전혀 그런 적이 없었음에도 지난 십 년 동안.

those years / he had only wished to forget him. Now, /
그 기간 동안 그는 아들을 잊으려고만 했다. 이제,

though he did not intend to think about him, / memories
그는 아들에 대해 생각하려 한 게 아님에도, 아들에 대한 기억은

of him / constantly drifted into his mind. He remembered
계속해서 그의 마음을 떠다녔다. 그는 그 캄캄했던 날들을

the black days / when he had raved like a madman /
기억했다 자신이 미치광이처럼 악을 썼던 때를

because the child was alive / and the mother was dead.
아들은 살아나고 엄마는 죽었기 때문에.

He had refused / to see it, / and when he had gone to look
그는 거부했다 그 아이를 보는 것을, 그리고 그가 보러 갔을 때

at it / at last / it had been, such a weak wretched thing /
마침내 그 아이는 너무 약하고 불쌍한 모습이어서

that everyone had been sure / it would die in a few days.
모든 사람들이 확신했다 얼마 후면 죽을 거라고.

But to the surprise / of those who took care of it / the
그러나 놀랍게도 그 아이를 돌보는 사람들이

days passed / and it lived / and then everyone believed / it
며칠이 지나자 아이는 살아났고 모든 사람들은 생각했다

would be a deformed and crippled creature.
아이는 기형이 되거나 장애자가 될 거라고.

Key Expression

to + one's + 감정 추상명사 : ~하게도

감정을 나타내는 형용사 앞에 to one's를 붙이면 '(~가) ~하게도'라는 뜻으로 부사의 의미를 갖게 됩니다.

to my surprise : 놀랍게도   to my sorrow : 슬프게도
to my delight : 즐겁게도   to my joy : 기쁘게도
to my satisfaction : 만족스럽게도   to my relief : 안심하게도
to my shame : 부끄럽게도   to my regret : 후회스럽게도

ex) But to the surprise of those who took care of it the days passed and it lived and then everyone believed ~.
(소유격 대신 of 사용)
하지만 그것을 돌보는 사람들이 놀라도록 날이 가고 그것이 살아나자 모두들 ~라고 믿었다.

He had not meant to be a bad father, / but he had not felt
크레이븐 씨가 나쁜 아빠가 되려 한 건 아니었지만, 그는 전혀 아빠임을 느낄 수 없

like a father at all. He had supplied doctors and nurses
었다. 그는 의사와 간호사와 사치품들을 주었지만,

and luxuries, / but he had shrunk / from the mere thought
 움츠려 들었다 아들을 생각하는 것만으로도

of the boy / and had buried himself / in his own misery.
 그래서 자신을 묻어버렸다 자신만의 비참함 속에.

The first time / after a year's absence / he returned to
처음으로 일 년 동안 집을 비우고 난 후 그는 미셀스와이트로

Misselthwaite / and the small miserable looking thing /
돌아왔을 때 그 작고 불쌍한 아이는

languidly and indifferently / lifted / to his face / the great
힘없이 그리고 무관심하게 들었다 그의 얼굴을 향해

gray eyes / with black lashes round them, / so like and yet
그 큰 회색 눈을 까만 속눈썹이 둘러싸고 있는, 매우 닮았지만

/ so horribly unlike / the happy eyes / he had adored, / he
 너무 무서울 정도로 달랐기 때문에 행복한 눈과는 그가 숭배했던,

could not bear / the sight of them / and turned away / pale
그는 참을 수 없어서 그 광경을 고개를 돌려버렸다 시체처럼

as death. After that / he scarcely ever saw him / except
창백한 얼굴로. 그 후로 그는 아들을 거의 보지 않았다

when he was asleep, / and all he knew of him / was that
잠들었을 때를 빼고, 그래서 그가 아는 거라곤

he was a confirmed invalid, / with a vicious, hysterical,
아들이 확실한 환자라는 것뿐이었다. 못되고, 히스테리를 부리며

/ half-insane temper. He could only be kept from furies
반쯤 미친 성격을 가진. 그는 겨우 화를 참을 수 있었다

/ dangerous to himself / by being given his own way / in
 자신에게 위험한 자기 마음대로 함으로써

every detail.
모든 면에서.

---

luxury 사치품 | shrunk 줄어든 | misery 고통 | absence 부재, 결석 | languidly 무기력하게 | indifferently 무관심하게 | lash 속눈썹 | adore 숭배하다 | invalid 병약자 | vicious 포악한 | temper (화내는) 성미 | fury 분노 | whirl 빙그르르 돌리다

224　The Secret Garden

All this was not an uplifting thing / to recall, / but as the
이 모든 일은 유쾌한 것은 아니었지만   기억하기에,

train whirled him / through mountain passes and golden
기차가 달리는 동안   산길과 황금 벌판을 지나

plains / the man who was "coming alive" / began to think
"되살아나고 있던" 그 남자는   새로운 길을 생각하기

in a new way / and he thought / long and steadily and
시작했다   그리고 생각했다   오래도록 꾸준히 깊게.

deeply.

"Perhaps / I have been all wrong / for ten years," / he said
"아마도   내가 모두 잘못한 거겠지   십 년 동안,"   그는 생각했다.

to himself. "Ten years is a long time. It may be too late / to
"십 년은 긴 시간이지.   너무 늦었을지도 몰라

do anything / —— quite too late. What have I been thinking
뭔가를 하기에   — 너무 많이 늦었어.   내가 무슨 생각을 하고 있었던 거야!"

of!"

Of course / this was the wrong Magic / —— to begin by
물론   이것은 잘못된 마법의 주문이었다   — "너무 늦었어"라고 말하는

saying "too late." Even Colin could have told him that.
것은.   심지어 콜린도 그렇게 말할 수 있었을 것이다.

> ### Key Expression
>
> #### either A or B : A 혹은 B
>
> 'either A or B'처럼 짝을 이루어 쓰는 접속사를 상관접속사라고 합니다. 이때, A와 B에는 같은 형태가 와야 합니다. 또한 상관접속사절이 주어로 쓰일 경우에는 단/복수 구별 및 수의 일치에도 주의하세요.
>
> ▶ both A and B : A와 B 둘 다 (항상 복수)
> ▶ either A or B : A 또는 B 둘 중의 하나 (단수 혹은 B에 일치)
> ▶ neither A nor B : A도 아니고 B도 아닌 (단수 혹은 B에 일치)
> ▶ not only A but also B : A뿐 아니라 B도(복수 혹은 B에 일치)
> ▶ A as well as B : B뿐 아니라 A도(복수 혹은 A에 일치)
> ▶ not A but B : A가 아니라 B(B에 일치)
>
> ex) But he knew nothing of Magic — either black or white.
> 그러나 그는 마술에 대해 아무것도 몰랐다 — 흑마술이든 백마술이든.

creature 존재, 생명체 | fatally 치명적으로 | spell 저주를 걸다 | possession 소유 | control 제어하다 | carriage 마차 | bob ~ curtsy 꾸벅 절을 하다

But he knew nothing of Magic / —— either black or white.
그러나 그는 마법에 대해 아는 게 없었다   — 흑마술이든 백마술이든.

This he had yet to learn. He wondered / if Susan Sowerby
이것은 그가 배워야 할 것이었다.   그는 궁금했다   수잔 소어비가 용기를 내서

had taken courage / and written to him / only because the
          편지를 쓴 건지

motherly creature had realized / that the boy was much
그 모성애 가득한 사람이 깨달았기 때문에   아이가 훨씬 더 나빠진 것을

worse / —— was fatally ill. If he had not been / under the
      — 치명적으로 나빴던.   만약 그가 있지 않다면

spell of the curious calmness / which had taken possession
그 이상한 고요함의 주문의 영향으로   그를 사로잡았던

of him / he would have been more wretched / than ever.
그는   훨씬 더 비참했을 것이다   그 어느 때보다.

But the calm had brought / a sort of courage and hope with
그러나 그 고요함은 가져다 주었다   어떤 용기와 희망을.

it. Instead of giving way / to thoughts of the worst / he
길을 내 주는 대신에   최악의 나쁜 생각에게

actually found / he was trying to believe in better things.
그는 정말로 알아차렸다   자신이 좋은 것들을 믿으려고 한다는 것을.

"Could it be possible / that she sees / that I may be able to
"그게 가능할까   그녀가 알아차리는 게   내가 아이에게 도움이 될 수 있고

do him good / and control him? " / he thought. "I will go
통제할 수 있을 거라고?"   그는 생각했다.   "가서 그녀를

and see her / on my way to Misselthwaite."
만나야겠다   미셀스와이트로 가는 길에."

But when on his way across the moor / he stopped the
그러나 황무지를 가로질러 가는 길에   그는 마차를 멈췄고

carriage / at the cottage, / seven or eight children / who
오두막에서,   7~8명의 아이들이

were playing about gathered in a group / and bobbing
무리 지어 놀고 있다가   허리를 숙여 싹싹하고 공손한

seven or eight / friendly and polite curtsies / told him / that
절을 하고는   그에게 말했다

their mother had gone / to the other side of the moor / early
어머니는 갔다고   황무지의 다른 쪽으로

in the morning / to help a woman / who had a new baby.
아침 일찍   여자를 돕기 위해   새로 아이를 낳은.

"Our Dickon," they volunteered, was over at the Manor working in one of the gardens where he went several days each week.

Mr. Craven looked over the collection of sturdy little bodies and round red-cheeked faces, each one grinning in its own particular way, and he awoke to the fact that they were a healthy likable lot. He smiled at their friendly grins and took a golden sovereign from his pocket and gave it to "our 'Lizabeth Ellen" who was the oldest.

"If you divide that into eight parts there will be half a crown for each of you," he said.

Then amid grins and chuckles and bobbing of curtsies he drove away, leaving ecstasy and nudging elbows and little jumps of joy behind.

The drive across the wonderfulness of the moor was a soothing thing. Why did it seem to give him a sense of homecoming which he had been sure he could never

volunteer 자원하다 | sturdy 튼튼한 | particular 특별히 | soverign 1파운드짜리 금화 | crown 1크라운(5실링, 현재 25펜스) | amid ~가운데 | ecstasy 환희 | nudge 쿡쿡 찌르다

feel again / —— that sense of the beauty / of land and sky
— 아름다움을 느끼는 감각이나

and purple bloom of distance / and a warming of the heart
땅과 하늘과 멀리 있는 자줏빛 꽃들의 그리고 따뜻한 마음을,

at drawing, / nearer to the great old house / which had
낡은 저택에 가까워질수록

held those of his blood / for six hundred years? How he
그의 조상이 머물러 온 600년 동안이나?

had driven away from it / the last time, / shuddering to
그가 어떻게 그곳을 달려 나왔는지를 지난번에는, 몸을 떨며 생각했다

think of / its closed rooms / and the boy / lying in the four-
그 굳게 닫힌 문들과 그 아이를 네 개의 기둥이 떠받치는

posted bed / with the brocaded hangings. Was it possible
침대에 누워 있던 양단의 장식품들이 걸려 있는. 가능할까

/ that perhaps he might find / him changed a little / for the
혹시 그가 발견하게 되어서 아이가 조금 변화한 것을 더 나은 쪽

better / and that he might overcome / his shrinking from
으로 그가 극복하는 것이 아이를 보고 몸을 움츠리게

him? How real / that dream had been / —— how wonderful
되는 걸? 얼마나 현실 같았던가 그 꿈은 — 얼마나 경이롭고 밝은 목

and clear the voice / which called back to him, / "In the
소리였나 그에게 대답하던 목소리는,

garden —— In the garden!"
"화원에 있어 — 화원에!"라고.

> ### Key Expression
>
> **while의 다양한 의미**
>
> while은 접속사와 명사로서 다양한 의미를 가지고 있어요.
>
> ▶ (시간) ~하는 동안
> ▶ (대조) ~하는 반면
> ▶ (문장 첫 부분) ~이긴 하지만
> ▶ (명사) 잠깐, 잠시, 동안 → for a while, a little while (잠시 동안)
>
> ex) Then they sat down under their tree — all but Colin, who wanted to stand while he told the story.
> 그리고 나서 그들은 나무 밑 의자에 앉았다 — 얘기하는 동안 서 있겠다는 콜린을 제외한 모두가.

shudder 떨다

"I will try to find the key," he said. "I will try to open the door. I must —— though I don't know why."

When he arrived at the Manor the servants who received him with the usual ceremony noticed that he looked better and that he did not go to the remote rooms where he usually lived attended by Pitcher. He went into the library and sent for Mrs. Medlock. She came to him somewhat excited and curious and flustered.

"How is Master Colin, Medlock?" he inquired.

"Well, sir," Mrs. Medlock answered, "he's —— he's different, in a manner of speaking."

"Worse?" he suggested.

Mrs. Medlock really was flushed.

"Well, you see, sir," she tried to explain, "neither Dr. Craven, nor the nurse, nor me can exactly make him out."

"Why is that?"

somewhat 다소 | curious 호기심 있는 | fluster 허둥지둥하다, 당황하다 | suggest 말하다, (뜻을) 비치다 | flush 얼굴을 붉히다

"To tell the truth, sir, / Master Colin might be better / and
"사실대로 말씀 드리면요, 주인님,   콜린 도련님은 나아지고 있는지 모릅니다   그리고

he might be changing / for the worse. His appetite, sir, / is
변하는 중인지도 모릅니다   더 나쁜 쪽으로.   그의 식욕은, 주인님,

past understanding / —— and his ways —— "
이해할 수 없습니다   — 그리고 방식들도 —"

"Has he become more —— more peculiar?" / her master,
"그가 더욱 — 더욱 이상해진 게요?"   주인이 물었다,

asked, / knitting his brows anxiously.
  걱정스레 눈살을 찌푸리며.

"That's it, sir. He's growing very peculiar —— when you
"그렇습니다, 주인님.   매우 특이하게 변하고 있습니다 — 비교해 보자면요

compare him / with what he used to be. He used to eat
  예전의 모습과.   아무것도 먹지 않았는데

nothing / and then suddenly he began / to eat something
  그리고 나서는 갑자기   엄청나게 먹기 시작했습니다

enormous / —— and then he stopped again all at once
  — 그리고 나서는 다시 갑자기 멈추고

/ and the meals were sent back / just as they used to
  식사를 되돌립니다   예전에 그랬던 것처럼.

be. You never knew, sir, / perhaps, / that out of doors
  주인님은 모르셨을 겁니다,   아마도,   도련님은 절대로 문 밖에 나가는

he never would let himself be taken. The things we've
법이 없었어요.   저희는 겪었어요

gone through / to get him to go out / in his chair / would
  도련님을 밖으로 데리고 나가려면   의자에서

leave a body trembling / like a leaf. He'd throw himself
벌벌 떨며 있곤 했지요   나뭇잎처럼.   도련님이 자신을 밀어 넣을지

/ into such a state / that Dr. Craven said / he couldn't
  어떤 상황에   크레이븐 박사 말로는   책임질 수 없을 거라고

be responsible / for forcing him. Well, sir, just without
했습니다   강제로 했다간.   그런데, 주인님, 아무 징후도 없이

---

appetite 입맛을 돋우다 | peculiar 이상한, 별난, 희한한, 특이한 | compare 비교하다 | enormous 엄청난, 막대한 | tremble 떨리다, 떨다 | leaf 나뭇잎

warning / —— not long after / one of his worst tantrums / he suddenly insisted on / being taken out every day / by Miss Mary / and Susan Sowerby's boy Dickon / that could push his chair. He took a fancy / to both Miss Mary and Dickon, / and Dickon brought his tame animals, / and, / if you'll credit it, sir, / out of doors / he will stay from morning until night."

"How does he look?" / was the next question.

"If he took his food natural, sir, / you'd think / he was putting on flesh / —— but we're afraid / it may be a sort of bloat. He laughs sometimes / in a queer way / when he's alone with Miss Mary. He never used to laugh at all. Dr. Craven is coming / to see you / at once, / if you'll allow him. He never was as puzzled / in his life."

---

warning 경고 | **tantrum** 발작, 악쓰고 성질내는 것 | **insist** 주장하다 | **tame** 길들은 | **credit** 칭찬, 인정, 자랑거리 | **flesh** 살, 고기, 피부 | **bloat** 부은 것, 부어오르다

"Where is Master Colin now?" / Mr. Craven asked.

"In the garden, sir. He's always in the garden / —— though not a human creature is allowed / to go near / for fear they'll look at him."

Mr. Craven scarcely heard her last words.

"In the garden," / he said, / and after he had sent Mrs. Medlock away / he stood and repeated it again and again. "In the garden!"

He had to make an effort / to bring himself back to the place / he was standing in / and when he felt / he was on earth again / he turned and went out of the room. He took his way, / as Mary had done, / through the door / in the shrubbery / and among the laurels and the fountain beds. The fountain was playing now / and was encircled / by beds of brilliant autumn flowers. He crossed the lawn / and turned into / the Long Walk / by the ivied walls. He did not walk quickly, / but slowly, / and his eyes were on the path. He felt / as if he were being drawn back / to the place

/ he had so long forsaken, / and he did not know why. As he drew near to it / his step became still more slow. He knew / where the door was / even though the ivy hung thick over it / —— but he did not know / exactly where it lay —— / that buried key.

So he stopped / and stood still, / looking around him, / and almost the moment / after he had paused / he startled and listened / —— asking himself / if he were walking in a dream.

Key Expression

to tell the truth : 사실을 말하자면

'to tell the truth(사실은, 사실을 말하자면)'이란 의미의 대표적인 독립부정사입니다.
독립부정사란 독립적으로 쓰이며 문장 전체를 수식하는 to 부정사구를 일컫는 용어입니다.

▶ to begin=start with : 우선
▶ to be honest=to tell the truth=to be frank with you : 솔직히 말해서
▶ not to mention=to say nothing of=not to speak of : ~는 말할 것도 없이
▶ to be short : 한마디로
▶ to make a long story short : 간단히 말하면
▶ to be sure : 분명히
▶ so to speak : 말하자면
▶ needless to say : 말할 필요도 없이
▶ strange to say : 이상한 말이지만
▶ to make matters worse : 설상가상으로

---

repeat 반복하다 | make an effort 노력하다 | shrubbery 관목 | encircle 둘러싸다 | forsake 저버리다, 그만두다

The ivy hung thick over the door, / the key was buried
담쟁이덩굴이 문 위로 빽빽하게 매달려 있었고, 열쇠는 관목들 아래에 묻혀 있었고,

under the shrubs, / no human being had passed that portal
 아무도 그 문을 통과하지 못했다

/ for ten lonely years / —— and yet inside the garden / there
그 고독의 십 년 동안 — 그러나 화원 안쪽에서

were sounds. They were the sounds / of running scuffling
소리가 들렸다. 그것은 소리였다 달리며 움직이는 발 소리

feet / seeming to chase round and round / under the
술래잡기를 하는 것 같은 나무 아래에서,

trees, / they were strange sounds / of lowered suppressed
이상한 소리였다 억지로 낮추는 듯한 목소리의

voices / —— exclamations and smothered joyous cries.
 — 탄성들과 숨죽인 환호성 소리들.

It seemed actually like the laughter / of young things, /
그것은 확실히 웃음 소리 같았다 어린 아이들의,

the uncontrollable laughter of children / who were trying
아이들의 통제할 수 없는 웃음 소리 들리지 않게 하려고 했지만

not to be heard / but who in a moment or so / —— as their
 한 순간

excitement mounted —— / would burst forth. What in
— 흥분이 올라서 — 확 터져버리기도 하는.

heaven's name was he dreaming of / —— what in heaven's
도대체 무슨 꿈을 꾸고 있는 걸까 — 도대체 무슨 소리를 들은 걸까?

name did he hear? Was he losing his reason / and thinking
 이성을 잃고 생각하는 건가

/ he heard things / which were not for human ears? Was it
소리를 들었다고 인간의 귀에는 들리지 않는 소리를? 저것이었을까?

that / the far clear voice had meant?
 멀리서 들린 맑은 목소리의 의미가?

And then / the moment came, / the uncontrollable moment
그리고 나서 그 순간이 왔다, 통제할 수 없는 순간이

/ when the sounds forgot to hush themselves. The feet
조용히 해야 한다는 사실을 잊어버린 순간이.

ran faster and faster / —— they were nearing the garden
발자국 소리가 점점 더 빨라져서 — 거의 화원 문 근처에 왔다

The Secret Garden

door / —— there was quick strong young breathing / and
— 빠르고 강하고 어린 숨소리와

a wild outbreak of laughing shows / which could not
크게 터지는 웃음 소리가   참을 수 없는 듯한

be contained / —— and the door in the wall was flung
— 그리고 문이 활짝 열렸다

wide open, / the sheet of ivy swinging back, / and a boy
담쟁이덩굴이 뒤로 젖혀지며,

burst through it / at full speed and, / without seeing the
소년이 그리로 달려 나왔다 전속력으로,   밖에 있는 사람을 보지 못한 채,

outsider, / dashed almost into his arms.
그의 팔로 달려들었다.

Mr. Craven had extended them / just in time / to save him
크레이븐 씨는 두 팔을 벌렸다   때맞춰   그를 구하기 위해

/ from falling / as a result of his unseeing dash against
넘어지는 것으로부터   보지 못하고 그와 부딪치는 될 경우,

him, / and when he held him away / to look at him / in
     그리고 그를 잡아 한 쪽에 놓았을 때   그를 보려고

amazement at his being there / he truly gasped for breath.
거기에 서 있던 존재에 놀라서   정말로 숨이 가빠졌다.

He was a tall boy / and a handsome one. He was glowing
그는 키가 크고   잘생긴 소년이었다.   생기로 빛나고 있었고

with life / and his running / had sent splendid color
          달리기는   달아오르게 했다

leaping / to his face. He threw the thick hair / back from
그의 얼굴을.   그는 숱 많은 머리를 넘기면서   이마에서 뒤로

his forehead / and lifted a pair of strange gray eyes / ——
              기묘한 회색 눈을 들었다

eyes full of boyish laughter / and rimmed with black
— 소년다운 웃음이 가득하고   술 장식처럼 까만 속눈썹으로 덮인 눈을.

lashes like a fringe. It was the eyes / which made Mr.
                     바로 그 눈이었다   크레이븐 씨를 숨가쁘게 만든 것은.

Craven gasp for breath.

shrub 관목숲 | portal 문 | scuffle 휙 움직이다 | suppress 억압하다, 참다 | smother 억누르다 |
uncontrollable 통제할 수 없는 | contain 억누르다 | flung 내던져진 | dash 달려들다 | extend 연장하다 | gasp
숨이 막히다 | splendid 훌륭한 | boyish 남자 아이 같은

"Who —— What? Who!" / he stammered.
"누구지 — 뭐야? 누구야!" 그는 더듬거렸다.

This was not / what Colin had expected —— this was not
이것은 아니었다 콜린이 기대 했던 상황은 — 이것은 달랐다

/ what he had planned. He had never thought of such a
그가 계획했던 것과도. 그는 그런 만남을 전혀 생각하지 않았었다.

meeting. And yet / to come dashing out / —— winning a
하지만 달려 나오는 바람에 — 달리기에서 이겨서 —

race —— / perhaps it was even better. He drew himself up
아마 더 좋을지도 몰랐다. 그는 몸을 쭉 들어 올렸다

/ to his very tallest. Mary, / who had been running with
키가 커 보이도록. 메리도, 그와 함께 달리던

him / and had dashed through the door too, / believed
역시 문으로 달려 나왔고, 믿었다

/ that he managed to make himself look taller / than he
그가 키가 커 보이려고 애쓰고 있다고 전보다

had ever looked before / —— inches taller.
— 몇 인치는 크게.

"Father," / he said, "I'm Colin. You can't believe it. I
"아버지," 그가 말했다, "저는 콜린이에요. 아버지는 못 믿으실 거예요.

scarcely can myself. I'm Colin."
저도 못 믿겠으니까요. 저는 콜린이에요."

Key Expression

it is ~ that… 강조구문

it is와 that 사이에 강조하는 말을 넣어 강조하는 구문을 만들 수 있습니다. '…한 것은 바로 ~이다'라고 해석하지요. 이때 ~ 자리에 들어갈 수 있는 말은 주어, 목적어, 부사구이며 동사는 강조할 수 없습니다.
강조구문의 that을 접속사나 관계대명사 등의 that과 구별하려면 문장에서 it is와 that을 지우고 문장이 성립하는지 확인하면 됩니다.

ex) It was the garden that did it. (주어 the garden 강조)
그 일을 한 것은 바로 정원이었다.
→ The garden did it. (원래 문장)

Like Mrs. Medlock, / he did not understand / what his father meant / when he said hurriedly:

"In the garden! In the garden!"

"Yes," / hurried on Colin. "It was the garden / that did it / —— and Mary and Dickon and the creatures —— / and the Magic. No one knows. We kept it / to tell you / when you came. I'm well, / I can beat Mary in a race. I'm going to be an athlete."

He said it all / so like a healthy boy / —— his face flushed, / his words tumbling over each other / in his eagerness —— / that Mr. Craven's soul shook / with unbelieving joy. Colin put out his hand / and laid it on his father's arm.

"Aren't you glad, Father?" / he ended.

"Aren't you glad? I'm going to live forever / and ever and ever!"

---

hurriedly 서둘러서 | athlete 운동선수 | flush 얼굴이 붉어진다 | tumble 시끌벅적하게 오르내리다

Mr. Craven put his hands / on both the boy's shoulders
크레이븐 씨는 손을 올리고 소년의 양 어깨 위에

/ and held him still. He knew / he dared not even try to
그를 꼭 잡았다. 그는 알았다 그는 감히 말을 꺼낼 수 없음을

speak / for a moment.
잠시 동안.

"Take me into the garden, my boy," / he said at last.
"나를 화원으로 데리고 가 다오, 아들아," 그가 마침내 말했다.

"And tell me all about it."
"그리고 전부에 대해 말해다오."

And so they led him in.
그래서 그들은 그를 안으로 이끌었다.

The place was a wilderness of autumn / gold and purple
그곳은 가을의 땅이었다 황금빛과 자줏빛과 청보라

and violet blue and flaming scarlet / and on every side /
빛과 불타는 선홍빛의 그리고 사방에

were sheaves of late lilies / standing together / —— lilies
늦은 백합 다발이 있었다 같이 서 있는 — 백합들이

/ which were white or white and ruby. He remembered
흰색이거나 흰색과 다홍색이 섞인. 그는 잘 기억하고 있었다

well / when the first of them had been planted / that just
그 꽃들을 맨 처음 여기 심었을 때를

at this season of the year / their late glories should reveal
그 때가 바로 이맘 때였다는 것을 지나간 그 꽃들의 영광의 순간이 스스로 드러날 거

themselves. Late roses climbed and hung and clustered
라는 사실을. 늦장미들은 타고 올라가 덩굴을 만들었고

/ and the sunshine deepening the hue of the yellowing
노랗게 되는 나무의 색조를 더 깊게 하는 햇빛은

trees / made one feel / that one, stood in an embowered
기분을 느끼도록 만들어 주었다 나무로 둘러싸인 황금 사원에 서 있는 듯한.

temple of gold. The newcomer stood silent / just as the
새로 온 방문자는 가만히 서 있었다

children had done / when they came into its grayness. He
아이들이 그랬던 것처럼 처음 이 회색 공간에 들어 왔을 때.

looked round and round.
그는 둘러보고 또 둘러 보았다.

"I thought / it would be dead," / he said."
"나는 생각했는데 이곳이 죽었을 거라고," 그가 말했다.

"Mary thought so / at first," / said Colin. "But it came alive."
"메리도 그렇게 생각했대요 처음에는," 콜린이 말했다. "그러나 살아났어요."

Then they sat down / under their tree / — all but Colin, / who wanted to stand / while he told the story.
그들은 앉았다 그들의 나무 아래에 — 콜린만 빼고 모두, 그는 서 있길 원했다 이야기를 하는 동안.

It was the strangest thing / he had ever heard, / Archibald Craven thought, / as it was poured forth / in headlong boy fashion. Mystery and Magic and wild creatures, / the weird midnight meeting / — the coming of the spring — / the passion of insulted pride / which had dragged the young Rajah / to his feet / to defy old Ben Weatherstaff to his face. The odd companionship, / the play acting, / the great secret so carefully kept. The listener laughed / until tears came into his eyes / and sometimes tears came into his eyes / when he was not laughing. The Athlete, the Lecturer, the Scientific Discoverer / was a laughable, lovable, / healthy young human thing.
그건 가장 이상한 이야기였다 그가 들어본 것 중에서, 아치볼드 크레이븐은 생각했다, 앞으로 쏟아질 것 같다고 서두가 긴 소년의 이야기에. 신비와 마법과 야생 동물들과, 기묘한 한밤 중의 만남 — 봄이 오는 것 — 모욕당한 자존심에 대한 열정 어린 라자를 이끌어 낸 그의 발로 걷도록 벤 웨더스태프 노인에게 반항하려고 그의 얼굴에 보였다. 별난 우정과, 연극놀이, 너무 조심스럽게 지켜진 위대한 비밀. 듣고 있던 사람은 웃음을 터뜨렸다 눈물이 맺힐 때까지 그리고 이따금 눈물을 흘렸다 웃지 않을 때는. 운동선수이자 강연자이자 과학적 발견자는 재미있고, 사랑스러우며, 건강하고 어린 남자애였다.

---

violet 보랏빛의 | flame 불꽃이 일다 | glory 영광 | reveal 드러내다 | embower 가리다, 나무로 둘러싸다 | headlong 성급한 | insulted 모욕받은 | defy 반항하다 | companionship 우정 | lovable 사랑스러운

"Now," / he said / at the end of the story, / "it need not be a secret any more. I dare say / it will frighten them / nearly into fits / when they see me / —— but I am never going to get into / the chair again. I shall walk back with you, Father / —— to the house."

Ben Weatherstaff's duties / rarely took him / away from the gardens, / but on this occasion / he made an excuse / to carry some vegetables / to the kitchen / and being invited into the servants' hall / by Mrs. Medlock / to drink a glass of beer / he was on the spot / —— as he had hoped to be —— / when the most dramatic event Misselthwaite Manor had seen / during the present generation / actually took place.

---

fit 발작 | rarely 거의 ~ 않다 | occasion 사건 | generation 세대 | take place 일어나다, 발생하다 | glimpse 흘끗 봄 | shrewdly 예리하게, 약삭빠르게 | sup up 훌쩍훌쩍 마시다 | overfill 넘치게 채우다

One of the windows / looking upon the courtyard / gave
한 창문으로는   마당이 보이는

also a glimpse of the lawn. Mrs. Medlock, / knowing
잔디밭도 조금 보였다.   메들록 부인은,   벤이 화원으로부터

Ben had come from the gardens, / hoped that he might
왔다는 것을 알고,   그가 보았기를 바랐다

have caught sight of / his master / and even by chance /
               주인님을   그리고 혹시 우연이라도

of his meeting with Master Colin.
주인님이 콜린 도련님과 만나는 것을.

"Did you see either of them, Weatherstaff?" / she asked.
"두 분 중 한 분이라도 봤나요, 벤?"   그녀가 물었다.

Ben took his beer-mug from his mouth / and wiped his
벤은 입에서 맥주잔을 떼고   입술을 닦았다

lips / with the back of his hand.
    손등으로.

"Aye, that I did," / he answered / with a shrewdly
"그럼요, 그랬죠,"   그는 대답했다   예리하고 의미심장한 분위기로.

significant air.

"Both of them?" / suggested Mrs. Medlock.
"둘 다요?"   메들록 부인이 물었다.

"Both of 'em," / returned Ben Weatherstaff. "Thank ye
"둘 다죠,"   벤 웨더스태프가 대답했다.   "친절함에 감사해요,

kindly, ma'am, / I could sup up / another mug of it."
부인,   마실 수 있을 것 같은데요 한 잔 더."

Key Expression

even의 다양한 의미

부사와 형용사로 다양하게 쓰이는 even의 의미를 살펴볼까요.

▶ 부사 : ~조차 / (비교급 강조) 훨씬 / 심지어 ~까지
▶ 형용사 : 평평한, 반반한 / 고른, 균등한 / 같은, 대등한 / 짝수의

ex) He thought he sprang to his feet not even startled.
그는 심지어 놀라지도 않고 벌떡 일어난 것 같았다.
Even Colin could have told him that.
콜린조차도 그에게 그걸 말할 수 없었다
Perhaps it was even better.
아마도 그게 훨씬 더 좋았다.

"Together?" / said Mrs. Medlock, / hastily overfilling / his beer-mug / in her excitement.

"Together, ma'am," / and Ben gulped down half of his new mug / at one gulp.

"Where was Master Colin? How did he look? What did they say to each other?"

"I didna' hear that," / said Ben, / "along o' only bein' on th' stepladder / lookin over th' wall. But I'll tell thee this. There's been things goin' on outside / as you house people knows nowt about. An' what tha'll find out / tha'll find out soon."

And it was not two minutes before / he swallowed the last of his beer / and waved his mug solemnly / toward the window / which took in through the shrubbery a piece of the lawn.

"Look there," / he said, / "if tha's curious. Look what's comin' / across th' grass."

gulp 벌컥 마시다 | each other 서로 | swallow 삼키다 | solemnly 근엄하게 | lawn 잔디 | shriek 비명소리, 비명지르다

When Mrs. Medlock looked / she threw up her hands
메들록 부인이 바라보았다 손을 들어서

/ and gave a little shriek / and every man and woman
그리고 짧은 비명을 질렀다 그리고 모든 남자 여자 하인들이

servant / within hearing bolted / across the servants' hall
그 소리를 듣고 하인들의 숙소로 가로질러와

/ and stood looking through the window / with their eyes
창문을 바라보며 섰다

almost starting out of their heads.
눈이 튀어나올 듯 한 표정으로.

Across the lawn / came the Master of Misselthwaite /
잔디밭을 가로질러 미셀스와이트의 주인이 오고 있었다

and he looked as many of them had never seen him. And
그리고 그는 대부분이 한 번도 본 적 없는 모습이었다.

by his side / with his head up in the air / and his eyes full
그리고 그 옆에는 고개를 꼿꼿이 들고 눈은 웃음으로 가득 찬 이가

of laughter / walked as strongly and steadily / as any boy
강하게 뚜벅뚜벅 걷고 있었다 요크셔의 여느

in Yorkshire / —— Master Colin.
남자 아이만큼이나 — 콜린 도련님이었다.

mini test 8

A. 다음 문장을 해석해 보세요.

(1) One of the new things / people began to find out / in the last century / was that thoughts are / as powerful as electric batteries.
→

(2) His scientific experiment / was quite practical and simple / and there was nothing weird about it at all.
→

(3) While the secret garden was coming alive / and two children were coming alive with it, / there was a man / wandering about certain far-away beautiful places.
→

(4) The door in the wall was flung wide open, / the sheet of ivy swinging back, / and a boy burst through it / at full speed and, / without seeing the outsider, / dashed almost into his arms.
→

B. 다음 주어진 문장이 되도록 빈칸에 써 넣으세요.

(1) 그는 얼마나 오래 그가 그곳에 앉아 있었는지 혹은 그에게 무슨 일이 일어났는지 몰랐다.

He did not know _____ or _____.

(2) 하지만 그에게는 이상하게 보일지라도, ~순간이 있었다.

But, _____, there were minutes ~.

(3) 그의 꿈은 너무도 생생해서 자신이 꿈을 꾸고 있는 것 같다는 느낌도 없었다.

His dream was _____ he did not feel _____.

A. (1) 지난 세기에 사람들이 발견하기 시작했던 새로운 것들 중에 하나는 사람의 생각이 전기 배터리만큼 이나 힘 있는 것이라는 사실이었다. (2) 그의 과학 실험은 꽤 실용적이고 간단했으며 거기에는 아무런 이상한 점이 없었다. (3) 비밀의 화원이 살아나고 두 아이들이 그와 함께 살아나는 동안, 멀리 떨어진 아름다

(4) <u>사실을 말하자면</u>, 콜린 도련님은 좋아지셨을지도 모릅니다.
　　　　　　　　　　　　, sir, Master Colin might be better.

C. 다음 주어진 문구가 알맞은 문장이 되도록 순서를 맞춰 보세요.

(1) 아무것도 아직 다른 누구도 하지 않았다.
 (anyone / yet / does / else / Neither)
 →

(2) 그것은 콜린이 기대했던 것이 아니었다.
 (what / Colin / not / This / expected / was / had)
 →

(3) 그 일은 한 것은 바로 정원이었어요.
 (the garden / that / It / it / did / was)
 →

(4) 그것은 그가 지금껏 들었던 가장 이상한 것이었다.
 (was / ever / It / had / strangest / the / thing / heard / he)
 →

D. 의미가 서로 비슷한 말끼리 연결해 보세요.

(1) detestation　▶　　　◀ ① peaceful
(2) reposeful　　▶　　　◀ ② cripple
(3) deform　　　▶　　　◀ ③ contain
(4) suppress　　▶　　　◀ ④ hatred

운 곳들을 배회하는 한 남자가 있었다. (4) 벽 속의 문이 활짝 열리고 담쟁이넝쿨이 뒤로 흔들리면서, 한 소년이 전속력으로 그곳을 통과해서 밖에 있는 사람을 보지도 못한 채 그의 팔 안으로 달려들었다. | B. (1) how long he sat there / what was happening to him (2) strange as it seemed to him (3) so real that / as if he were dreaming (4) To tell the truth | C. (1) Neither does anyone else yet. (2) This was not what Colin had expected. (3) It was the garden that did it. (4) It was the strangest thing he had ever heard. | D. (1) ③ (2) ① (3) ② (4) ④

The Secret Garden을 다시 읽어 보세요.

1

THERE IS NO ONE LEFT

When Mary Lennox was sent to Misselthwaite Manor to live with her uncle everybody said she was the most disagreeable-looking child ever seen. It was true, too. She had a little thin face and a little thin body, thin light hair and a sour expression. Her hair was yellow, and her face was yellow because she had been born in India and had always been ill in one way or another. Her father had held a position under the English Government and had always been busy and ill himself, and her mother had been a great beauty who cared only to go to parties and amuse herself with gay people. She had not wanted a little girl at all, and when Mary was born she handed her over to the care of an Ayah, who was made to understand that if she wished to please the Mem Sahib she must keep the child out of sight as much as possible. So when she was a sickly, fretful, ugly little baby she was kept out of the way, and when she became a sickly, fretful, toddling thing she was kept out of the way also. She never remembered seeing familiarly anything but the dark faces of her Ayah and the other native servants, and as they always obeyed her and gave her her own way in everything, because the Mem Sahib would be angry if she was disturbed by her crying, by the time she was six years old she was as tyrannical and selfish a little pig as ever lived. The young English governess who came to teach her to read and write disliked her so much that she gave up her place in three months, and when other governesses came to try to fill it they always went away in a shorter time than the first one. So if Mary had not chosen to really want to know how to read books she would never have learned her letters at all.

One frightfully hot morning, when she was about nine years old, she awakened feeling very cross, and she became crosser still when she saw that the servant who stood by her bedside was not her Ayah. "Why did you come?" she said to the strange woman. "I will not let you stay. Send my Ayah to me."

The woman looked frightened, but she only stammered that the Ayah could not come and when Mary threw herself into a passion and beat and kicked her, she looked only more frightened and repeated that it was not possible for the Ayah to come to Missie Sahib.

There was something mysterious in the air that morning. Nothing was done in its regular order and several of the native servants seemed missing, while those whom Mary saw slunk or hurried about with ashy and scared faces. But no one would tell her anything and her Ayah did not come. She was actually left alone as the morning went on, and at last she wandered out into the garden and began to play by herself under a tree near the veranda. She pretended that she was making a flower-bed, and she stuck big scarlet hibiscus blossoms into little heaps of earth, all the time growing more and more angry and muttering to herself the things she would say and the names she would call Saidie when she returned.

"Pig! Pig! Daughter of Pigs!" she said, because to call a native a pig is the worst insult of all.

She was grinding her teeth and saying this over and over again when she heard her mother come out on the veranda with someone. She was with a fair young man and they stood talking together in low strange voices. Mary knew the fair young man who looked like a boy. She had heard that he was a very young officer who had just come from England.

The child stared at him, but she stared most at her mother. She always did this when she had a chance to see her, because the Mem Sahib —— Mary used to call her that oftener than anything else —— was such a tall, slim, pretty person and wore such lovely clothes. Her hair was like curly silk and she had a delicate little nose which seemed to be disdaining things, and she had large laughing eyes. All her clothes were thin and floating, and Mary said they were "full of lace." They looked fuller of lace than ever this morning, but her eyes were not laughing at all. They were large and scared and lifted imploringly to the fair boy officer's face.

"Is it so very bad? Oh, is it?" Mary heard her say.

"Awfully," the young man answered in a trembling voice. "Awfully, Mrs. Lennox. You ought to have gone to the hills two weeks ago."

The Mem Sahib wrung her hands.

"Oh, I know I ought!" she cried. "I only stayed to go to that silly dinner party. What a fool I was!"

At that very moment such a loud sound of wailing broke out from the servants' quarters that she clutched the young man's arm, and Mary stood shivering from head to foot. The wailing grew wilder and wilder.

"What is it? What is it?" Mrs. Lennox gasped.

"Someone has died," answered the boy officer. "You did not say it had broken out among your servants."

"I did not know!" the Mem Sahib cried. "Come with me! Come with me!" and she turned and ran into the house.

After that, appalling things happened, and the mysteriousness of the morning was explained to Mary. The cholera had broken out in its most fatal form and people were dying like flies. The Ayah had been taken ill in the night, and it was because she had just died that the servants had wailed in the huts. Before the next day three other servants were dead and others had run away in terror. There was

panic on every side, and dying people in all the bungalows.
During the confusion and bewilderment of the second day Mary hid herself in the nursery and was forgotten by everyone. Nobody thought of her, nobody wanted her, and strange things happened of which she knew nothing. Mary alternately cried and slept through the hours. She only knew that people were ill and that she heard mysterious and tightening sounds. Once she crept into the dining-room and found it empty, though a partly finished meal was on the table and chairs and plates looked as if they had been hastily pushed back when the diners rose suddenly for some reason. The child ate some fruit and biscuits, and being thirsty she drank a glass of wine which stood nearly filled. It was sweet, and she did not know how strong it was. Very soon it made her intensely drowsy, and she went back to her nursery and shut herself in again, frightened by cries she heard in the huts and by the hurrying sound of feet. The wine made her so sleepy that she could scarcely keep her eyes open and she lay down on her bed and knew nothing more for a long time.
Many things happened during the hours in which she slept so heavily, but she was not disturbed by the wails and the sound of things being carried in and out of the bungalow.
When she awakened she lay and stared at the wall. The house was perfectly still. She had never known it to be so silent before. She heard neither voices nor footsteps, and wondered if everybody had got well of the cholera and all the trouble was over. She wondered also who would take care of her now her Ayah was dead. There would be a new Ayah, and perhaps she would know some new stories. Mary had been rather tired of the old ones. She did not cry because her nurse had died. She was not an affectionate child and had never cared much for any one. The noise and hurrying about and wailing over the cholera had frightened her, and she

had been angry because no one seemed to remember that she was alive. Everyone was too panic-stricken to think of a little girl no one was fond of. When people had the cholera it seemed that they remembered nothing but themselves. But if everyone had got well again, surely someone would remember and come to look for her. But no one came, and as she lay waiting the house seemed to grow more and more silent. She heard something rustling on the matting and when she looked down she saw a little snake gliding along and watching her with eyes like jewels. She was not frightened, because he was a harmless little thing who would not hurt her and he seemed in a hurry to get out of the room. He slipped under the door as she watched him.

"How queer and quiet it is," she said. "It sounds as if there were no one in the bungalow but me and the snake."

Almost the next minute she heard footsteps in the compound, and then on the veranda. They were men's footsteps, and the men entered the bungalow and talked in low voices. No one went to meet or speak to them and they seemed to open doors and look into rooms.

What desolation!" she heard one voice say. "That pretty, pretty woman! I suppose the child, too. I heard there was a child, though no one ever saw her."

Mary was standing in the middle of the nursery when they opened the door a few minutes later. She looked an ugly, cross little thing and was frowning because she was beginning to be hungry and feel disgracefully neglected. The first man who came in was a large officer she had once seen talking to her father. He looked tired and troubled, but when he saw her he was so startled that he almost jumped back.

"Barney!" he cried out. "There is a child here! A child alone! In a place like this! Mercy on us, who is she!"

"I am Mary Lennox," the little girl said, drawing herself up stiffly. She thought the man was very rude to call her father's bungalow "A place like this!" "I fell asleep when everyone had the cholera and I have only just wakened up. Why does nobody come?"

"It is the child no one ever saw!" exclaimed the man, turning to his companions. "She has actually been forgotten!"

"Why was I forgotten?" Mary said, stamping her foot. "Why does no one come?"

The young man whose name was Barney looked at her very sadly. Mary even thought she saw him wink his eyes as if to wink tears away.

"Poor little kid!" he said. "There is nobody left to come."

It was in that strange and sudden way that Mary found out that she had neither father nor mother left; that they had died and been carried away in the night, and that the few native servants who had not died also had left the house as quickly as they could get out of it, none of them even remembering that there was a Missie Sahib. That was why the place was so quiet. It was true that there was no one in the bungalow but herself and the little rustling snake.

2

MISTRESS MARY QUITE CONTRARY

Mary had liked to look at her mother from a distance and she had thought her very pretty, but as she knew very little of her she could scarcely have been expected to love her or to miss her very much when she was gone. She did not miss her at all, in fact, and as she was a self-absorbed child she gave her entire thought to herself, as she had always done. If she had been older she would no doubt have been very anxious at being left alone in the world, but she was very young, and as she had always been taken care of, she supposed she always would be. What she thought was that she would like to know if she was going to nice people, who would be polite to her and give her her own way as her Ayah and the other native servants had done.

She knew that she was not going to stay at the English clergyman's house where she was taken at first. She did not want to stay. The English clergyman was poor and he had five children nearly all the same age and they wore shabby clothes and were always quarreling and snatching toys from each other. Mary hated their untidy bungalow and was so disagreeable to them that after the first day or two nobody would play with her. By the second day they had given her a nickname which made her furious.

It was Basil who thought of it first. Basil was a little boy with impudent blue eyes and a turned-up nose, and Mary hated him. She was playing by herself under a tree, just as she had been playing the day the cholera broke out. She was making heaps of earth and paths for a garden and Basil came and stood near to watch her. Presently he got rather interested and suddenly made a suggestion.

"Why don't you put a heap of stones there and pretend it is a rockery?" he said. "There in the middle," and he leaned over her to point.

"Go away!" cried Mary. "I don't want boys. Go away!"

For a moment Basil looked angry, and then he began to tease. He was always teasing his sisters. He danced round and round her and made faces and sang and laughed.

"Mistress Mary, quite contrary,

How does your garden grow?
With silver bells, and cockle shells,
And marigolds all in a row."

He sang it until the other children heard and laughed, too; and the crosser Mary got, the more they sang "Mistress Mary, quite contrary"; and after that as long as she stayed with them they called her "Mistress Mary Quite Contrary" when they spoke of her to each other, and often when they spoke to her.

"You are going to be sent home," Basil said to her, "at the end of the week. And we're glad of it."

"I am glad of it, too," answered Mary. "Where is home?"

"She doesn't know where home is!" said Basil, with seven-year-old scorn. "It's England, of course. Our grandmama lives there and our sister Mabel was sent to her last year. You are not going to your grandmama. You have none. You are going to your uncle. His name is Mr. Archibald Craven."

"I don't know anything about him," snapped Mary.

"I know you don't," Basil answered. "You don't know anything. Girls never do. I heard father and mother talking about him. He lives in a great, big, desolate old house in the country and no one goes near him. He's so cross he won't let them, and they wouldn't come if he would let them. He's a hunchback, and he's horrid."

"I don't believe you," said Mary; and she turned her back and stuck her fingers in her ears, because she would not listen any more. But she thought over it a great deal afterward; and when Mrs. Crawford told her that night that she was going to sail away to England in a few days and go to her uncle, Mr. Archibald Craven, who lived at Misselthwaite Manor, she looked so stony and stubbornly uninterested that they did not know what to think about her. They tried to be kind to her, but she only turned her face away when Mrs. Crawford attempted to kiss her, and held herself stiffly when Mr. Crawford patted her shoulder.

"She is such a plain child," Mrs. Crawford said pityingly, afterward. "And her mother was such a pretty creature. She had a very pretty manner, too, and Mary has the most unattractive ways I ever saw in a child. The children call her 'Mistress Mary Quite Contrary,' and though it's naughty of them, one can't help understanding it."

"Perhaps if her mother had carried her pretty face and her pretty manners oftener into the nursery Mary might have learned some pretty ways too. It is very sad, now the poor beautiful thing is gone, to remember that many people never even knew that she had a child at all."

"I believe she scarcely ever looked at her," sighed Mrs. Crawford. "When her Ayah was dead there was no one to give a thought to the little thing. Think of the servants running away and leaving her all alone in that deserted bungalow. Colonel McGrew said he nearly jumped out of his skin when he opened the door and found her standing by herself in the middle of the room."

Mary made the long voyage to England under the care of an officer's wife, who was taking her children to leave them in a boarding-school. She was very much absorbed in her own little boy and girl, and was rather glad to hand the child over to the woman Mr. Archibald Craven sent to meet her, in London. The woman was his housekeeper at Misselthwaite Manor, and her name was Mrs. Medlock. She was a stout woman, with very red cheeks and sharp black eyes. She wore a very purple dress, a black silk mantle with jet fringe on it and a black bonnet with purple velvet flowers which stuck up and trembled when she moved her head. Mary did not like her at all, but as she very seldom liked people there was nothing remarkable in that; besides which it was very evident Mrs. Medlock did not think much of her.

"My word! She's a plain little piece of goods!" she said. "And we'd heard that her mother was a beauty. She hasn't handed much of it down, has she, ma'am?"

"Perhaps she will improve as she grows older," the officer's wife said good-naturedly. "If she were not so sallow and had a nicer expression, her features are rather good. Children alter so much."

"She'll have to alter a good deal," answered Mrs. Medlock. "And, there's nothing likely to improve children at Misselthwaite ⎯ if you ask me!" They thought Mary was not listening because she was standing a little apart from them at the window of the private hotel they had gone to. She was watching the passing buses and cabs and people, but she heard quite well and was made very curious about her uncle and the place he lived in. What sort of a place was it, and what would he be like? What was a hunchback? She had never seen one. Perhaps there were none in India.

Since she had been living in other people's houses and had had no Ayah, she had begun to feel lonely and to think queer thoughts which were new to her. She had begun to wonder why she had never seemed to belong to anyone even when her father and mother had been alive. Other children seemed to belong to their fathers and mothers, but she had never seemed to really be anyone's little girl. She had had servants, and food and clothes, but no one had taken any notice of her. She did not know that this was because she was a disagreeable child; but then, of course, she did not know she was disagreeable. She often thought that other people were, but she did not know that she was so herself.

She thought Mrs. Medlock the most disagreeable person she had ever seen, with her common, highly colored face and her common fine bonnet. When the next day they set out on their journey to

Yorkshire, she walked through the station to the railway carriage with her head up and trying to keep as far away from her as she could, because she did not want to seem to belong to her. It would have made her angry to think people imagined she was her little girl.

But Mrs. Medlock was not in the least disturbed by her and her thoughts. She was the kind of woman who would "stand no nonsense from young ones." At least, that is what she would have said if she had been asked. She had not wanted to go to London just when her sister Maria's daughter was going to be married, but she had a comfortable, well paid place as housekeeper at Misselthwaite Manor and the only way in which she could keep it was to do at once what Mr. Archibald Craven told her to do. She never dared even to ask a question.

"Captain Lennox and his wife died of the cholera,"
Mr. Craven had said in his short, cold way. "Captain Lennox was my wife's brother and I am their daughter's guardian. The child is to be brought here. You must go to London and bring her yourself."
So she packed her small trunk and made the journey.

Mary sat in her corner of the railway carriage and looked plain and fretful. She had nothing to read or to look at, and she had folded her thin little black-gloved hands in her lap. Her black dress made her look yellower than ever, and her limp light hair straggled from under her black crepe hat.

"A more marred-looking young one I never saw in my life," Mrs. Medlock thought. (Marred is a Yorkshire word and means spoiled and pettish.) She had never seen a child who sat so still without doing anything; and at last she got tired of watching her and began to talk in a brisk, hard voice.

"I suppose I may as well tell you something about where you are going to," she said. "Do you know anything about your uncle?"

"No," said Mary.

"Never heard your father and mother talk about him?"

"No," said Mary frowning. She frowned because she remembered that her father and mother had never talked to her about anything in particular. Certainly they had never told her things.

"Humph," muttered Mrs. Medlock, staring at her queer, unresponsive little face. She did not say any more for a few moments and then she began again.

"I suppose you might as well be told something —— to prepare you. You are going to a queer place."

Mary said nothing at all, and Mrs. Medlock looked rather discomfited by her apparent indifference, but, after taking a breath, she went on.

"Not but that it's a grand big place in a gloomy way, and Mr. Craven's proud of it in his way —— and that's gloomy enough, too. The house is six hundred years old and it's on the edge of the moor, and there's near a hundred rooms in it, though most of them's shut up and locked. And there's pictures and fine old furniture and things that's been there for ages, and there's a big park round it and gardens and trees with branches trailing to the ground —— some of them." She paused and took another breath. "But there's nothing else," she ended suddenly.

Mary had begun to listen in spite of herself. It all sounded so unlike India, and anything new rather attracted her. But she did not intend to look as if she were interested. That was one of her unhappy, disagreeable ways. So she sat still.

"Well," said Mrs. Medlock. "What do you think of it?"

"Nothing," she answered. "I know nothing about such places."

That made Mrs. Medlock laugh a short sort of laugh.

"Eh!" she said, "but you are like an old woman. Don't you care?"

"It doesn't matter" said Mary, "whether I care or not."

"You are right enough there," said Mrs. Medlock. "It doesn't. What you're to be kept at Misselthwaite Manor for I don't know, unless because it's the easiest way. He's not going to trouble himself about you, that's sure and certain. He never troubles himself about no one."

She stopped herself as if she had just remembered something in time.

"He's got a crooked back," she said. "That set him wrong. He was a sour young man and got no good of all his money and big place till he was married."

Mary's eyes turned toward her in spite of her intention not to seem to care. She had never thought of the hunchback's being married and she was a trifle surprised. Mrs. Medlock saw this, and as she was a talkative woman she continued with more interest. This was one way of passing some of the time, at any rate.

"She was a sweet, pretty thing and he'd have walked the world over to get her a blade o' grass she wanted. Nobody thought she'd marry him, but she did, and people said she married him for his money. But she didn't —— she didn't," positively. "When she died —— "

Mary gave a little involuntary jump.

"Oh! Did she die!" she exclaimed, quite without meaning to. She had just remembered a French fairy story she had once read called "Riquet a la Houppe." It had been about a poor hunchback and a beautiful princess and it had made her suddenly sorry for Mr. Archibald Craven.

"Yes, she died," Mrs. Medlock answered. "And it made him queerer than ever. He cares about nobody. He won't see people. Most of the time he goes away, and when he is at Misselthwaite he shuts himself up in the West Wing and won't let any one but Pitcher see him. Pitcher's an old fellow, but he took care of him when he was a child and he knows his ways."

It sounded like something in a book and it did not make Mary feel cheerful. A house with a hundred rooms, nearly all shut up and with their doors locked —— a house on the edge of a moor —— whatsoever a moor was —— sounded dreary. A man with a crooked back who shut himself up also! She stared out of the window with her lips pinched together, and it seemed quite natural that the rain should have begun to pour down in gray slanting lines and splash and stream down the window-panes. If the pretty wife had been alive she might have made things cheerful by being something like her own mother and by running in and out and going to parties as she had done in frocks "full of lace." But she was not there any more.

"You needn't expect to see him, because ten to one you won't," said Mrs. Medlock. "And you mustn't expect that there will be people to talk to you. You'll have to play about and look after yourself. You'll be told what rooms you can go into and what rooms you're to keep out of. There's gardens enough. But when you're in the house don't go wandering and poking about. Mr. Craven won't have it."

"I shall not want to go poking about," said sour little Mary and just as suddenly as she had begun to be rather sorry for Mr. Archibald Craven she began to cease to be sorry and to think he was unpleasant enough to deserve all that had happened to him.

And she turned her face toward the streaming panes of the window of the railway carriage and gazed out at the gray rain-storm which looked as if it would go on forever and ever. She watched it so long and steadily that the grayness grew heavier and heavier before her eyes and she fell asleep.

3

THE CRY IN THE CORRIDOR

At first each day which passed by for Mary Lennox was exactly like the others. Every morning she awoke in her tapestried room and found Martha kneeling upon the hearth building her fire; every morning she ate her breakfast in the nursery which had nothing amusing in it; and after each breakfast she gazed out of the window across to the huge moor which seemed to spread out on all sides and climb up to the sky, and after she had stared for a while she realized that if she did not go out she would have to stay in and do nothing —— and so she went out. She did not know that this was the best thing she could have done, and she did not know that, when she began to walk quickly or even run along the paths and down the avenue, she was stirring her slow blood and making herself stronger by fighting with the wind which swept down from the moor. She ran only to make herself warm, and she hated the wind which rushed at her face and roared and held her back as if it were some giant she could not see.

But the big breaths of rough fresh air blown over the heather filled her lungs with something which was good for her whole thin body and whipped some red color into her cheeks and brightened her dull eyes when she did not know anything about it.

But after a few days spent almost entirely out of doors she wakened one morning knowing what it was to be hungry, and when she sat down to her breakfast she did not glance disdainfully at her porridge and push it away, but took up her spoon and began to eat it and went on eating it until her bowl was empty.

"Tha' got on well enough with that this mornin', didn't tha'?" said Martha.

"It tastes nice today," said Mary, feeling a little surprised herself.
"It's th' air of th' moor that's givin' thee stomach for tha' victuals," answered Martha. "It's lucky for thee that tha's got victuals as well as appetite. There's been twelve in our cottage as had th' stomach an' nothin' to put in it. You go on playin' you out o' doors every day an' you'll get some flesh on your bones an' you won't be so yeller."

"I don't play," said Mary. "I have nothing to play with."

"Nothin' to play with!" exclaimed Martha. "Our children plays with sticks and stones. They just runs about an' shouts an' looks at things." Mary did not shout, but she looked at things. There was nothing else to do. She walked round and round the gardens and wandered about the paths in the park. Sometimes she looked for Ben Weatherstaff, but though several times she saw him at work he was too busy to look at her or was too surly. Once when she was walking toward him he picked up his spade and turned away as if he did it on purpose.

One place she went to oftener than to any other. It was the long walk outside the gardens with the walls round them. There were bare flower-beds on either side of it and against the walls ivy grew thickly. There was one part of the wall where the creeping dark green leaves were more bushy than elsewhere. It seemed as if for a long time that part had been neglected. The rest of it had been clipped and made to look neat, but at this lower end of the walk it had not been trimmed at all.

A few days after she had talked to Ben Weatherstaff, Mary stopped to notice this and wondered why it was so. She had just paused and was looking up at a long spray of ivy swinging in the wind when she saw a gleam of scarlet and heard a brilliant chirp, and there, on the top of the wall, forward perched Ben Weatherstaff's robin redbreast, tilting forward to look at her with his small head on one side.

"Oh!" she cried out, "is it you ⎯ is it you?" And it did not seem at all queer to her that she spoke to him as if she were sure that he would understand and answer her.

He did answer. He twittered and chirped and hopped along the wall as if he were telling her all sorts of things. It seemed to Mistress Mary as if she understood him, too, though he was not speaking in words. It was as if he said:

"Good morning! Isn't the wind nice? Isn't the sun nice? Isn't everything nice? Let us both chirp and hop and twitter. Come on! Come on!"

Mary began to laugh, and as he hopped and took little flights along the wall she ran after him. Poor little thin, sallow, ugly Mary ⎯ she actually looked almost pretty for a moment.

"I like you! I like you!" she cried out, pattering down the walk; and she chirped and tried to whistle, which last she did not know how to do in the least. But the robin seemed to be quite satisfied and chirped and whistled back at her. At last he spread his wings and made a darting flight to the top of a tree, where he perched and sang loudly.

That reminded Mary of the first time she had seen him. He had been swinging on a tree-top then and she had been standing in the orchard. Now she was on the other side of the orchard and standing in the path outside a wall ⎯ much lower down ⎯ and there was the same tree inside.

"It's in the garden no one can go into," she said to herself. "It's the garden without a door. He lives in there. How I wish I could see what it is like!"

She ran up the walk to the green door she had entered the first morning. Then she ran down the path through the other door and then into the orchard, and when she stood and looked up there was the tree on the other side of the wall, and there was the robin just finishing his song and, beginning to preen his feathers with his beak.

"It is the garden," she said. "I am sure it is."

She walked round and looked closely at that side of the orchard wall, but she only found what she had found before —— that there was no door in it. Then she ran through the kitchen-gardens again and out into the walk outside the long ivy-covered wall, and she walked to the end of it and looked at it, but there was no door; and then she walked to the other end, looking again, but there was no door.

"It's very queer," she said. "Ben Weatherstaff said there was no door and there is no door. But there must have been one ten years ago, because Mr. Craven buried the key."

This gave her so much to think of that she began to be quite interested and feel that she was not sorry that she had come to Misselthwaite Manor. In India she had always felt hot and too languid to care much about anything. The fact was that the fresh wind from the moor had begun to blow the cobwebs out of her young brain and to waken her up a little.

She stayed out of doors nearly all day, and when she sat down to her supper at night she felt hungry and drowsy and comfortable. She did not feel cross when Martha chattered away. She felt as if she rather liked to hear her, and at last she thought she would ask her a question. She asked it after she had finished her supper and had sat down on the hearth-rug before the fire.

"Why did Mr. Craven hate the garden?" she said.

She had made Martha stay with her and Martha had not objected at all. She was very young, and used to a crowded cottage full of brothers and sisters, and she found it dull in the great servants' hall down-stairs where the footman and upper-housemaids made fun of her Yorkshire speech and looked upon her as a common little thing, and sat and whispered among themselves. Martha liked to talk, and the strange child who had lived in India, and been waited upon by "blacks," was novelty enough to attract her.

She sat down on the hearth herself without waiting to be asked.

"Art tha' thinkin' about that garden yet?" she said. "I knew tha' would. That was just the way with me when I first heard about it."

"Why did he hate it?" Mary persisted.

Martha tucked her feet under her and made herself quite comfortable.

"Listen to th' wind wutherin' round the house," she said. "You could bare stand up on the moor if you was out on it tonight."

Mary did not know what "wutherin'" meant until she listened, and then she understood. It must mean that hollow shuddering sort of roar which rushed round and round the house as if the giant no one could see were buffeting it and beating at the walls and windows to try to break in. But one knew he could not get in, and somehow it made one feel very safe and warm inside a room with a red coal fire.

"But why did he hate it so?" she asked, after she had listened. She intended to know if Martha did.

Then Martha gave up her store of knowledge.

"Mind," she said, "Mrs. Medlock said it's not to be talked about. There's lots o' things in this place that's not to be talked over. That's Mr. Craven's orders. His troubles are none servants' business, he says. But for th' garden he wouldn't be like he is. It was Mrs. Craven's garden that she had made when first they were married an' she just loved it, an' they used to 'ttend the flowers themselves. An' none o' th' gardeners was ever let to go in. Him an' her used to go in an' shut th' door an' stay there hours an' hours, readin' and talkin'. An, she was just a bit of a girl an' there was an old tree with a branch bent like a seat on it. An' she made roses grow over it an' she used to sit there. But one day when she was sittin' there th' branch broke an' she fell on th' ground an' was hurt so bad that next day she died. Th' doctors thought he'd go out o' his mind an' die, too. That's why he hates it. No one's never gone in since, an' he won't let anyone talk about it."

Mary did not ask any more questions. She looked at the red fire and listened to the wind "wutherin'." It seemed to be "wutherin'" louder than ever.

At that moment a very good thing was happening to her. Four good things had happened to her, in fact, since she came to Misselthwaite Manor. She had felt as if she had understood a robin and that he had understood her; she had run in the wind until her blood had grown warm; she had been healthily hungry for the first time in her life; and she had found out what it was to be sorry for someone.

But as she was listening to the wind she began to listen to something else. She did not know what it was, because at first she could scarcely distinguish it from the wind itself. It was a curious sound ___ it seemed almost as if a child were crying somewhere. Sometimes the wind sounded rather like a child crying, but presently Mistress Mary felt quite sure this sound was inside the house, not outside it. It was far away, but it was inside. She turned round and looked at Martha.

"Do you hear any one crying?" she said.

Martha suddenly looked confused.

"No," she answered. "It's th' wind. Sometimes it sounds like as if someone was lost on th' moor an' wailin'. It's got all sorts o' sounds."

"But listen," said Mary. "It's in the house ⎯⎯ down one of those long corridors."

And at that very moment a door must have been opened somewhere down-stairs; for a great rushing draft blew along the passage and the door of the room they sat in was blown open with a crash, and as they both jumped to their feet the light was blown out and the crying sound was swept down the far corridor so that it was to be heard more plainly than ever.

"There!" said Mary. "I told you so! It is someone crying ⎯⎯ and it isn't a grown-up person."

Martha ran and shut the door and turned the key, but before she did it they both heard the sound of a door in some far passage shutting with a bang, and then everything was quiet, for even the wind ceased "wutherin'" for a few moments.

"It was th' wind," said Martha stubbornly. "An' if it wasn't, it was little Betty Butterworth, th' scullery-maid. She's had th' toothache all day."

But something troubled and awkward in her manner made Mistress Mary stare very hard at her. She did not believe she was speaking the truth.

THE KEY TO THE GARDEN

Two days after this, when Mary opened her eyes she sat upright in bed immediately, and called to Martha.

"Look at the moor! Look at the moor!"

The rainstorm had ended and the gray mist and clouds had been swept away in the night by the wind. The wind itself had ceased and a brilliant, deep blue sky arched high over the moorland. Never, never had Mary dreamed of a sky so blue. In India skies were hot and blazing; this was of a deep cool blue which almost seemed to sparkle like the waters of some lovely bottomless lake, and here and there, high, high in the arched blueness floated small clouds of snow-white fleece. The far-reaching world of the moor itself looked softly blue instead of gloomy purple-black or awful dreary gray.

"Aye," said Martha with a cheerful grin. "Th' storm's over for a bit. It does like this at this time o' th' year. It goes off in a night like it was pretendin' it had never been here an' never meant to come again. That's because th' springtime's on its way. It's a long way off yet, but it's comin'."

"I thought perhaps it always rained or looked dark in England," Mary said.

"Eh! No!" said Martha, sitting up on her heels among her black lead brushes. "Nowt o' th' soart!"

"What does that mean?" asked Mary seriously. In India the natives spoke different dialects which only a few people understood, so she was not surprised when Martha used words she did not know.

Martha laughed as she had done the first morning.

"There now," she said. "I've talked broad Yorkshire again like Mrs. Medlock said I mustn't. 'Nowt o' th' soart' means 'nothin'-of-the-sort,'" slowly and carefully, "but it takes so long to say it. Yorkshire's th' sunniest place on earth when it is sunny. I told thee tha'd like th' moor after a bit. Just you wait till you see th' gold-colored gorse blossoms an' th' blossoms o' th' broom, an' th' heather flowerin', all purple bells, an' hundreds o' butterflies flutterin' an' bees hummin' an' skylarks soarin' up an' singin'. You'll want to get out on it as sunrise an' live out on it all day like

Dickon does."

"Could I ever get there?" asked Mary wistfully, looking through her window at the far-off blue. It was so new and big and wonderful and such a heavenly color.

"I don't know," answered Martha. "Tha's never used tha' legs since tha' was born, it seems to me. Tha' couldn't walk five mile. It's five mile to our cottage."

"I should like to see your cottage."

Martha stared at her a moment curiously before she took up her polishing brush and began to rub the grate again. She was thinking that the small plain face did not look quite as sour at this moment as it had done the first morning she saw it. It looked just a trifle like little Susan Ann's when she wanted something very much.

"I'll ask my mother about it," she said. "She's one o' them that nearly always sees a way to do things. It's my day out today an' I'm goin' home. Eh! I am glad. Mrs. Medlock thinks a lot o' mother. Perhaps she could talk to her."

"I like your mother," said Mary.

"I should think tha' did," agreed Martha, polishing away.

"I've never seen her," said Mary.

"No, tha' hasn't," replied Martha.

She sat up on her heels again and rubbed the end of her nose with the back of her hand as if puzzled for a moment, but she ended quite positively.

"Well, she's that sensible an' hard workin' an' goodnatured an' clean that no one could help likin' her whether they'd seen her or not. When I'm goin' home to her on my day out I just jump for joy when I'm crossin' the moor."

"I like Dickon," added Mary. "And I've never seen him."

"Well," said Martha stoutly, "I've told thee that th' very birds likes him an' th' rabbits an' wild sheep an' ponies, an' th' foxes themselves. I wonder," staring at her reflectively, "what Dickon would think of thee?"

"He wouldn't like me," said Mary in her stiff, cold little way. "No one does."

Martha looked reflective again.

"How does tha' like thysel'?" she inquired, really quite as if she were curious to know.

Mary hesitated a moment and thought it over.

"Not at all —— really," she answered. "But I never thought of that before."

Martha grinned a little as if at some homely recollection.

"Mother said that to me once," she said. "She was at her wash-tub an' I was in a bad temper an' talkin' ill of folk, an' she turns round on me an' says: `Tha' young vixen, tha'! There tha' stands sayin' tha' doesn't like this one an' tha' doesn't like that one. How does tha' like thysel'?' It made me laugh an' it brought me to my senses in a minute."

She went away in high spirits as soon as she had given Mary her breakfast. She was going to walk five miles across the moor to the cottage, and she was going to help her mother with the washing and do the week's baking and enjoy herself thoroughly.

Mary felt lonelier than ever when she knew she was no longer in the house. She went out into the garden as quickly as possible, and the first thing she did was to run round and round the fountain flower garden ten times. She counted the times carefully and when she had finished she felt in better spirits. The sunshine made the whole place look different. The high, deep, blue sky arched over Misselthwaite as well as over the moor, and she kept lifting her face and looking up into it, trying to imagine what it would be like to lie down on one of the little snow-white clouds and float about. She went into the first kitchen-garden and found Ben Weatherstaff working there with two other gardeners. The change in the weather seemed to have done him good. He spoke to her of his own accord.

"Springtime's comin,'" he said. "Cannot tha' smell it?"

Mary sniffed and thought she could.

"I smell something nice and fresh and damp," she said.

"That's th' good rich earth," he answered, digging away. "It's in a good humor makin' ready to grow things. It's glad when plantin' time comes. It's dull in th' winter when it's got nowt to do. In th' flower gardens out there things will be stirrin' down below in th' dark. Th' sun's warmin' 'em. You'll see bits o' green spikes stickin' out o' th' black earth after a bit."

"What will they be?" asked Mary.

"Crocuses an' snowdrops an' daffydowndillys. Has tha' never seen them?"

"No. Everything is hot, and wet, and green after the rains in India," said Mary. "And I think things grow up in a night."

"These won't grow up in a night," said Weatherstaff. "Tha'll have to wait for 'em. They'll poke up a bit higher here, an' push out a spike more there, an' uncurl a leaf this day an' another that. You watch 'em."

"I am going to," answered Mary.

Very soon she heard the soft rustling flight of wings again and she knew at once that the robin had come again. He was very pert and lively, and hopped about so close to her feet, and put his head on one side and looked at her so slyly that she asked Ben Weatherstaff a question.

"Do you think he remembers me?" she said.

"Remembers thee!" said Weatherstaff indignantly. "He knows every cabbage stump in th' gardens, let alone th' people. He's never seen a little wench here before, an' he's bent on findin' out all about thee. Tha's no need to try to hide anything from him."

"Are things stirring down below in the dark in that garden where he lives?" Mary inquired.

"What garden?" grunted Weatherstaff, becoming surly again.

"The one where the old rose-trees are." She could not help asking, because she wanted so much to know. "Are all the flowers dead, or do some of them come again in the summer? Are there ever any roses?"

"Ask him," said Ben Weatherstaff, hunching his shoulders toward the robin. "He's the only one as knows. No one else has seen inside it for ten year'."

Ten years was a long time, Mary thought. She had been born ten years ago.

She walked away, slowly thinking. She had begun to like the garden just as she had begun to like the robin and Dickon and Martha's mother.

She was beginning to like Martha, too. That seemed a good many people to like ___ when you were not used to liking. She thought of the robin as one of the people. She went to her walk outside the long, ivy-covered wall over which she could see the tree-tops; and the second time she walked up and down the most interesting and exciting thing happened to her, and it was all through Ben Weatherstaff's robin.

She heard a chirp and a twitter, and when she looked at the bare flower-bed at her left side there he was hopping about and pretending to peck things out of the earth to persuade her that he had not followed her. But she knew he had followed her and the surprise so filled her with delight that she almost trembled a little.

"You do remember me!" she cried out. "You do! You are prettier than anything else in the world!"

She chirped, and talked, and coaxed and he hopped, and flirted his tail and twittered. It was as if he were talking. His red waistcoat was like satin and he puffed his tiny breast out and was so fine and so grand and so pretty that it was really as if he were showing her how important and like a human person a robin could be. Mistress Mary forgot that she had ever been contrary in her life when he allowed her to draw closer and closer to him, and bend down and talk and try to make something like robin sounds.

Oh! To think that he should actually let her come as near to him as that! He knew nothing in the world would make her put out her hand toward him or startle him in the least tiniest way. He knew it because he was a real person ___ only nicer than any other person in the world. She was so happy that she scarcely dared to breathe.

The flower-bed was not quite bare. It was bare of flowers because the perennial plants had been cut down for their winter rest, but there were tall shrubs and low ones which grew together at the back of the bed, and as the robin hopped about under them she saw him hop over a small pile of freshly turned up earth. He stopped on it to look for a worm. The earth had been turned up because a dog had been trying to dig up a mole and he had scratched quite a deep hole. Mary looked at it, not really knowing why the hole was there, and as she looked she saw something almost buried in the newly-turned soil. It was something like a ring of rusty iron or brass and when the robin flew up into a tree nearby she put out her hand and picked the ring up. It was more than a ring, however; it was an old key which looked as if it had been buried a long time.

Mistress Mary stood up and looked at it with an almost frightened face as it hung from her finger.

"Perhaps it has been buried for ten years," she said in a whisper. "Perhaps it is the key to the garden!"

THE ROBIN WHO SHOWED THE WAY

She looked at the key quite a long time. She turned it over and over, and thought about it. As I have said before, she was not a child who had been trained to ask permission or consult her elders about things. All she thought about the key was that if it was the key to the closed garden, and she could find out where the door was, she could perhaps open it and see what was inside the walls, and what had happened to the old rose-trees. It was because it had been shut up so long that she wanted to see it. It seemed as if it must be different from other places and that something strange must have happened to it during ten years. Besides that, if she liked it she could go into it every day and shut the door behind her, and she could make up some play of her own and play it quite alone, because nobody would ever know where she was, but would think the door was still locked and the key buried in the earth. The thought of that pleased her very much.

Living as it were, all by herself in a house with a hundred mysteriously closed rooms and having nothing whatever to do to amuse herself, had set her inactive brain to working and was actually awakening her imagination. There is no doubt that the fresh, strong, pure air from the moor had a great deal to do with it. Just as it had given her an appetite, and fighting with the wind had stirred her blood, so the same things had stirred her mind. In India she had always been too hot and languid and weak to care much about anything, but in this place she was beginning to care and to want to do new things. Already she felt less "contrary," though she did not know why.

She put the key in her pocket and walked up and down her walk. No one but herself ever seemed to come there, so she could walk slowly and look at the wall, or, rather, at the ivy growing on it. The ivy was the baffling thing. Howsoever carefully she looked she could see nothing but thickly growing, glossy, dark green leaves. She was very much disappointed. Something of her contrariness came back to her as she paced the walk and looked over it at the tree-tops inside. It seemed so silly, she said to herself, to be near it and not be able to get in. She took the key in her pocket when she went back to the house, and she made up her mind that she would always carry it with her when she went out, so that if she ever should find the hidden door she would be ready.

Mrs. Medlock had allowed Martha to sleep all night at the cottage, but she was back at her work in the morning with cheeks redder than ever and in the best of spirits.

"I got up at four o'clock," she said. "Eh! It was pretty on th' moor with th' birds gettin' up an' th' rabbits scamperin' about an' th' sun risin'. I didn't walk all th' way. A man gave me a ride in his cart an' I did enjoy myself."

She was full of stories of the delights of her day out. Her mother had been glad to see her and they had got the baking and washing all out of the way. She had even made each of the children a doughcake with a bit of brown sugar in it.

"I had 'em all pipin' hot when they came in from playin' on th' moor. An' th' cottage all smelt o' nice, clean hot bakin' an' there was a good fire, an' they just shouted for joy. Our Dickon he said our cottage was good enough for a king."

In the evening they had all sat round the fire, and Martha and her mother had sewed patches on torn clothes and mended stockings and Martha had told them about the little girl who had come from India and who had been waited on all her life by what Martha called "blacks" until she didn't know how to put on her own stockings.

"Eh! They did like to hear about you," said Martha. "They wanted to know all about th' blacks an' about th' ship you came in. I couldn't tell 'em enough."

Mary reflected a little.

"I'll tell you a great deal more before your next day out," she said, "so that you will have more to talk about. I dare say they would like to hear about riding on elephants and camels, and about the officers going to hunt tigers."

"My word!" cried delighted Martha. "It would set 'em clean off their heads. Would tha' really do that, Miss? It would be same as a wild beast show like we heard they had in York once."

"India is quite different from Yorkshire," Mary said slowly, as she thought the matter over. "I never thought of that. Did Dickon and your mother like to hear you talk about me?"

"Why, our Dickon's eyes nearly started out o' his head, they got that round," answered Martha. "But mother, she was put out about your seemin' to be all by yourself like. She said, 'Hasn't Mr. Craven got no governess for her, nor no nurse?' and I said, 'No, he hasn't, though Mrs. Medlock says he will when he thinks of it, but she says he mayn't think of it for two or three years.'"

"I don't want a governess," said Mary sharply.

"But mother says you ought to be learnin' your book by this time an' you ought to have a woman to look after you, an' she says: 'Now, Martha, you just think how you'd feel yourself, in a big place like that, wanderin' about all alone, an' no mother. You do your best to cheer her up,' she says, an' I said I would."

Mary gave her a long, steady look.

"You do cheer me up," she said. "I like to hear you talk."

Presently Martha went out of the room and came back with something held in her hands under her apron.

"What does tha' think," she said, with a cheerful grin. "I've brought thee a present."

"A present!" exclaimed Mistress Mary. How could a cottage full of fourteen hungry people give any one a present!

"A man was drivin' across the moor peddlin'," Martha explained. "An' he stopped his cart at our door. He had pots an' pans an' odds an' ends, but mother had no money to buy anythin'. Just as he was goin' away our 'Lizabeth Ellen called out, 'Mother, he's got skippin'-ropes with red an' blue handles.' An' mother she calls out quite sudden, 'Here, stop, mister! How much are they?' An' he says 'Tuppence', an' mother she began fumblin' in her pocket an' she says to me, 'Martha, tha's brought me thy wages like a good lass, an' I've got four places to put every penny, but I'm just goin' to take tuppence out of it to buy that child a skippin'-rope,' an' she bought one an' here it is."

She brought it out from under her apron and exhibited it quite proudly. It was a strong, slender rope with a striped red and blue handle at each end, but Mary Lennox had never seen a skipping-rope before. She gazed at it with a mystified expression.

"What is it for?" she asked curiously.

"For!" cried out Martha. "Does tha' mean that they've not got skippin'-ropes in India, for all they've got elephants and tigers and camels! No wonder most of 'em's black. This is what it's for; just watch me."

And she ran into the middle of the room and, taking a handle in each hand, began to skip, and skip, and skip, while Mary turned in her chair to stare at her, and the queer faces in the old portraits seemed to stare at her, too, and wonder what on earth this common little cottager had the impudence to be doing under their very noses. But Martha did not even see them. The interest and curiosity in Mistress Mary's face delighted her, and she went on skipping and counted as she skipped until she had reached a hundred.

"I could skip longer than that," she said when she stopped. "I've skipped as much as five hundred when I was twelve, but I wasn't as fat then as I am now, an' I was in practice."

Mary got up from her chair beginning to feel excited herself.

"It looks nice," she said. "Your mother is a kind woman. Do you think I could ever skip like that?"

"You just try it," urged Martha, handing her the skipping-rope. "You can't skip a hundred at first, but if you practice you'll mount up. That's what mother said. She says, 'Nothin' will do her more good than skippin' rope. It's th' sensiblest toy a child can have. Let her play out in th' fresh air skippin' an' it'll stretch her legs an' arms an' give her some strength in 'em.'"

It was plain that there was not a great deal of strength in Mistress Mary's arms and legs when she first began to skip. She was not very clever at it, but she liked it so much that she did not want to stop.

"Put on tha' things and run an' skip out o' doors," said Martha. "Mother said I must tell you to keep out o' doors as much as you could, even when it rains a bit, so as tha' wrap up warm."

Mary put on her coat and hat and took her skipping-rope over her arm. She opened the door to go out, and then suddenly thought of something and turned back rather slowly.

"Martha," she said, "they were your wages. It was your two-pence really. Thank you." She said it stiffly because she was not used to thanking people or noticing that they did things for her. "Thank you," she said, and held out her hand because she did not know what else to do.

Martha gave her hand a clumsy little shake, as if she was not accustomed to this sort of thing either. Then she laughed.

"Eh! Th' art a queer, old-womanish thing," she said. "If tha'd been our 'Lizabeth Ellen tha'd have given me a kiss."

Mary looked stiffer than ever.

"Do you want me to kiss you?"

Martha laughed again.

"Nay, not me," she answered. "If tha' was different, p'raps tha'd want to thysel'. But tha' isn't. Run off outside an' play with thy rope."

Mistress Mary felt a little awkward as she went out of the room. Yorkshire people seemed strange, and Martha was always rather a puzzle to her. At first she had disliked her very much, but now she did not.

The skipping-rope was a wonderful thing. She counted and skipped, and skipped and counted, until her cheeks were quite red, and she was more interested than she had ever been since she was born. The sun was shining and a little wind was blowing —— not a rough wind, but one which came in delightful little gusts and brought a fresh scent of newly turned earth with it. She skipped round the fountain garden, and up one walk and down another. She skipped at last into the kitchen-garden and saw Ben Weatherstaff digging and talking to his robin, which was hopping about him. She skipped down the walk toward him and he lifted his head and looked at her with a curious expression. She had wondered if he would notice her. She wanted him to see her skip.

"Well!" he exclaimed. "Upon my word. P'raps tha' art a young 'un, after all, an' p'raps tha's got child's blood in thy veins instead of sour buttermilk. Tha's skipped red into thy cheeks as sure as my name's Ben Weatherstaff. I wouldn't have believed tha' could do it."

"I never skipped before," Mary said. "I'm just beginning. I can only go up to twenty."

"Tha' keep on," said Ben. "Tha' shapes well enough at it for a young 'un that's lived with heathen. Just see how he's watchin' thee," jerking his head toward the robin. "He followed after thee yesterday. He'll be at it again today. He'll be bound to find out what th' skippin'-rope is. He's never seen one. Eh!" shaking his head at the bird, "tha' curiosity will be th' death of thee sometime if tha' doesn't look sharp."

Mary skipped round all the gardens and round the orchard, resting every few minutes. At length she went to her own special walk and made up her mind to try if she could skip the whole length of it. It was a good long skip and she began slowly, but before she had gone half-way down the path she was so hot and breathless that she was obliged to stop. She did not mind much, because she had already counted up to thirty. She stopped with a little laugh of pleasure, and there, lo and behold, was the robin swaying on a long branch of ivy. He had followed her and he greeted her with a chirp. As Mary had skipped toward him she felt something heavy in her pocket strike against her at each jump, and when she saw the robin she laughed again.

"You showed me where the key was yesterday," she said. "You ought to show me the door today; but I don't believe you know!"

The robin flew from his swinging spray of ivy on to the top of the wall and he opened his beak and sang a loud, lovely trill, merely to show off. Nothing in the world is quite as adorably lovely as a robin when he shows off —— and they are nearly always doing it.

Mary Lennox had heard a great deal about Magic in her Ayah's stories, and she always said that what happened almost at that moment was Magic.

One of the nice little gusts of wind rushed down the walk, and it was a stronger one than the rest. It was strong enough to wave the branches of the trees, and it was more than strong enough to sway the trailing sprays of untrimmed ivy hanging from the wall. Mary had stepped close to the robin, and suddenly the gust of wind swung aside some loose ivy trails, and more suddenly still she jumped toward it and caught it in her hand. This she did because she had seen something under it —— a round knob which had been covered by the leaves hanging over it. It was the knob of a door.

She put her hands under the leaves and began to pull and push them aside. Thick as the ivy hung, it nearly all was a loose and swinging curtain, though some had crept over wood and iron. Mary's heart began to thump and her hands to shake a little in her delight and excitement. The robin kept singing and twittering away and tilting his head on one side, as if he were as excited as she was. What was this under her hands which was square and made of iron and which her fingers found a hole in?

It was the lock of the door which had been closed ten years and she put her hand in her pocket, drew out the key and found it fitted the keyhole. She put the key in and turned it. It took two hands to do it, but it did turn.

And then she took a long breath and looked behind her up the long walk to see if any one was coming. No one was coming. No one ever did come, it seemed, and she took another long breath, because she could not help it, and she held back the swinging curtain of ivy and pushed back the door which opened slowly —— slowly.

Then she slipped through it, and shut it behind her, and stood with her back against it, looking about her and breathing quite fast with excitement, and wonder, and delight.

She was standing inside the secret garden.

6

DICKON

The sun shone down for nearly a week on the secret garden. The Secret Garden was what Mary called it when she was thinking of it. She liked the name, and she liked still more the feeling that when its beautiful old walls shut her in no one knew where she was. It seemed almost like being shut out of the world in some fairy place. The few books she had read and liked had been fairy-story books, and she had read of secret gardens in some of the stories. Sometimes people went to sleep in them for a hundred years, which she had thought must be rather stupid. She had no intention of going to sleep, and, in fact, she was becoming wider awake every day which passed at Misselthwaite. She was beginning to like to be out of doors; she no longer hated the wind, but enjoyed it. She could run faster, and longer, and she could skip up to a hundred. The bulbs in the secret garden must have been much astonished. Such nice clear places were made round them that they had all the breathing space they wanted, and really, if Mistress Mary had known it, they began to cheer up under the dark earth and work tremendously. The sun could get at them and warm them, and when the rain came down it could reach them at once, so they began to feel very much alive. Mary was an odd, determined little person, and now she had something interesting to be determined about, she was very much absorbed, indeed. She worked and dug and pulled up weeds steadily, only becoming more pleased with her work every hour instead of tiring of it. It seemed to her like a fascinating sort of play. She found many more of the sprouting pale green points than she had ever hoped to find. They seemed to be starting up everywhere and each day she was sure she found tiny new ones, some so tiny that they barely peeped above the earth. There were so many that she remembered what Martha had said about the "snowdrops by the thousands," and about bulbs spreading and making new ones. These had been left to themselves for ten years and perhaps they had spread, like the snowdrops, into thousands. She wondered how long it would be before they showed that they were flowers. Sometimes she stopped digging to look at the garden and try to imagine what it would be like when it was covered with thousands of lovely things in bloom.

During that week of sunshine, she became more intimate with Ben Weatherstaff. She surprised him several times by seeming to start up beside him as if she sprang out of the earth. The truth was that she was afraid that he would pick up his tools and go away if he saw her coming, so she always walked toward him as silently as possible. But, in fact, he did not object to her as strongly as he had at first. Perhaps he was secretly rather flattered by her evident desire for his elderly company. Then, also, she was more civil than she had been. He did not know that when she first saw him she spoke to him as she would have spoken to a native, and had not known that a cross, sturdy old Yorkshire man was not accustomed to salaam to his masters, and be merely commanded by them to do things.

"Tha'rt like th' robin," he said to her one morning when he lifted his head and saw her standing by him. "I never knows when I shall see thee or which side tha'll come from."

"He's friends with me now," said Mary.

"That's like him," snapped Ben Weatherstaff. "Makin' up to th' women folk just for vanity an' flightiness. There's nothin' he wouldn't do for th' sake o' showin' off an' flirtin' his tail-feathers. He's as full o' pride as an egg's full o' meat."

He very seldom talked much and sometimes did not even answer Mary's questions except by a grunt, but this morning he said more than usual. He stood up and rested one hobnailed boot on the top of his spade while he looked her over.

"How long has tha' been here?" he jerked out.

"I think it's about a month," she answered.

"Tha's beginnin' to do Misselthwaite credit," he said. "Tha's a bit fatter than tha' was an' tha's not quite so yeller. Tha' looked like a young plucked crow when tha' first came into this garden. Thinks I to myself I never set eyes on an uglier, sourer faced young 'un."

Mary was not vain and as she had never thought much of her looks she was not greatly disturbed.

"I know I'm fatter," she said. "My stockings are getting tighter. They used to make wrinkles. There's the robin, Ben Weatherstaff."

There, indeed, was the robin, and she thought he looked nicer than ever. His red waistcoat was as glossy as satin and he flirted his wings and tail and tilted his head and hopped about with all sorts of lively graces. He seemed determined to make Ben Weatherstaff admire him. But Ben was sarcastic.

"Aye, there tha' art!" he said. "Tha' can put up with me for a bit sometimes when tha's got no one better. Tha's been reddenin' up thy waistcoat an' polishin' thy feathers this two weeks. I know what tha's up to. Tha's courtin' some bold young madam somewhere tellin' thy lies to her about bein' th' finest cock robin on Missel

Moor an' ready to fight all th' rest of 'em."

"Oh! Look at him!" exclaimed Mary.

The robin was evidently in a fascinating, bold mood. He hopped closer and closer and looked at Ben Weatherstaff more and more engagingly. He flew on to the nearest currant bush and tilted his head and sang a little song right at him.

"Tha' thinks tha'll get over me by doin' that," said Ben, wrinkling his face up in such a way that Mary felt sure he was trying not to look pleased. "Tha' thinks no one can stand out against thee ____ that's what tha' thinks."

The robin spread his wings ____ Mary could scarcely believe her eyes. He flew right up to the handle of Ben Weatherstaff's spade and alighted on the top of it. Then the old man's face wrinkled itself slowly into a new expression. He stood still as if he were afraid to breathe ____ as if he would not have stirred for the world, lest his robin should start away. He spoke quite in a whisper.

"Well, I'm danged!" he said as softly as if he were saying something quite different. "Tha' does know how to get at a chap ____ tha' does! Tha's fair unearthly, tha's so knowin'."

And he stood without stirring ____ almost without drawing his breath ____ until the robin gave another flirt to his wings and flew away. Then he stood looking at the handle of the spade as if there might be Magic in it, and then he began to dig again and said nothing for several minutes.

But because he kept breaking into a slow grin now and then, Mary was not afraid to talk to him.

"Have you a garden of your own?" she asked.

"No. I'm bachelder an' lodge with Martin at th' gate."

"If you had one," said Mary, "what would you plant?"

"Cabbages an' 'taters an' onions."

"But if you wanted to make a flower garden," persisted Mary, "what would you plant?"

"Bulbs an' sweet-smellin' things —— but mostly roses."

Mary's face lighted up.

"Do you like roses?" she said.

Ben Weatherstaff rooted up a weed and threw it aside before he answered.

"Well, yes, I do. I was learned that by a young lady I was gardener to. She had a lot in a place she was fond of, an' she loved 'em like they was children —— or robins. I've seen her bend over an' kiss 'em." He dragged out another weed and scowled at it. "That were as much as ten year' ago."

"Where is she now?" asked Mary, much interested.

"Heaven," he answered, and drove his spade deep into the soil, "'cording to what parson says."

"What happened to the roses?" Mary asked again, more interested than ever.

"They was left to themselves."

Mary was becoming quite excited.

"Did they quite die? Do roses quite die when they are left to themselves?" she ventured.

"Well, I'd got to like 'em —— an' I liked her —— an' she liked 'em," Ben Weatherstaff admitted reluctantly. "Once or twice a year I'd go an' work at 'em a bit —— prune 'em an' dig about th' roots. They run wild, but they was in rich soil, so some of 'em lived."

"When they have no leaves and look gray and brown and dry, how can you tell whether they are dead or alive?" inquired Mary.

"Wait till th' spring gets at 'em —— wait till th' sun shines on th' rain and th' rain falls on th' sunshine an' then tha'll find out."

"How —— how?" cried Mary, forgetting to be careful.

"Look along th' twigs an' branches an' if tha' see a bit of a brown lump swelling here an' there, watch it after th' warm rain an' see what happens." He stopped suddenly and looked curiously at her eager face. "Why does tha' care so much about roses an' such, all of a sudden?" he demanded.

Mistress Mary felt her face grow red. She was almost afraid to answer.

"I ⎯ I want to play that ⎯ that I have a garden of my own," she stammered. "I ⎯ there is nothing for me to do. I have nothing ⎯ and no one."

"Well," said Ben Weatherstaff slowly, as he watched her, "that's true. Tha' hasn't."

He said it in such an odd way that Mary wondered if he was actually a little sorry for her. She had never felt sorry for herself; she had only felt tired and cross, because she disliked people and things so much. But now the world seemed to be changing and getting nicer. If no one found out about the secret garden, she should enjoy herself always.

She stayed with him for ten or fifteen minutes longer and asked him as many questions as she dared. He answered every one of them in his queer grunting way and he did not seem really cross and did not pick up his spade and leave her.

He said something about roses just as she was going away and it reminded her of the ones he had said he had been fond of.

"Do you go and see those other roses now?" she asked.

"Not been this year. My rheumatics has made me too stiff in th' joints."

He said it in his grumbling voice, and then quite suddenly he seemed to get angry with her, though she did not see why he should.

"Now look here!" he said sharply. "Don't tha' ask so many

questions. Tha'rt th' worst wench for askin' questions I've ever come a cross. Get thee gone an' play thee. I've done talkin' for today."

And he said it so crossly that she knew there was not the least use in staying another minute. She went skipping slowly down the outside walk, thinking him over and saying to herself that, queer as it was, here was another person whom she liked in spite of his crossness. She liked old Ben Weatherstaff. Yes, she did like him. She always wanted to try to make him talk to her. Also she began to believe that he knew everything in the world about flowers.

There was a laurel-hedged walk which curved round the secret garden and ended at a gate which opened into a wood, in the park. She thought she would skip round this walk and look into the wood and see if there were any rabbits hopping about. She enjoyed the skipping very much and when she reached the little gate she opened it and went through because she heard a low, peculiar whistling sound and wanted to find out what it was.

It was a very strange thing indeed. She quite caught her breath as she stopped to look at it. A boy was sitting under a tree, with his back against it, playing on a rough wooden pipe. He was a funny looking boy about twelve. He looked very clean and his nose turned up and his cheeks were as red as poppies and never had Mistress Mary seen such round and such blue eyes in any boy's face. And on the trunk of the tree he leaned against, a brown squirrel was clinging and watching him, and from behind a bush nearby a cock pheasant was delicately stretching his neck to peep out, and quite near him were two rabbits sitting up and sniffing with tremulous noses ___ and actually it appeared as if they were all drawing near to watch him and listen to the strange low little call his pipe seemed to make.

When he saw Mary he held up his hand and spoke to her in a voice almost as low as and rather like his piping.

"Don't tha' move," he said. "It'd flight 'em."

Mary remained motionless. He stopped playing his pipe and began to rise from the ground. He moved so slowly that it scarcely seemed as though he were moving at all, but at last he stood on his feet and then the squirrel scampered back up into the branches of his tree, the pheasant withdrew his head and the rabbits dropped on all fours and began to hop away, though not at all as if they were frightened.

"I'm Dickon," the boy said. "I know tha'rt Miss Mary."

Then Mary realized that somehow she had known at first that he was Dickon. Who else could have been charming rabbits and pheasants as the natives charm snakes in India? He had a wide, red, curving mouth and his smile spread all over his face.

"I got up slow," he explained, "because if tha' makes a quick move it startles 'em. A body 'as to move gentle an' speak low when wild things is about."

He did not speak to her as if they had never seen each other before but as if he knew her quite well. Mary knew nothing about boys and she spoke to him a little stiffly because she felt rather shy.

"Did you get Martha's letter?" she asked.

He nodded his curly, rust-colored head.

"That's why I come."

He stooped to pick up something which had been lying on the ground beside him when he piped.

"I've got th' garden tools. There's a little spade an' rake an' a fork an' hoe. Eh! They are good 'uns. There's a trowel, too. An' th' woman in th' shop threw in a packet o' white poppy an' one o' blue larkspur when I bought th' other seeds."

"Will you show the seeds to me?" Mary said.

She wished she could talk as he did. His speech was so quick and easy. It sounded as if he liked her and was not the least afraid she would not like him, though he was only a common moor boy, in patched clothes and with a funny face and a rough, rusty-red head. As she came closer to him she noticed that there was a clean fresh scent of heather and grass and leaves about him, almost as if he were made of them. She liked it very much and when she looked into his funny face with the red cheeks and round blue eyes she forgot that she had felt shy.

"Let us sit down on this log and look at them," she said.

They sat down and he took a clumsy little brown paper package out of his coat pocket. He untied the string and inside there were ever so many neater and smaller packages with a picture of a flower on each one.

"There's a lot o' mignonette an' poppies," he said. "Mignonette's th' sweetest smellin' thing as grows, an' it'll grow wherever you cast it, same as poppies will. Them as'll come up an' bloom if you just whistle to 'em, them's th' nicest of all." He stopped and turned his head quickly, his poppy-cheeked face lighting up.

"Where's that robin as is callin' us?" he said.

The chirp came from a thick holly bush, bright with scarlet berries, and Mary thought she knew whose it was.

"Is it really calling us?" she asked.

"Aye," said Dickon, as if it was the most natural thing in the world, "he's callin' some one he's friends with. That's same as sayin' 'Here I am. Look at me. I wants a bit of a chat.' There he is in the bush. Whose is he?"

"He's Ben Weatherstaff's, but I think he knows me a little," answered Mary.

"Aye, he knows thee," said Dickon in his low voice again. "An' he likes thee. He's took thee on. He'll tell me all about thee in a minute."

He moved quite close to the bush with the slow movement Mary had noticed before, and then he made a sound almost like the robin's own twitter. The robin listened a few seconds, intently, and then answered quite as if he were replying to a question.

"Aye, he's a friend o' yours," chuckled Dickon.

"Do you think he is?" cried Mary eagerly. She did so want to know. "Do you think he really likes me?"

"He wouldn't come near thee if he didn't," answered Dickon. "Birds is rare choosers an' a robin can flout a body worse than a man. See, he's making up to thee now. 'Cannot tha' see a chap?' he's sayin'."

And it really seemed as if it must be true. He so sidled and twittered and tilted as he hopped on his bush.

"Do you understand everything birds say?" said Mary.

Dickon's grin spread until he seemed all wide, red, curving mouth, and he rubbed his rough head.

"I think I do, and they think I do," he said. "I've lived on th' moor with 'em so long. I've watched 'em break shell an' come out an' fledge an' learn to fly an' begin to sing, till I think I'm one of 'em. Sometimes I think p'raps I'm a bird, or a fox, or a rabbit, or a squirrel, or even a beetle, an' I don't know it."

He laughed and came back to the log and began to talk about the flower seeds again. He told her what they looked like when they were flowers; he told her how to plant them, and watch them, and feed and water them.

"See here," he said suddenly, turning round to look at her. "I'll plant them for thee myself. Where is tha' garden?"

Mary's thin hands clutched each other as they lay on her lap. She did not know what to say, so for a whole minute she said nothing.

She had never thought of this. She felt miserable. And she felt as if she went red and then pale.

"Tha's got a bit o' garden, hasn't tha'?" Dickon said.

It was true that she had turned red and then pale. Dickon saw her do it, and as she still said nothing, he began to be puzzled.

"Wouldn't they give thee a bit?" he asked. "Hasn't tha' got any yet?"

She held her hands tighter and turned her eyes toward him.

"I don't know anything about boys," she said slowly. "Could you keep a secret, if I told you one? It's a great secret. I don't know what I should do if anyone found it out. I believe I should die!" She said the last sentence quite fiercely.

Dickon looked more puzzled than ever and even rubbed his hand over his rough head again, but he answered quite good-humoredly.

"I'm keepin' secrets all th' time," he said. "If I couldn't keep secrets from th' other lads, secrets about foxes' cubs, an' birds' nests, an' wild things' holes, there'd be naught safe on th' moor. Aye, I can keep secrets."

Mistress Mary did not mean to put out her hand and clutch his sleeve but she did it.

"I've stolen a garden," she said very fast. "It isn't mine. It isn't anybody's. Nobody wants it, nobody cares for it, nobody ever goes into it. Perhaps everything is dead in it already. I don't know."

She began to feel hot and as contrary as she had ever felt in her life.

"I don't care, I don't care! Nobody has any right to take it from me when I care about it and they don't. They're letting it die, all shut in by itself," she ended passionately, and she threw her arms over her face and burst out crying-poor little Mistress Mary.

Dickon's curious blue eyes grew rounder and rounder. "Eh-h-h!" he said, drawing his exclamation out slowly, and the way he did it meant both wonder and sympathy.

"I've nothing to do," said Mary. "Nothing belongs to me. I found it myself and I got into it myself. I was only just like the robin, and they wouldn't take it from the robin."

"Where is it?" asked Dickon in a dropped voice.

Mistress Mary got up from the log at once. She knew she felt contrary again, and obstinate, and she did not care at all. She was imperious and Indian, and at the same time hot and sorrowful.

"Come with me and I'll show you," she said.

She led him round the laurel path and to the walk where the ivy grew so thickly. Dickon followed her with a queer, almost pitying, look on his face. He felt as if he were being led to look at some strange bird's nest and must move softly. When she stepped to the wall and lifted the hanging ivy he started. There was a door and Mary pushed it slowly open and they passed in together, and then Mary stood and waved her hand round defiantly.

"It's this," she said. "It's a secret garden, and I'm the only one in the world who wants it to be alive."

Dickon looked round and round about it, and round and round again.

"Eh!" he almost whispered, "it is a queer, pretty place! It's like as if a body was in a dream."

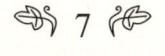

"I AM COLIN"

Mary took the picture back to the house when she went to her supper and she showed it to Martha.

"Eh!" said Martha with great pride. "I never knew our Dickon was as clever as that. That there's a picture of a missel thrush on her nest, as large as life an' twice as natural."

Then Mary knew Dickon had meant the picture to be a message. He had meant that she might be sure he would keep her secret. Her garden was her nest and she was like a missel thrush. Oh, how she did like that queer, common boy!

She hoped he would come back the very next day and she fell asleep looking forward to the morning.

But you never know what the weather will do in Yorkshire, particularly in the springtime. She was awakened in the night by the sound of rain beating with heavy drops against her window. It was pouring down in torrents and the wind was "wuthering" round the corners and in the chimneys of the huge old house. Mary sat up in bed and felt miserable and angry.

"The rain is as contrary as I ever was," she said. "It came because it knew I did not want it."

She threw herself back on her pillow and buried her face. She did not cry, but she lay and hated the sound of the heavily beating rain, she hated the wind and its "wuthering." She could not go to sleep again. The mournful sound kept her awake because she felt mournful herself. If she had felt happy it would probably have lulled her to sleep. How it "wuthered" and how the big raindrops poured down and beat against the pane!

"It sounds just like a person lost on the moor and wandering on and on crying," she said.

She had been lying awake turning from side to side for about an hour, when suddenly something made her sit up in bed and turn her head toward the door listening. She listened and she listened.

"It isn't the wind now," she said in a loud whisper. "That isn't the wind. It is different. It is that crying I heard before."

The door of her room was ajar and the sound came down the corridor, a far-off faint sound of fretful crying. She listened for a few minutes and each minute she became more and more sure. She felt as if she must find out what it was. It seemed even stranger than the secret garden and the buried key. Perhaps the fact that she was in a rebellious mood made her bold. She put her foot out of bed and stood on the floor.

"I am going to find out what it is," she said. "Everybody is in bed and I don't care about Mrs. Medlock ____ I don't care!"

There was a candle by her bedside and she took it up and went softly out of the room. The corridor looked very long and dark, but she was too excited to mind that. She thought she remembered the corners she must turn to find the short corridor with the door covered with tapestry ____ the one Mrs. Medlock had come through the day she lost herself. The sound had come up that passage. So she went on with her dim light, almost feeling her way, her heart beating so loud that she fancied she could hear it. The far-off faint crying went on and led her. Sometimes it stopped for a moment or so and then began again. Was this the right corner to turn? She stopped and thought. Yes it was. Down this passage and then to the left, and then up two broad steps, and then to the right again. Yes, there was the tapestry door.

She pushed it open very gently and closed it behind her, and she stood in the corridor and could hear the crying quite plainly, though it was not loud. It was on the other side of the wall at her left and a few yards farther on there was a door. She could see a glimmer of light coming from beneath it. The Someone was crying in that room, and it was quite a young Someone.

So she walked to the door and pushed it open, and there she was standing in the room!

It was a big room with ancient, handsome furniture in it. There was a low fire glowing faintly on the hearth and a night light burning by the side of a carved four-posted bed hung with brocade, and on the bed was lying a boy, crying fretfully.

Mary wondered if she was in a real place or if she had fallen asleep again and was dreaming without knowing it.

The boy had a sharp, delicate face the color of ivory and he seemed to have eyes too big for it. He had also a lot of hair which tumbled over his forehead in heavy locks and made his thin face seem smaller. He looked like a boy who had been ill, but he was crying more as if he were tired and cross than as if he were in pain.

Mary stood near the door with her candle in her hand, holding her breath. Then she crept 'WHO ARE YOU? ___ ARE YOU A GHOST?' across the room, and, as she drew nearer, the light attracted the boy's attention and he turned his head on his pillow and stared at her, his gray eyes opening so wide that they seemed immense.

"Who are you?" he said at last in a half-frightened whisper. "Are you a ghost?"

"No, I am not," Mary answered, her own whisper sounding half frightened. "Are you one?"

He stared and stared and stared. Mary could not help noticing what strange eyes he had. They were agate gray and they looked too big for his face because they had black lashes all round them.

"No," he replied after waiting a moment or so. "I am Colin."

"Who is Colin?" she faltered.

"I am Colin Craven. Who are you?"

"I am Mary Lennox. Mr. Craven is my uncle."

"He is my father," said the boy.

"Your father!" gasped Mary. "No one ever told me he had a boy!

Why didn't they?"

"Come here," he said, still keeping his strange eyes fixed on her with an anxious expression.

She came close to the bed and he put out his hand and touched her.

"You are real, aren't you?" he said. "I have such real dreams very often. You might be one of them."

Mary had slipped on a woolen wrapper before she left her room and she put a piece of it between his fingers.

"Rub that and see how thick and warm it is," she said. "I will pinch you a little if you like, to show you how real I am. For a minute I thought you might be a dream too."

"Where did you come from?" he asked.

"From my own room. The wind wuthered so I couldn't go to sleep and I heard someone crying and wanted to find out who it was. What were you crying for?"

"Because I couldn't go to sleep either and my head ached. Tell me your name again."

"Mary Lennox. Did no one ever tell you I had come to live here?"

He was still fingering the fold of her wrapper, but he began to look a little more as if he believed in her reality.

"No," he answered. "They daren't."

"Why?" asked Mary.

"Because I should have been afraid you would see me. I won't let people see me and talk me over."

"Why?" Mary asked again, feeling more mystified every moment.

"Because I am like this always, ill and having to lie down. My father won't let people talk me over either. The servants are not allowed to speak about me. If I live I may be a hunchback, but I shan't live. My father hates to think I may be like him."

"Oh, what a queer house this is!" Mary said. "What a queer house!

Everything is a kind of secret. Rooms are locked up and gardens are locked up ____ and you! Have you been locked up?"

"No. I stay in this room because I don't want to be moved out of it. It tires me too much."

"Does your father come and see you?" Mary ventured.

"Sometimes. Generally when I am asleep. He doesn't want to see me."

"Why?" Mary could not help asking again.

A sort of angry shadow passed over the boy's face.

"My mother died when I was born and it makes him wretched to look at me. He thinks I don't know, but I've heard people talking. He almost hates me."

"He hates the garden, because she died," said Mary half speaking to herself.

"What garden?" the boy asked.

"Oh! Just ____ just a garden she used to like," Mary stammered. "Have you been here always?"

"Nearly always. Sometimes I have been taken to places at the seaside, but I won't stay because people stare at me. I used to wear an iron thing to keep my back straight, but a grand doctor came from London to see me and said it was stupid. He told them to take it off and keep me out in the fresh air. I hate fresh air and I don't want to go out."

"I didn't when first I came here," said Mary. "Why do you keep looking at me like that?"

"Because of the dreams that are so real," he answered rather fretfully. "Sometimes when I open my eyes I don't believe I'm awake."

"We're both awake," said Mary. She glanced round the room with its high ceiling and shadowy corners and dim fire-light. "It looks quite like a dream, and it's the middle of the night, and everybody in the house is asleep —— everybody but us. We are wide awake."

"I don't want it to be a dream," the boy said restlessly.

Mary thought of something all at once.

"If you don't like people to see you," she began, "do you want me to go away?"

He still held the fold of her wrapper and he gave it a little pull.

"No," he said. "I should be sure you were a dream if you went. If you are real, sit down on that big footstool and talk. I want to hear about you."

Mary put down her candle on the table near the bed and sat down on the cushioned stool. She did not want to go away at all. She wanted to stay in the mysterious hidden-away room and talk to the mysterious boy.

"What do you want me to tell you?" she said.

He wanted to know how long she had been at Misselthwaite; he wanted to know which corridor her room was on; he wanted to know what she had been doing; if she disliked the moor as he disliked it; where she had lived before she came to Yorkshire. She answered all these questions and many more and he lay back on his pillow and listened. He made her tell him a great deal about India and about her voyage across the ocean. She found out that because he had been an invalid he had not learned things as other children had. One of his nurses had taught him to read when he was quite little and he was always reading and looking at pictures in splendid books.

Though his father rarely saw him when he was awake, he was given all sorts of wonderful things to amuse himself with. He never seemed to have been amused, however. He could have anything he asked for and was never made to do anything he did not like to do.

"Everyone is obliged to do what pleases me," he said indifferently. "It makes me ill to be angry. No one believes I shall live to grow up."

He said it as if he was so accustomed to the idea that it had ceased to matter to him at all. He seemed to like the sound of Mary's voice. As she went on talking he listened in a drowsy, interested way. Once or twice she wondered if he were not gradually falling into a doze. But at last he asked a question which opened up a new subject.

"How old are you?" he asked.

"I am ten," answered Mary, forgetting herself for the moment, "and so are you."

"How do you know that?" he demanded in a surprised voice.

"Because when you were born the garden door was locked and the key was buried. And it has been locked for ten years."

Colin half sat up, turning toward her, leaning on his elbows.

"What garden door was locked? Who did it? Where was the key buried?" he exclaimed as if he were suddenly very much interested.

"It ___ it was the garden Mr. Craven hates," said Mary nervously. "He locked the door. No one ___ no one knew where he buried the key."

"What sort of a garden is it?" Colin persisted eagerly.

"No one has been allowed to go into it for ten years," was Mary's careful answer.

But it was too late to be careful. He was too much like herself. He too had had nothing to think about and the idea of a hidden garden attracted him as it had attracted her. He asked question after question. Where was it? Had she never looked for the door? Had she never asked the gardeners?

"They won't talk about it," said Mary. "I think they have been told not to answer questions."

"I would make them," said Colin.

"Could you?" Mary faltered, beginning to feel frightened. If he could make people answer questions, who knew what might happen!

"Everyone is obliged to please me. I told you that," he said. "If I were to live, this place would sometime belong to me. They all know that. I would make them tell me."

Mary had not known that she herself had been spoiled, but she could see quite plainly that this mysterious boy had been. He thought that the whole world belonged to him. How peculiar he was and how coolly he spoke of not living.

"Do you think you won't live?" she asked, partly because she was curious and partly in hope of making him forget the garden.

"I don't suppose I shall," he answered as indifferently as he had spoken before. "Ever since I remember anything I have heard people say I shan't. At first they thought I was too little to understand and now they think I don't hear. But I do. My doctor is my father's cousin. He is quite poor and if I die he will have all Misselthwaite when my father is dead. I should think he wouldn't want me to live."

"Do you want to live?" inquired Mary.

"No," he answered, in a cross, tired fashion. "But I don't want to die. When I feel ill I lie here and think about it until I cry and cry."

"I have heard you crying three times," Mary said, "but I did not know who it was. Were you crying about that?" She did so want him to forget the garden.

"I dare say," he answered. "Let us talk about something else. Talk about that garden. Don't you want to see it?"

"Yes," answered Mary, in quite a low voice.

"I do," he went on persistently. "I don't think I ever really wanted to see anything before, but I want to see that garden. I want the key dug up. I want the door unlocked. I would let them take me there in my chair. That would be getting fresh air. I am going to make them open the door."

He had become quite excited and his strange eyes began to shine like stars and looked more immense than ever.

"They have to please me," he said. "I will make them take me there and I will let you go, too."

Mary's hands clutched each other. Everything would be spoiled ____ everything! Dickon would never come back. She would never again feel like a missel thrush with a safe-hidden nest.

"Oh, don't ____ don't ____ don't ____ don't do that!" she cried out.

He stared as if he thought she had gone crazy!

"Why?" he exclaimed. "You said you wanted to see it."

"I do," she answered almost with a sob in her throat, "but if you make them open the door and take you in like that it will never be a secret again."

He leaned still farther forward.

"A secret," he said. "What do you mean? Tell me."

Mary's words almost tumbled over one another.

"You see ____ you see," she panted, "if no one knows but ourselves ____ if there was a door, hidden somewhere under the ivy ____ if there was ____ and we could find it; and if we could slip through it together and shut it behind us, and no one knew any one was inside and we called it our garden and pretended that ____ that we were missel thrushes and it was our nest, and if we played there almost every day and dug and planted seeds and made it all come alive ____ "

"Is it dead?" he interrupted her.

"It soon will be if no one cares for it," she went on. "The bulbs will live but the roses ____ "

304   The Secret Garden

He stopped her again as excited as she was herself.

"What are bulbs?" he put in quickly.

"They are daffodils and lilies and snowdrops. They are working in the earth now ⎯ pushing up pale green points because the spring is coming."

"Is the spring coming?" he said. "What is it like? You don't see it in rooms if you are ill."

"It is the sun shining on the rain and the rain falling on the sunshine, and things pushing up and working under the earth," said Mary. "If the garden was a secret and we could get into it we could watch the things grow bigger every day, and see how many roses are alive. Don't you. see? Oh, don't you see how much nicer it would be if it was a secret?"

He dropped back on his pillow and lay there with an odd expression on his face.

"I never had a secret," he said, "except that one about not living to grow up. They don't know I know that, so it is a sort of secret. But I like this kind better."

"If you won't make them take you to the garden," pleaded Mary, "perhaps ⎯ I feel almost sure I can find out how to get in sometime. And then ⎯ if the doctor wants you to go out in your chair, and if you can always do what you want to do, perhaps ⎯ perhaps we might find some boy who would push you, and we could go alone and it would always be a secret garden."

"I should ⎯ like ⎯ that," he said very slowly, his eyes looking dreamy. "I should like that. I should not mind fresh air in a secret garden."

Mary began to recover her breath and feel safer because the idea of keeping the secret seemed to please him. She felt almost sure that if she kept on talking and could make him see the garden in his mind as she had seen it he would like it so much that he could not bear to think that everybody might tramp in to it when they chose.

"I'll tell you what I think it would be like, if we could go into it," she said. "It has been shut up so long things have grown into a tangle perhaps."

He lay quite still and listened while she went on talking about the roses which might have clambered from tree to tree and hung down ___ about the many birds which might have built their nests there because it was so safe. And then she told him about the robin and Ben Weatherstaff, and there was so much to tell about the robin and it was so easy and safe to talk about it that she ceased to be afraid. The robin pleased him so much that he smiled until he looked almost beautiful, and at first Mary had thought that he was even plainer than herself, with his big eyes and heavy locks of hair.

"I did not know birds could be like that," he said. "But if you stay in a room you never see things. What a lot of things you know. I feel as if you had been inside that garden."

She did not know what to say, so she did not say anything. He evidently did not expect an answer and the next moment he gave her a surprise.

"I am going to let you look at something," he said. "Do you see that rose-colored silk curtain hanging on the wall over the mantel-piece?"

Mary had not noticed it before, but she looked up and saw it. It was a curtain of soft silk hanging over what seemed to be some picture.

"Yes," she answered.

"There is a cord hanging from it," said Colin. "Go and pull it."

Mary got up, much mystified, and found the cord. When she pulled it the silk curtain ran back on rings and when it ran back it uncovered a picture. It was the picture of a girl with a laughing face.

She had bright hair tied up with a blue ribbon and her gay, lovely eyes were exactly like Colin's unhappy ones, agate gray and looking twice as big as they really were because of the black lashes all round them.

"She is my mother," said Colin complainingly. "I don't see why she died. Sometimes I hate her for doing it."

"How queer!" said Mary.

"If she had lived I believe I should not have been ill always," he grumbled. "I dare say I should have lived, too. And my father would not have hated to look at me. I dare say I should have had a strong back. Draw the curtain again."

Mary did as she was told and returned to her footstool.

"She is much prettier than you," she said, "but her eyes are just like yours —— at least they are the same shape and color. Why is the curtain drawn over her?"

He moved uncomfortably.

"I made them do it," he said. "Sometimes I don't like to see her looking at me. She smiles too much when I am ill and miserable. Besides, she is mine and I don't want everyone to see her."

There were a few moments of silence and then Mary spoke.

"What would Mrs. Medlock do if she found out that I had been here?" she inquired.

"She would do as I told her to do," he answered. "And I should tell her that I wanted you to come here and talk to me every day. I am glad you came."

"So am I," said Mary. "I will come as often as I can, but" —— she hesitated —— "I shall have to look every day for the garden door."

"Yes, you must," said Colin, "and you can tell me about it afterward."

He lay thinking a few minutes, as he had done before, and then he spoke again.

"I think you shall be a secret, too," he said. "I will not tell them until they find out. I can always send the nurse out of the room and say that I want to be by myself. Do you know Martha?"

"Yes, I know her very well," said Mary. "She waits on me."

He nodded his head toward the outer corridor.

"She is the one who is asleep in the other room. The nurse went away yesterday to stay all night with her sister and she always makes Martha attend to me when she wants to go out. Martha shall tell you when to come here."

Then Mary understood Martha's troubled look when she had asked questions about the crying.

"Martha knew about you all the time?" she said.

"Yes; she often attends to me. The nurse likes to get away from me and then Martha comes."

"I have been here a long time," said Mary. "Shall I go away now? Your eyes look sleepy."

"I wish I could go to sleep before you leave me," he said rather shyly.

"Shut your eyes," said Mary, drawing her footstool closer, "and I will do what my Ayah used to do in India. I will pat your hand and stroke it and sing something quite low."

"I should like that perhaps," he said drowsily.

Somehow she was sorry for him and did not want him to lie awake, so she leaned against the bed and began to stroke and pat his hand and sing a very low little chanting song in Hindustani.

"That is nice," he said more drowsily still, and she went on chanting and stroking, but when she looked at him again his black lashes were lying close against his cheeks, for his eyes were shut and he was fast asleep. So she got up softly, took her candle and crept away without making a sound.

8

MAGIC

Dr. Craven had been waiting some time at the house when they returned to it. He had indeed begun to wonder if it might not be wise to send someone out to explore the garden paths. When Colin was brought back to his room the poor man looked him over seriously.

"You should not have stayed so long," he said. "You must not overexert yourself."

"I am not tired at all," said Colin. "It has made me well. Tomorrow I am going out in the morning as well as in the afternoon."

"I am not sure that I can allow it," answered Dr. Craven. "I am afraid it would not be wise."

"It would not be wise to try to stop me," said Colin quite seriously. "I am going."

Even Mary had found out that one of Colin's chief peculiarities was that he did not know in the least what a rude little brute he was with his way of ordering people about. He had lived on a sort of desert island all his life and as he had been the king of it he had made his own manners and had had no one to compare himself with. Mary had indeed been rather like him herself and since she had been at Misselthwaite had gradually discovered that her own manners had not been of the kind which is usual or popular. Having made this discovery she naturally thought it of enough interest to communicate to Colin. So she sat and looked at him curiously for a few minutes after Dr. Craven had gone. She wanted to make him ask her why she was doing it and of course she did.

"What are you looking at me for?" he said.

"I'm thinking that I am rather sorry for Dr. Craven."

"So am I," said Colin calmly, but not without an air of some satisfaction. "He won't get Misselthwaite at all now I'm not going to die."

"I'm sorry for him because of that, of course," said Mary, "but I was thinking just then that it must have been very horrid to have had to be polite for ten years to a boy who was always rude. I would never have done it."

"Am I rude?" Colin inquired undisturbedly.

"If you had been his own boy and he had been a slapping sort of man," said Mary, "he would have slapped you."

"But he daren't," said Colin.

"No, he daren't," answered Mistress Mary, thinking the thing out quite without prejudice. "Nobody ever dared to do anything you didn't like ⎯ because you were going to die and things like that. You were such a poor thing."

"But," announced Colin stubbornly, "I am not going to be a poor thing. I won't let people think I'm one. I stood on my feet this afternoon."

"It is always having your own way that has made you so queer," Mary went on, thinking aloud.

Colin turned his head, frowning.

"Am I queer?" he demanded.

"Yes," answered Mary, "very. But you needn't be cross," she added impartially, "because so am I queer ⎯ and so is Ben Weatherstaff. But I am not as queer as I was before I began to like people and before I found the garden."

"I don't want to be queer," said Colin. "I am not going to be," and he frowned again with determination.

He was a very proud boy. He lay thinking for a while and then Mary saw his beautiful smile begin and gradually change his whole face.

"I shall stop being queer," he said, "if I go every day to the garden. There is Magic in there —— good Magic, you know, Mary. I am sure there is."

"So am I," said Mary.

"Even if it isn't real Magic," Colin said, "we can pretend it is. Something is there —— something!"

"It's Magic," said Mary, "but not black. It's as white as snow."

They always called it Magic and indeed it seemed like it in the months that followed —— the wonderful months —— the radiant months —— the amazing ones. Oh! The things which happened in that garden! If you have never had a garden you cannot understand, and if you have had a garden you will know that it would take a whole book to describe all that came to pass there. At first it seemed that green things would never cease pushing their way through the earth, in the grass, in the beds, even in the crevices of the walls. Then the green things began to show buds and the buds began to unfurl and show color, every shade of blue, every shade of purple, every tint and hue of crimson. In its happy days flowers had been tucked away into every inch and hole and corner. Ben Weatherstaff had seen it done and had himself scraped out mortar from between the bricks of the wall and made pockets of earth for lovely clinging things to grow on. Iris and white lilies rose out of the grass in sheaves, and the green alcoves filled themselves with amazing armies of the blue and white flower lances of tall delphiniums or columbines or campanulas.

"She was main fond o' them —— she was," Ben Weatherstaff said.

"She liked them things as was allus pointin' up to th' blue sky, she used to tell. Not as she was one o' them as looked down on th' earth —— not her. She just loved it but she said as th' blue sky allus looked so joyful."

The seeds Dickon and Mary had planted grew as if fairies had tended them. Satiny poppies of all tints danced in the breeze by the score, gaily defying flowers which had lived in the garden for years and which it might be confessed seemed rather to wonder how such new people had got there. And the roses —— the roses! Rising out of the grass, tangled round the sun-dial, wreathing the tree trunks and hanging from their branches, climbing up the walls and spreading over them with long garlands falling in cascades —— they came alive day by day, hour by hour. Fair fresh leaves, and buds —— and buds —— tiny at first but swelling and working Magic until they burst and uncurled into cups of scent delicately spilling themselves over their brims and filling the garden air.

Colin saw it all, watching each change as it took place. Every morning he was brought out and every hour of each day when it didn't rain he spent in the garden. Even gray days pleased him. He would lie on the grass "watching things growing," he said. If you watched long enough, he declared, you could see buds unsheath themselves. Also you could make the acquaintance of strange busy insect things running about on various unknown but evidently serious errands, sometimes carrying tiny scraps of straw or feather or food, or climbing blades of grass as if they were trees from whose tops one could look out to explore the country. A mole throwing up its mound at the end of its burrow and making its way out at last with the long-nailed paws which looked so like elfish hands, had absorbed him one whole morning. Ants' ways, beetles' ways, bees' ways, frogs' ways, birds' ways, plants' ways, gave him a new world to explore and when Dickon revealed them all and added foxes' ways, otters' ways, ferrets' ways, squirrels' ways, and trout' and water-rats' and badgers' ways, there was no end to the things to talk about and think over.

And this was not the half of the Magic. The fact that he had really once stood on his feet had set Colin thinking tremendously and when Mary told him of the spell she had worked he was excited and approved of it greatly. He talked of it constantly.

"Of course there must be lots of Magic in the world," he said wisely one day, "but people don't know what it is like or how to make it. Perhaps the beginning is just to say nice things are going to happen until you make them happen. I am going to try and experiment"

The next morning when they went to the secret garden he sent at once for Ben Weatherstaff. Ben came as quickly as he could and found the Rajah standing on his feet under a tree and looking very grand but also very beautifully smiling.

"Good morning, Ben Weatherstaff," he said. "I want you and Dickon and Miss Mary to stand in a row and listen to me because I am going to tell you something very important."

"Aye, aye, sir!" answered Ben Weatherstaff, touching his forehead. (One of the long concealed charms of Ben Weatherstaff was that in his boyhood he had once run away to sea and had made voyages. So he could reply like a sailor.)

"I am going to try a scientific experiment," explained the Rajah. "When I grow up I am going to make great scientific discoveries and I am going to begin now with this experiment"

"Aye, aye, sir!" said Ben Weatherstaff promptly, though this was the first time he had heard of great scientific discoveries.

It was the first time Mary had heard of them, either, but even at this stage she had begun to realize that, queer as he was, Colin had read about a great many singular things and was somehow a very convincing sort of boy. When he held up his head and fixed his strange eyes on you it seemed as if you believed him almost in spite of yourself though he was only ten years old —— going on eleven. At this moment he was especially convincing because he suddenly felt the fascination of actually making a sort of speech like a grown-up person.

"The great scientific discoveries I am going to make," he went on, "will be about Magic. Magic is a great thing and scarcely any one knows anything about it except a few people in old books —— and Mary a little, because she was born in India where there are fakirs. I believe Dickon knows some Magic, but perhaps he doesn't know he knows it. He charms animals and people. I would never have let him come to see me if he had not been an animal charmer —— which is a boy charmer, too, because a boy is an animal. I am sure there is Magic in everything, only we have not sense enough to get hold of it and make it do things for us —— like electricity and horses and steam."

This sounded so imposing that Ben Weatherstaff became quite excited and really could not keep still.

"Aye, aye, sir," he said and he began to stand up quite straight.

"When Mary found this garden it looked quite dead," the orator proceeded. "Then something began pushing things up out of the soil and making things out of nothing. One day things weren't there and another they were. I had never watched things before and it made me feel very curious. Scientific people are always curious and I am going to be scientific. I keep saying to myself, 'What is it? What is it?' It's something. It can't be nothing! I don't know its name so I call it Magic. I have never seen the sun rise but Mary and Dickon have and from what they tell me I am sure that is Magic too.

Something pushes it up and draws it. Sometimes since I've been in the garden I've looked up through the trees at the sky and I have had a strange feeling of being happy as if something were pushing and drawing in my chest and making me breathe fast. Magic is always pushing and drawing and making things out of nothing. Everything is made out of Magic, leaves and trees, flowers and birds, badgers and foxes and squirrels and people. So it must be all around us. In this garden ___ in all the places. The Magic in this garden has made me stand up and know I am going to live to be a man. I am going to make the scientific experiment of trying to get some and put it in myself and make it push and draw me and make me strong. I don't know how to do it but I think that if you keep thinking about it and calling it perhaps it will come. Perhaps that is the first baby way to get it. When I was going to try to stand that first time Mary kept saying to herself as fast as she could, 'You can do it! You can do it!' and I did. I had to try myself at the same time, of course, but her Magic helped me ___ and so did Dickon's. Every morning and evening and as often in the daytime as I can remember I am going to say, 'Magic is in me! Magic is making me well! I am going to be as strong as Dickon, as strong as Dickon!' And you must all do it, too. That is my experiment Will you help, Ben Weatherstaff?"

"Aye, aye, sir!" said Ben Weatherstaff. "Aye, aye!"

"If you keep doing it every day as regularly as soldiers go through drill we shall see what will happen and find out if the experiment succeeds. You learn things by saying them over and over and thinking about them until they stay in your mind forever and I think it will be the same with Magic. If you keep calling it to come to you and help you it will get to be part of you and it will stay and do things."

"I once heard an officer in India tell my mother that there were

fakirs who said words over and over thousands of times," said Mary.
"I've heard Jem Fettleworth's wife say th' same thing over thousands o' times —— callin' Jem a drunken brute," said Ben Weatherstaff dryly. "Summat allus come o' that, sure enough. He gave her a good hidin' an' went to th' Blue Lion an' got as drunk as a lord."

Colin drew his brows together and thought a few minutes. Then he cheered up.

"Well," he said, "you see something did come of it. She used the wrong Magic until she made him beat her. If she'd used the right Magic and had said something nice perhaps he wouldn't have got as drunk as a lord and perhaps —— perhaps he might have bought her a new bonnet."

Ben Weatherstaff chuckled and there was shrewd admiration in his little old eyes.

"Tha'rt a clever lad as well as a straight-legged one, Mester Colin," he said. "Next time I see Bess Fettleworth I'll give her a bit of a hint o' what Magic will do for her. She'd be rare an' pleased if th' sinetifik 'speriment worked —— an' so 'ud Jem."

Dickon had stood listening to the lecture, his round eyes shining with curious delight. Nut and Shell were on his shoulders and he held a long-eared white rabbit in his arm and stroked and stroked it softly while it laid its ears along its back and enjoyed itself.

"Do you think the experiment will work?" Colin asked him, wondering what he was thinking. He so often wondered what Dickon was thinking when he saw him looking at him or at one of his "creatures" with his happy wide smile.

He smiled now and his smile was wider than usual.

"Aye," he answered, "that I do. It'll work same as th' seeds do when th' sun shines on 'em. It'll work for sure. Shall us begin it now?"

Colin was delighted and so was Mary. Fired by recollections of fakirs and devotees in illustrations Colin suggested that they should all sit cross-legged under the tree which made a canopy.

"It will be like sitting in a sort of temple," said Colin. "I'm rather tired and I want to sit down."

"Eh!" said Dickon, "tha' mustn't begin by sayin' tha'rt tired. Tha' might spoil th' Magic."

Colin turned and looked at him ⎯ into his innocent round eyes.

"That's true," he said slowly. "I must only think of the Magic."

It all seemed most majestic and mysterious when they sat down in their circle. Ben Weatherstaff felt as if he had somehow been led into appearing at a prayer-meeting. Ordinarily he was very fixed in being what he called "agen' prayer-meetin's" but this being the Rajah's affair he did not resent it and was indeed inclined to be gratified at being called upon to assist. Mistress Mary felt solemnly enraptured. Dickon held his rabbit in his arm, and perhaps he made some charmer's signal no one heard, for when he sat down, cross-legged like the rest, the crow, the fox, the squirrels and the lamb slowly drew near and made part of the circle, settling each into a place of rest as if of their own desire.

"The 'creatures' have come," said Colin gravely. "They want to help us."

Colin really looked quite beautiful, Mary thought. He held his head high as if he felt like a sort of priest and his strange eyes had a wonderful look in them. The light shone on him through the tree canopy.

"Now we will begin," he said. "Shall we sway backward and forward, Mary, as if we were dervishes?"

"I canna' do no swayin' back'ard and for'ard," said Ben Weatherstaff. "I've got th' rheumatics."

"The Magic will take them away," said Colin in a High Priest tone, "but we won't sway until it has done it. We will only chant."

"I canna' do no chantin'" said Ben Weatherstaff a trifle testily. "They turned me out o' th' church choir th' only time I ever tried it."

No one smiled. They were all too much in earnest. Colin's face was not even crossed by a shadow. He was thinking only of the Magic. "Then I will chant," he said. And he began, looking like a strange boy spirit. "The sun is shining —— the sun is shining. That is the Magic. The flowers are growing —— the roots are stirring. That is the Magic. Being alive is the Magic —— being strong is the Magic. The Magic is in me —— the Magic is in me. It is in me —— it is in me. It's in every one of us. It's in Ben Weatherstaff's back. Magic! Magic! Come and help!"

He said it a great many times —— not a thousand times but quite a goodly number. Mary listened entranced. She felt as if it were at once queer and beautiful and she wanted him to go on and on. Ben Weatherstaff began to feel soothed into a sort of dream which was quite agreeable. The humming of the bees in the blossoms mingled with the chanting voice and drowsily melted into a doze. Dickon sat cross-legged with his rabbit asleep on his arm and a hand resting on the lamb's back. Soot had pushed away a squirrel and huddled close to him on his shoulder, the gray film dropped over his eyes. At last Colin stopped.

"Now I am going to walk round the garden," he announced.

Ben Weatherstaff's head had just dropped forward and he lifted it with a jerk.

"You have been asleep," said Colin.

"Nowt o' th' sort," mumbled Ben. "Th' sermon was good enow —— but I'm bound to get out afore th' collection."

He was not quite awake yet.

"You're not in church," said Colin.

"Not me," said Ben, straightening himself. "Who said I were? I heard every bit of it. You said th' Magic was in my back. Th' doctor calls it rheumatics."

The Rajah waved his hand.

"That was the wrong Magic," he said. "You will get better. You have my permission to go to your work. But come back tomorrow."

"I'd like to see thee walk round the garden," grunted Ben.

It was not an unfriendly grunt, but it was a grunt. In fact, being a stubborn old party and not having entire faith in Magic he had made up his mind that if he were sent away he would climb his ladder and look over the wall so that he might be ready to hobble back if there were any stumbling.

The Rajah did not object to his staying and so the procession was formed. It really did look like a procession. Colin was at its head with Dickon on one side and Mary on the other. Ben Weatherstaff walked behind, and the "creatures" trailed after them, the lamb and the fox cub keeping close to Dickon, the white rabbit hopping along or stopping to nibble and Soot following with the solemnity of a person who felt himself in charge.

It was a procession which moved slowly but with dignity. Every few yards it stopped to rest. Colin leaned on Dickon's arm and privately Ben Weatherstaff kept a sharp lookout, but now and then Colin took his hand from its support and walked a few steps alone. His head was held up all the time and he looked very grand.

"The Magic is in me!" he kept saying. "The Magic is making me strong! I can feel it! I can feel it!"

It seemed very certain that something was upholding and uplifting him. He sat on the seats in the alcoves, and once or twice he sat down on the grass and several times he paused in the path and leaned on Dickon, but he would not give up until he had gone all round the garden. When he returned to the canopy tree his cheeks were flushed and he looked triumphant.

"I did it! The Magic worked!" he cried. "That is my first scientific discovery."

"What will Dr. Craven say?" broke out Mary.

"He won't say anything," Colin answered, "because he will not be told. This is to be the biggest secret of all. No one is to know anything about it until I have grown so strong that I can walk and run like any other boy. I shall come here every day in my chair and I shall be taken back in it. I won't have people whispering and asking questions and I won't let my father hear about it until the experiment has quite succeeded. Then sometime when he comes back to Misselthwaite I shall just walk into his study and say 'Here I am; I am like any other boy. I am quite well and I shall live to be a man. It has been done by a scientific experiment.'"

"He will think he is in a dream," cried Mary. "He won't believe his eyes."

Colin flushed triumphantly. He had made himself believe that he was going to get well, which was really more than half the battle, if he had been aware of it. And the thought which stimulated him more than any other was this imagining what his father would look like when he saw that he had a son who was as straight and strong as other fathers' sons. One of his darkest miseries in the unhealthy morbid past days had been his hatred of being a sickly weak-backed boy whose father was afraid to look at him.

"He'll be obliged to believe them," he said.

"One of the things I am going to do, after the Magic works and before I begin to make scientific discoveries, is to be an athlete."

"We shall have thee takin' to boxin' in a week or so," said Ben Weatherstaff. "Tha'lt end wi' winnin' th' Belt an' bein' champion prize-fighter of all England."

Colin fixed his eyes on him sternly.

"Weatherstaff," he said, "that is disrespectful. You must not take liberties because you are in the secret. However much the Magic works I shall not be a prize-fighter. I shall be a Scientific Discoverer."

"Ax pardon —— ax pardon, sir" answered Ben, touching his forehead in salute. "I ought to have seed it wasn't a jokin' matter," but his eyes twinkled and secretly he was immensely pleased. He really did not mind being snubbed since the snubbing meant that the lad was gaining strength and spirit.

9

IN THE GARDEN

In each century since the beginning of the world wonderful things have been discovered. In the last century more amazing things were found out than in any century before. In this new century hundreds of things still more astounding will be brought to light. At first people refuse to believe that a strange new thing can be done, then they begin to hope it can be done, then they see it can be done —— then it is done and all the world wonders why it was not done centuries ago. One of the new things people began to find out in the last century was that thoughts —— just mere thoughts —— are as powerful as electric batteries —— as good for one as sunlight is, or as bad for one as poison. To let a sad thought or a bad one get into your mind is as dangerous as letting a scarlet fever germ get into your body. If you let it stay there after it has got in you may never get over it as long as you live.

So long as Mistress Mary's mind was full of disagreeable thoughts about her dislikes and sour opinions of people and her determination not to be pleased by or interested in anything, she was a yellow-faced, sickly, bored and wretched child. Circumstances, however, were very kind to her, though she was not at all aware of it. They began to push her about for her own good. When her mind gradually filled itself with robins, and moorland cottages crowded with children, with queer crabbed old gardeners and common little Yorkshire housemaids, with springtime and with secret gardens coming alive day by day, and also with a moor boy and his "creatures," there was no room left for the disagreeable thoughts which affected her liver and her digestion and made her yellow and tired.

So long as Colin shut himself up in his room and thought only of his fears and weakness and his detestation of people who looked at him and reflected hourly on humps and early death, he was a hysterical half-crazy little hypochondriac who knew nothing of the sunshine and the spring and also did not know that he could get well and could stand upon his feet if he tried to do it. When new beautiful thoughts began to push out the old hideous ones, life began to come back to him, his blood ran healthily through his veins and strength poured into him like a flood. His scientific experiment was quite practical and simple and there was nothing weird about it at all. Much more surprising things can happen to any one who, when a disagreeable or discouraged thought comes into his mind, just has the sense to remember in time and push it out by putting in an agreeable determinedly courageous one. Two things cannot be in one place.

"Where, you tend a rose, my lad,
A thistle cannot grow."

While the secret garden was coming alive and two children were coming alive with it, there was a man wandering about certain far-away beautiful places in the Norwegian fiords and the valleys and mountains of Switzerland and he was a man who for ten years had kept his mind filled with dark and heart-broken thinking. He had not been courageous; he had never tried to put any other thoughts in the place of the dark ones. He had wandered by blue lakes and thought them; he had lain on mountain-sides with sheets of deep blue gentians blooming all about him and flower breaths filling all the air and he had thought them. A terrible sorrow had fallen upon him when he had been happy and he had let his soul fill itself with blackness and had refused obstinately to allow any rift of light to pierce through. He had forgotten and deserted his home and his duties. When he traveled about, darkness so brooded over him that the sight of him was a wrong done to other people because it was as if he poisoned the air about him with gloom. Most strangers thought he must be either half mad or a man with some hidden crime on his soul. He, was a tall man with a drawn face and crooked shoulders and the name he always entered on hotel registers was, "Archibald Craven, Misselthwaite Manor, Yorkshire, England."

He had traveled far and wide since the day he saw Mistress Mary in his study and told her she might have her "bit of earth." He had been in the most beautiful places in Europe, though he had remained nowhere more than a few days. He had chosen the quietest and remotest spots. He had been on the tops of mountains whose heads were in the clouds and had looked down on other mountains when the sun rose and touched them with such light as made it seem as if the world were just being born.

But the light had never seemed to touch himself until one day when he realized that for the first time in ten years a strange thing had happened. He was in a wonderful valley in the Austrian Tyrol and he had been walking alone through such beauty as might have lifted, any man's soul out of shadow. He had walked a long way and it had not lifted his. But at last he had felt tired and had thrown himself down to rest on a carpet of moss by a stream. It was a clear little stream which ran quite merrily along on its narrow way through the luscious damp greenness. Sometimes it made a sound rather like very low laughter as it bubbled over and round stones. He saw birds come and dip their heads to drink in it and then flick their wings and fly away. It seemed like a thing alive and yet its tiny voice made the stillness seem deeper. The valley was very, very still.

As he sat gazing into the clear running of the water, Archibald Craven gradually felt his mind and body both grow quiet, as quiet as the valley itself. He wondered if he were going to sleep, but he was not. He sat and gazed at the sunlit water and his eyes began to see things growing at its edge. There was one lovely mass of blue forget-me-nots growing so close to the stream that its leaves were wet and at these he found himself looking as he remembered he had looked at such things years ago. He was actually thinking tenderly how lovely it was and what wonders of blue its hundreds of little blossoms were. He did not know that just that simple thought was slowly filling his mind ___ filling and filling it until other things were softly pushed aside. It was as if a sweet clear spring had begun to rise in a stagnant pool and had risen and risen until at last it swept the dark water away. But of course he did not think of this himself. He only knew that the valley seemed to grow quieter and quieter as he sat and stared at the bright delicate blueness. He did not know how long he sat there or what was happening to him, but at last he moved as if he were awakening and he got up slowly and stood on the moss carpet, drawing a long, deep, soft breath and wondering at himself. Something seemed to have been unbound and released in him, very quietly.

"What is it?" he said, almost in a whisper, and he passed his hand over his forehead. "I almost feel as if ___ I were alive!"

I do not know enough about the wonderfulness of undiscovered things to be able to explain how this had happened to him. Neither does anyone else yet. He did not understand at all himself ___ but he remembered this strange hour months afterward when he was at Misselthwaite again and he found out quite by accident that on this very day Colin had cried out as he went into the secret garden:

"I am going to live forever and ever and ever!"

The singular calmness remained with him the rest of the evening and he slept a new reposeful sleep; but it was not with him very long. He did not know that it could be kept. By the next night he had opened the doors wide to his dark thoughts and they had come trooping and rushing back. He left the valley and went on his wandering way again. But, strange as it seemed to him, there were minutes ___ sometimes half-hours ___ when, without his knowing why, the black burden seemed to lift itself again and he knew he was a living man and not a dead one. Slowly ___ slowly ___ for no reason that he knew of ___ he was "coming alive" with the garden. As the golden summer changed into the deep golden autumn he went to the Lake of Como. There he found the loveliness of a dream. He spent his days upon the crystal blueness of the lake or he walked back into the soft thick verdure of the hills and tramped until he was tired so that he might sleep. But by this time he had begun to sleep better, he knew, and his dreams had ceased to be a terror to him. "Perhaps," he thought, "my body is growing stronger."

It was growing stronger but ___ because of the rare peaceful hours when his thoughts were changed ___ his soul was slowly growing stronger, too. He began to think of Misselthwaite and wonder if he should not go home. Now and then he wondered vaguely about his boy and asked himself what he should feel when he went and stood by the carved four-posted bed again and looked down at the sharply chiseled ivory-white face while it slept and, the black lashes rimmed so startlingly the close-shut eyes. He shrank from it.

One marvel of a day he had walked so far that when he returned the moon was high and full and all the world was purple shadow and silver. The stillness of lake and shore and wood was so wonderful that he did not go into the villa he lived in. He walked down to a little bowered terrace at the water's edge and sat upon a seat and breathed in all the heavenly scents of the night. He felt the strange calmness stealing over him and it grew deeper and deeper until he fell asleep.

He did not know when he fell asleep and when he began to dream; his dream was so real that he did not feel as if he were dreaming. He remembered afterward how intensely wide awake and alert he had thought he was. He thought that as he sat and breathed in the scent of the late roses and listened to the lapping of the water at his feet he heard a voice calling. It was sweet and clear and happy and far away. It seemed very far, but he heard it as distinctly as if it had been at his very side.

"Archie! Archie! Archie!" it said, and then again, sweeter and clearer than before, "Archie! Archie!"

He thought he sprang to his feet not even startled. It was such a real voice and it seemed so natural that he should hear it.

"Lilias! Lilias!" he answered. "Lilias! Where are you?"

"In the garden," it came back like a sound from a golden flute. "In the garden!"

And then the dream ended. But he did not awaken. He slept soundly and sweetly all through the lovely night. When he did awake at last it was brilliant morning and a servant was standing staring at him. He was an Italian servant and was accustomed, as all the servants of the villa were, to accepting without question any strange thing his foreign master might do. No one ever knew when he would go out or come in or where he would choose to sleep or if he would roam about the garden or lie in the boat on the lake all night. The man held a salver with some letters on it and he waited quietly until Mr. Craven took them. When he had gone away Mr. Craven sat a few moments holding them in his hand and looking at the lake. His strange calm was still upon him and something more ___ a lightness as if the cruel thing which had been done had not happened as he thought ___ as if something had changed. He was remembering the dream ___ the real ___ real dream.

"In the garden!" he said, wondering at himself. "In the garden! But the door is locked and the key is buried deep."

When he glanced at the letters a few minutes later he saw that the one lying at the top of the rest was an English letter and came from Yorkshire. It was directed in a plain woman's hand but it was not a hand he knew. He opened it, scarcely thinking of the writer, but the first words attracted his attention at once.

"Dear Sir:

I am Susan Sowerby that made bold to speak to you once on the moor. It was about Miss Mary I spoke. I will make bold to speak again. Please, sir, I would come home if I was you. I think you would be glad to come and ___ if you will excuse me, sir ___ I think your lady would ask you to come if she was here.

"Your obedient servant,

" Susan Sowerby."

Mr. Craven read the letter twice before he put it back in its envelope. He kept thinking about the dream.

"I will go back to Misselthwaite," he said. "Yes, I'll go at once."

And he went through the garden to the villa and ordered Pitcher to prepare for his return to England.

In a few days he was in Yorkshire again, and on his long railroad journey he found himself thinking of his boy as he had never thought in all the ten years past. During those years he had only wished to forget him. Now, though he did not intend to think about him, memories of him constantly drifted into his mind. He remembered the black days when he had raved like a madman because the child was alive and the mother was dead. He had refused to see it, and when he had gone to look at it at last it had been, such a weak wretched thing that everyone had been sure it would die in a few days. But to the surprise of those who took care of it the days passed and it lived and then everyone believed it would be a deformed and crippled creature.

He had not meant to be a bad father, but he had not felt like a father at all. He had supplied doctors and nurses and luxuries, but he had shrunk from the mere thought of the boy and had buried himself in his own misery. The first time after a year's absence he returned to Misselthwaite and the small miserable looking thing languidly and indifferently lifted to his face the great gray eyes with black lashes round them, so like and yet so horribly unlike the happy eyes he had adored, he could not bear the sight of them and turned away pale as death. After that he scarcely ever saw him except when he was asleep, and all he knew of him was that he was a confirmed invalid, with a vicious, hysterical, half-insane temper. He could only be kept from furies dangerous to himself by being given his own way in every detail.

All this was not an uplifting thing to recall, but as the train whirled him through mountain passes and golden plains the man who was "coming alive" began to think in a new way and he thought long and steadily and deeply.

"Perhaps I have been all wrong for ten years," he said to himself. "Ten years is a long time. It may be too late to do anything —— quite too late. What have I been thinking of!"

Of course this was the wrong Magic —— to begin by saying "too late." Even Colin could have told him that. But he knew nothing of Magic —— either black or white. This he had yet to learn. He wondered if Susan Sowerby had taken courage and written to him only because the motherly creature had realized that the boy was much worse —— was fatally ill. If he had not been under the spell of the curious calmness which had taken possession of him he would have been more wretched than ever. But the calm had brought a sort of courage and hope with it. Instead of giving way to thoughts of the worst he actually found he was trying to believe in better things.

"Could it be possible that she sees that I may be able to do him good and control him? " he thought. "I will go and see her on my way to Misselthwaite."

But when on his way across the moor he stopped the carriage at the cottage, seven or eight children who were playing about gathered in a group and bobbing seven or eight friendly and polite curtsies told him that their mother had gone to the other side of the moor early in the morning to help a woman who had a new baby. "Our Dickon," they volunteered, was over at the Manor working in one of the gardens where he went several days each week.

Mr. Craven looked over the collection of sturdy little bodies and round red-cheeked faces, each one grinning in its own particular way, and he awoke to the fact that they were a healthy likable lot. He smiled at their friendly grins and took a golden sovereign from his pocket and gave it to "our 'Lizabeth Ellen'" who was the oldest. "If you divide that into eight parts there will be half a crown for each of, you," he said.

Then amid grins and chuckles and bobbing of curtsies he drove away, leaving ecstasy and nudging elbows and little jumps of joy behind.

The drive across the wonderfulness of the moor was a soothing thing. Why did it seem to give him a sense of homecoming which he had been sure he could never feel again —— that sense of the beauty of land and sky and purple bloom of distance and a warming of the heart at drawing, nearer to the great old house which had held those of his blood for six hundred years? How he had driven away from it the last time, shuddering to think of its closed rooms and the boy lying in the four-posted bed with the brocaded hangings. Was it possible that perhaps he might find him changed a little for the better and that he might overcome his shrinking from him? How real that dream had been —— how wonderful and clear the voice which called back to him, "In the garden —— In the garden!"

"I will try to find the key," he said. "I will try to open the door. I must —— though I don't know why."

When he arrived at the Manor the servants who received him with the usual ceremony noticed that he looked better and that he did not go to the remote rooms where he usually lived attended by Pitcher. He went into the library and sent for Mrs. Medlock. She came to him somewhat excited and curious and flustered.

"How is Master Colin, Medlock?" he inquired.

"Well, sir," Mrs. Medlock answered, "he's ⎯ he's different, in a manner of speaking."

"Worse?" he suggested.

Mrs. Medlock really was flushed.

"Well, you see, sir," she tried to explain, "neither Dr. Craven, nor the nurse, nor me can exactly make him out."

"Why is that?"

"To tell the truth, sir, Master Colin might be better and he might be changing for the worse. His appetite, sir, is past understanding ⎯ and his ways ⎯ "

"Has he become more ⎯ more peculiar?" her master, asked, knitting his brows anxiously.

"That's it, sir. He's growing very peculiar ⎯ when you compare him with what he used to be. He used to eat nothing and then suddenly he began to eat something enormous ⎯ and then he stopped again all at once and the meals were sent back just as they used to be. You never knew, sir, perhaps, that out of doors he never would let himself be taken. The things we've gone through to get him to go out in his chair would leave a body trembling like a leaf. He'd throw himself into such a state that Dr. Craven said he couldn't be responsible for forcing him. Well, sir, just without warning ⎯ not long after one of his worst tantrums he suddenly insisted on being taken out every day by Miss Mary and Susan Sowerby's boy Dickon that could push his chair. He took a fancy to both Miss Mary and Dickon, and Dickon brought his tame animals, and, if you'll credit it, sir, out of doors he will stay from morning until night."

"How does he look?" was the next question.

"If he took his food natural, sir, you'd think he was putting on flesh ⎯ but we're afraid it may be a sort of bloat. He laughs sometimes in a queer way when he's alone with Miss Mary. He never used to laugh at all. Dr. Craven is coming to see you at once, if you'll allow him. He never was as puzzled in his life."

"Where is Master Colin now?" Mr. Craven asked.

"In the garden, sir. He's always in the garden —— though not a human creature is allowed to go near for fear they'll look at him."

Mr. Craven scarcely heard her last words.

"In the garden," he said, and after he had sent Mrs. Medlock away he stood and repeated it again and again. "In the garden!"

He had to make an effort to bring himself back to the place he was standing in and when he felt he was on earth again he turned and went out of the room. He took his way, as Mary had done, through the door in the shrubbery and among the laurels and the fountain beds. The fountain was playing now and was encircled by beds of brilliant autumn flowers. He crossed the lawn and turned into the Long Walk by the ivied walls. He did not walk quickly, but slowly, and his eyes were on the path. He felt as if he were being drawn back to the place he had so long forsaken, and he did not know why. As he drew near to it his step became still more slow. He knew where the door was even though the ivy hung thick over it —— but he did not know exactly where it lay —— that buried key.

So he stopped and stood still, looking about him, and almost the moment after he had paused he started and listened —— asking himself if he were walking in a dream.

The ivy hung thick over the door, the key was buried under the shrubs, no human being had passed that portal for ten lonely years —— and yet inside the garden there were sounds. They were the sounds of running scuffling feet seeming to chase round and round under the trees, they were strange sounds of lowered suppressed voices —— exclamations and smothered joyous cries. It seemed actually like the laughter of young things, the uncontrollable laughter of children who were trying not to be heard but who in a moment or so ⸺ as their excitement mounted ⸺ would burst forth. What in heaven's name was he dreaming of ⸺ what in heaven's name did he hear? Was he losing his reason and thinking he heard things which were not for human ears? Was it that the far clear voice had meant?

And then the moment came, the uncontrollable moment when the sounds forgot to hush themselves. The feet ran faster and faster ⸺ they were nearing the garden door ⸺ there was quick strong young breathing and a wild outbreak of laughing shows which could not be contained ⸺ and the door in the wall was flung wide open, the sheet of ivy swinging back, and a boy burst through it at full speed and, without seeing the outsider, dashed almost into his arms. Mr. Craven had extended them just in time to save him from falling as a result of his unseeing dash against him, and when he held him away to look at him in amazement at his being there he truly gasped for breath.

He was a tall boy and a handsome one. He was glowing with life and his running had sent splendid color leaping to his face. He threw the thick hair back from his forehead and lifted a pair of strange gray eyes ⸺ eyes full of boyish laughter and rimmed with black lashes like a fringe. It was the eyes which made Mr. Craven gasp for breath.

"Who ⸺ What? Who!" he stammered.

This was not what Colin had expected ⸺ this was not what he had planned. He had never thought of such a meeting. And yet to come dashing out ⸺ winning a race ⸺ perhaps it was even better. He drew himself up to his very tallest. Mary, who had been running with him and had dashed through the door too, believed that he managed to make himself look taller than he had ever looked before

____ inches taller.

"Father," he said, "I'm Colin. You can't believe it. I scarcely can myself. I'm Colin."

Like Mrs. Medlock, he did not understand what his father meant when he said hurriedly:

"In the garden! In the garden!"

"Yes," hurried on Colin. "It was the garden that did it ____ and Mary and Dickon and the creatures ____ and the Magic. No one knows. We kept it to tell you when you came. I'm well, I can beat Mary in a race. I'm going to be an athlete."

He said it all so like a healthy boy ____ his face flushed, his words tumbling over each other in his eagerness ____ that Mr. Craven's soul shook with unbelieving joy.

Colin put out his hand and laid it on his father's arm.

"Aren't you glad, Father?" he ended.

"Aren't you glad? I'm going to live forever and ever and ever!"

Mr. Craven put his hands on both the boy's shoulders and held him still. He knew he dared not even try to speak for a moment.

"Take me into the garden, my boy," he said at last. "And tell me all about it."

And so they led him in.

The place was a wilderness of autumn gold and purple and violet blue and flaming scarlet and on every side were sheaves of late lilies standing together ____ lilies which were white or white and ruby. He remembered well when the first of them had been planted that just at this season of the year their late glories should reveal themselves. Late roses climbed and hung and clustered and the sunshine deepening the hue of the yellowing trees made one feel that one, stood in an embowered temple of gold. The newcomer stood silent just as the children had done when they came into its grayness. He looked round and round.

"I thought it would be dead," he said."

"Mary thought so at first," said Colin. "But it came alive."

Then they sat down under their tree ___ all but Colin, who wanted to stand while he told the story.

It was the strangest thing he had ever heard, Archibald Craven thought, as it was poured forth in headlong boy fashion. Mystery and Magic and wild creatures, the weird midnight meeting ___ the coming of the spring ___ the passion of insulted pride which had dragged the young Rajah to his feet to defy old Ben Weatherstaff to his face. The odd companionship, the play acting, the great secret so carefully kept. The listener laughed until tears came into his eyes and sometimes tears came into his eyes when he was not laughing. The Athlete, the Lecturer, the Scientific Discoverer was a laughable, lovable, healthy young human thing.

"Now," he said at the end of the story, "it need not be a secret any more. I dare say it will frighten them nearly into fits when they see me ___ but I am never going to get into the chair again. I shall walk back with you, Father ___ to the house."

Ben Weatherstaff's duties rarely took him away from the gardens, but on this occasion he made an excuse to carry some vegetables to the kitchen and being invited into the servants' hall by Mrs. Medlock to drink a glass of beer he was on the spot ___ as he had hoped to be ___ when the most dramatic event Misselthwaite Manor had seen during the present generation actually took place. One of the windows looking upon the courtyard gave also a glimpse of the lawn. Mrs. Medlock, knowing Ben had come from the gardens, hoped that he might have caught sight of his master and even by chance of his meeting with Master Colin.

"Did you see either of them, Weatherstaff?" she asked.

Ben took his beer-mug from his mouth and wiped his lips with the back of his hand.

"Aye, that I did," he answered with a shrewdly significant air.

"Both of them?" suggested Mrs. Medlock.

"Both of 'em," returned Ben Weatherstaff. "Thank ye kindly, ma'am, I could sup up another mug of it."

"Together?" said Mrs. Medlock, hastily overfilling his beer-mug in her excitement.

"Together, ma'am," and Ben gulped down half of his new mug at one gulp.

"Where was Master Colin? How did he look? What did they say to each other?"

"I didna' hear that," said Ben, "along o' only bein' on th' stepladder lookin, over th' wall. But I'll tell thee this. There's been things goin' on outside as you house people knows nowt about. An' what tha'll find out tha'll find out soon."

And it was not two minutes before he swallowed the last of his beer and waved his mug solemnly toward the window which took in through the shrubbery a piece of the lawn.

"Look there," he said, "if tha's curious. Look what's comin' across th' grass."

When Mrs. Medlock looked she threw up her hands and gave a little shriek and every man and woman servant within hearing bolted across the servants' hall and stood looking through the window with their eyes almost starting out of their heads.

Across the lawn came the Master of Misselthwaite and he looked as many of them had never seen him. And by his, side with his head up in the air and his eyes full of laughter walked as strongly and steadily as any boy in Yorkshire ___Master Colin.